The Cruel Country

The Cruel Country

Judith Ortiz Cofer

THE UNIVERSITY OF GEORGIA PRESS *Athens & London*

© 2015 by the University of Georgia Press
Athens, Georgia 30602
www.ugapress.org
All rights reserved
Designed by Erin Kirk New
Set in Galliard
Printed and bound by Sheridan Books
The paper in this book meets the guidelines for
permanence and durability of the Committee on
Production Guidelines for Book Longevity of the
Council on Library Resources.

Most University of Georgia Press titles are
available from popular e-book vendors.

Printed in the United States of America
19 18 17 16 15 C 5 4 3 2 1

Library of Congress Control Number 2014958942

ISBN-13: 978-0-8203-4763-9 (hardcover)
ISBN-13: 978-0-8203-4764-6 (e-book)

British Library Cataloging-in-Publication Data available

This book is dedicated to

the memory of my mother,

Fanny Morot Ortiz,

and my father-in-law,

C. H. Cofer Jr.

"Mourning: a cruel country where I am *no longer afraid.*"

—ROLAND BARTHES, *Mourning Diary*

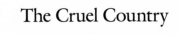

The Cruel Country

This summer, the summer of 2011, is the time when the dominoes fall around me—one collapsing after another, a row of tombstones—and the earth trembles and shakes beneath my family's feet. I try to imagine an end to this summer, as if it is a neat work of short fiction. But I know that the best stories aren't so neatly tied up.

The day before Father's Day, June 18, John's father dies. I call my mother, and although her weak voice and unenergetic demeanor worry me, I shut down my concern for her because next I have to give our daughter the terrible news of her grandfather's death. My daughter's grief intensifies my own. She feels cheated out of time at the farm with her grandfather, of time for him to get to know his great-grandson, Eli. I do not tell her that I am concerned for my mother. I am learning the alchemy of grief—how it must be carefully measured and doled out, inflicted—but I have not yet mastered this art. What seems like gold can transform to molten lead. Unshared suspicions and pain may double the grief. The weight of a secret revealed too late is a heavy burden to bear.

The night I get the phone call from my relatives in Puerto Rico letting me know that my mother is gravely ill, I have a dream that I would have shared with her. I've always told her my most interesting dreams because she takes delight in looking them up in her much-used, completely unscientific book of dream interpretation, *Los Sueños*, a copy of which she once sent me and which I used in writing a number of poems. I dream that my front teeth have come out and I am choking on them, and then I wake up choking on a cough drop. My mother's book of dreams says that to dream of teeth means an imminent death. Teeth in dreams are the little headstones foretelling the end for someone close to you. My mother would cross herself and reassure me that I am probably channeling the news of death for someone else because *Eres muy sensitiva*. Later she would call her friends to ask if anyone in their circle had died. If someone had died around the time of my dream, she'd say "¿Recuerdas?" Do you remember when you had that dream and I told you it meant *la muerte* was nearby? She's always claimed to have prescient feelings about imminent death, as well as luck, and she always knew when any *pruebas* were forthcoming in her life.

I know I dream of choking on my own teeth not because I am clairvoyant but because my mother is so much a part of my unconscious and subconscious life. It is no mere cliché or coincidence, this airway obstruction. I place my hands on my chest to feel the convulsions, and I know that I am suffering from some sort of empathic reaction, that I am trying to breathe for both of us. *Anticipatory grief*—I believe that's what the medical texts call it.

Notebook One

I *The black word: el cáncer*

I am headed to the west coast of our tiny island, toward my mother, who has been hospitalized with a mysterious combination of symptoms that include tachycardia, respiratory distress, and trembling—symptoms she's had before, but this time they are uncontrollable. The sound of the black word still tastes bitter on my tongue: cancer. *El cáncer.* The cousin of mine with the best grasp of English in the family had been assigned the task of calling and e-mailing me, as everyone assumed I'd need some words of explanation in English. *El cáncer*, however, is a cognate, pronounced almost exactly the same in both tongues. It creates a vacuum in both languages, a sinkhole.

I take an *avioneta* from San Juan to Mayagüez. The eight-passenger propeller plane is not big enough to even qualify as a small plane; the diminutive *avioneta* as opposed to *avión*, airplane, implies its minuscule size, smaller-than-small—advance notice to all potential occupants who will be suspended above the earth in an (almost) toy-sized plane. The pilot's elbow hangs out of his open window, like a driver's before the advent of signal lights, as we taxi down the runway. I get the impression that this maneuver is somehow necessary to lifting us off the ground. Or maybe he's just showing off. My seat is so close behind the pilot's that I can see the sweat on his neck and the reflection of the burning tropical sun on his shaved head.

My first response to the news, after I emerged from the initial shock, was anger. Rage at the so-called specialists who found reasons for endless cardiological tests and a CT scan of her abdomen but did not think to check her lungs, although she was a life-long cigarette smoker. When my aunt took the phone after my cousin had run out of words that would satisfy me, she finally said that the primary care physician's opinion was that my mother had hidden the truth from her family. It appears that my beloved mother, Mami, the inspiration for many of my poems, stories, and essays, had lied so convincingly to her doctors that she managed to evade inspection of the area that would reveal her darkest secret. She had claimed and proclaimed to have cut back on her smoking, to have nearly quit. I had occasionally caught her with a cigarette when I visited her on the Island, but it was always "I'm down to two a day, Hija." And always she'd repeat the old stories of her father, mother-in-law, and other relatives who had lived as smokers to a great old age. I lectured, questioned, and cajoled, but because we lived so far apart and always had so much else to discuss during our phone conversations—our talks were filled with news of my daughter, the granddaughter whom she adored, and my new grandson, her great-grandchild, whom, it turned out, she'd never get to meet—that I was unable to see the truth.

The avioneta rounds the Island at such low altitude that I get to see the Island's full natural beauty from the vantage point of a seabird. I look beyond the huge tracts of houses, the great metropolitan spread of San Juan, and focus on the stunning turquoise of the seashore and, ahead, mountains so lush that in spite of the weight of the word *cancer* growing in my chest cavity, the poisonous taste of it on my tongue, and the bubble of sobs on the verge of choking me, I let out a mighty sigh. A Puerto Rican sigh. Loud enough that the pilot hears it above the propeller's noise and turns around to wink at me. "Quite a sight, huh?" He's American and younger than I imagined from the gray shadow of hair on his shaved head. He is earning his wings on these taxi rides across my country, I heard him tell the shotgun seat passenger. "Yes, it's beautiful," I reply and he smiles again at the emotion in my voice. I can practically hear his thoughts: "These mainland Puerto Ricans are a sentimental lot about this crazy place. They should try living here for a while." Or maybe I'm just projecting. At this moment, still distanced, flying above my mother's island, I have no idea that I will soon be trying to do just that, to live in this foreign land that is my native country, while also learning to separate myself from all that has ever connected me to it—my mother.

2   Before my trip, while still in the peaceful setting of our home in the Georgia countryside, I made a plan for getting her the best care possible. I downloaded several e-books to my iPad, including *Cancer Caregiving A-to-Z* and *The Emperor of All Maladies: A Biography of Cancer*. During the long days and nights sitting by my mother's hospital bed, and afterward, only a total immersion in words and scientific facts will keep me from drowning as the shoreline recedes from view.

The hospital, La Inmaculada Concepción, has the appearance and ambience of a Catholic chapel, with a large statue of Mary in front and blue-and-white-toned décor punctuated by murals and portraits of a peaceful-looking and apparently hopeful Holy Family: the Holy Family before they knew what was coming; before torment, pain, and death; before Calvary.

I have already been to the Island to visit my mother twice this year because she'd been experiencing a decline in her health. Tiny to begin with, not quite five feet tall and never weighing more than 112 pounds, she was down to only 98. No appetite, a grayish pallor over her honey-colored skin. Alarmed by her sickly appearance and unusual lethargy, I had accompanied her and her husband, Ángel, from specialist to specialist, arguing in my basic-to-weak Spanish (weaker as the vocabulary for her symptoms and treatment got more technical) with bureaucrats who refused one doctor's request of a CT scan of her abdomen without signatures from several other doctors who had insisted on return appointments weeks in the future. Finally, she got the scan and we got some answers: she had stones in her bile duct, which could be pulverized with a laser! With this good news, I finally left the Island, flying out of the warmth into two winter storms, one at my Newark connection and another, a rare southern snowstorm, in Atlanta. I managed to get home just as everything was shutting down. I felt good about having helped my mother and felt even better, after her endoscopy was over, hearing her tell me over the phone in her familiar, strong voice that she was eating again. In the next few months her recovery seemed real enough. She claimed to be almost back to her usual busy schedule of church and civic activities and the endless round of celebrations that is common in a family the size of hers, with seven out of eight living brothers and sisters and all the related baptisms, birthdays, and anniversaries that had to be marked with fiestas. Not as much dancing as before, she admitted, but she was on her way.

Along with the other two books, I also downloaded a Spanish-English dictionary and looked up the translations for certain key words: *quimioterapia*, *decaída de salud*, and *cuidado en un hospicio*. I've practiced the pronunciations. I recall one of the things my mother often complained about during the many years of what she always called her *exilio* in the United States as a navy wife, before she returned to her Island to live her real life: that when she tried speaking in English, people treated her as if she were stupid. In the eyes and ears of others, her intelligence was indicated by her thick accent, her mispronunciations, and her limited vocabulary. In Spanish, however, she was a powerful woman. All during her last year, I heard how her voice weakened, how words began to be cut off by the little breaks in her breathing that were slowly becoming more pronounced. How could I not have known?

3 *Estoy aquí*

I enter that other place, the kingdom of the sick, on this white-hot day when the tropical sun seems to be burning a hole in the sky. Last night, at home in Georgia, I lay awake, trying to imagine my mother as she must now be, so ill that she could not speak to me on the phone. This has never happened before in the long history of our separation. Her voice has been a constant in my life during all manner of crises on either side of the Atlantic.

I'd heard many other voices the night before. Ángel's voice was hardly understandable, it was so low on the voicemail message, saying hesitantly in Spanish that he thought I should come to her. She had been asking for my brother and me but was very weak. My oldest uncle advised me in a stronger voice to come soon and to let my brother know that she *estaba muy malita*, the diminutive used when you want to avoid saying "gravely ill." The cousin who knows English repeated their messages to make sure I understood the situation. But she too said *muy malita* in Spanish, unable to come up with the equivalent words in English. I know that much about the dialect—the worse the situation gets, the littler everything becomes, almost baby talk: *Tu mami está muy malita*. Not *muy mal*, very bad, but a little bit very bad.

Susan Sontag has called illness "the night side of life" and said that we enter the kingdom of the sick "as citizens with a dual passport." On June 30, 2011, I walk into the place where my mother will die fully experiencing what I used to think of as a cliché, a sinking heart, but someone long ago got it right. There is no better way to express that physiological plunge, much like the sensation I feel when the *avioneta* from San Juan begins its descent—a sinking of all my inner organs, a need to take deep breaths, the sensation of vertigo at the approaching downfall, the landscape turning and turning. I am going to be okay, I tell myself, but as soon as my aunt reaches for me in the lobby of La Concepción, I collapse into her arms. She and my uncle let me empty my chest of the sobs I have carried with me as dead weight since the phone call. Then they sit me down in front of the mural of the Holy Family and tell me that I have to prepare myself for what I will see. My mother is on oxygen and an IV for morphine and nutrition, as she is eating less and less every day. She has lost a lot of weight. Her eyes are mostly closed, and she does not remain conscious for long.

Her doctor has shown them her chest X-rays. I insist that my uncle tell me exactly what they saw.

Oscuros con manchas en la placa, he says. Dark with plaque. But I know from the careful way he speaks the words that there had been much more to see in that stark landscape of her lungs.

What can be done, I want to know. Surgery? Chemo? *Quimioterapia*?

This is something I will have to discuss with the pulmonologist, the oncologist, and her primary care physician.

How did this happen? How could she have gotten so ill so quickly?

Shaking of heads. Then my aunt, carefully, gently, "Fanny fumaba mucho."

She smoked. She smoked a lot. No, I say, she had cut down, had almost quit. She told me so herself.

Silence.

The kingdom of the sick is very small and keeps shrinking the longer you stay within its boundaries. There are at least six people around her bed: her four sisters, her sister-in-law, and my oldest uncle. Four or five of her nieces and nephews are in the hallway. No, there are seven people in the room. Ángel, her husband, is in a chair very close to her bed. His head is sunken into his chest, his hand near her hand, which he can't hold because it has so many tubes attached to it. I am hugged by each of my aunts and then gently, respectfully, by the man who replaced my father over two decades ago. My mother was a widow then, still beautiful in her forties, and had gone back to the Island to reinvent herself as an independent woman who had spent most of her life in the United States. She had kept her Puertoricanness intact, paying for it with loneliness and good-wife servitude. Ángel was divorced, six years her junior, a former minor-league baseball player with Latin-lover poise, dark good looks, and a gentle disposition that matched his name. He had been immediately struck by her sophistication, her intelligence, her wit, and most of all by the fact that she loved to dance as much as he. He was the opposite of my intellectual, taciturn father and perfect as a partner in part two of the narrative my mother was creating for herself. With her Ángel, she began a life so different from her exilio that I drew from it again and again in my poems, essays, and stories. She had taught me something about reinvention and transformation.

My mother was a performance artist; she had re-created herself by sheer will and perseverance. Once a timid immigrant wife who needed her husband and children to lead her through the labyrinth of life on the mainland—a lonely navy wife who read romance novels as she waited for her eventual release from exile—she had made herself into a sassy, bold, and fully engaged woman who had returned to her rightful place in the world. I watched her grow and change with amazement and pride, as if she were *my* offspring. I recorded in my poems how I saw the light return to her eyes—the light that had been dimmed by her loneliness and the demands of life away from her beloved Island and the support of her extended family, the little fire she had stoked with dreams of eventually returning home. For almost twenty-five years she had managed to keep faith in her dream of return. Over the years of her developing liberation, I observed that although she was involved in politics, charity work, the church, and her large extended family, she expressed her recovery of the best in herself most fluently on the dance floor with her Ángel. In the days and weeks to follow, I will hear from their friends and acquaintances that Fanny and Ángel were *dos trompos* on the dance floor. Like two spinning tops.

A phrase from Shakespeare comes to mind as I look at my mother lying on her hospital bed with an oxygen mask over her long "Roman" nose and full lips, gasping so hard for breaths that her thin chest literally jumps at the intake, almost like she wants to wake herself up from a bad dream. "Fly away, fly away, breath." I can't imagine her never getting up from this bed. I will myself to think of her as resting between salsa numbers while the band is taking a break. She is catching her breath.

4   *The kingdom of the sick is very cold.*

I spend the first night in the hospital room. The family has tried to dissuade me. I have been traveling for twelve hours: I look exhausted. "She knows you're here. Ángel will stay." But Ángel has already been by her side for over a week, ever since I talked her into going to the ER. Her voice had been so weak. The few steps from her rocker to the phone had made her dizzy. For once, she had admitted that she was not feeling very well. She did not say, "Estoy malita," which would have alarmed me even more. She said, "No me siento bien hoy." Not feeling well today. I asked to speak to Ángel, who was obviously right by her side, possibly holding her up. He said, "Está malita." She is a little bit sick. So sick that words had to be moderated. She began to protest, and I used my translator voice, the commanding voice I had learned to use as a child when I needed to make her see that I knew the situation better than she could; I was the interpreter. If the landlord had said we had to pay the rent this week, it meant *this* week and not "horita." Not the vague sometime soon. If the teacher scheduled a conference for next Monday, in America, it really meant "el lunes" and not "I will see your teacher when your father comes home. She's not going anywhere, right?" The day of her breathlessness, I said, "I am going to call you back in thirty minutes. Please be on your way to the clinic. Do you want me to go down there again to make sure you take care of yourself?" She had agreed, although she took a shallow breath and said something that seems ominous now but sounded only like a protestation then. She said, "I know what they will say." That day, I began the inexorable gallop toward this night in the cold hospital room looking at my mother, no bigger than a child under her favorite pink blanket, which Ángel had brought her, and with her head resting on a pillowcase she had embroidered with multicolored flowers and vines. The embroidery once done for food money by her mother and sisters during the World War II years had become a relaxing, meditative activity for her. She'd called her hours working the intricate patterns on cloth *mi terapia*, her therapy sessions. I have a shelf in my linen closet stacked with pillowcases, tablecloths, and towels embroidered by her and her sisters. I also keep a treasured tablecloth intricately embroidered by my abuela, now dead for fifteen years. Embroidery was a family female activity. They gathered in the afternoons to sew and talk. In my childhood it was a magical time of eavesdropping on gossip and listening to *cuentos* that would seed my imagination.

Her hands are swollen from the ivs and she is barely conscious. I lean close to her ear and say, "Mami, estoy aquí." I put my hand on her head and stroke her hair, noting that her roots are showing. She has never allowed any gray to show. This gives me a clue to how long she has been really sick—several inches of illness. Like many Island women of her generation she had decided not to go gray by going brownish copper instead; at least her hair was not red like many others'. I had always disliked this trend of older Latinas bleaching and coloring their once-dark hair to emulate the fair-skinned models they saw on TV. In my mind's eye my mother has ebony black hair, lots of it. It's hair I inherited, and I am still fighting the urge to let it go gray naturally, but black or gray—never red. Why am I thinking this now?

My mother responds to my touch with a flutter of her eyelids, moves her fingers a little. Keeping my left hand on her head, I take her hand in my right. I look at it. My hand looks more wrinkled and fingers more bent with our family arthritis than hers; the swelling has rejuvenated hers. I speak the words that I will repeat to her until the last breath she takes:

"Estoy aquí, Mami."

As people file out at the end of visiting hours, the room grows colder. Crowds of people are the norm in this country. No one seems to require much personal space except for the overworked doctors, who can be seen backing away out of rooms, separating themselves from the anxious relatives who surround the beds of their loved ones and always have a thousand questions. There are always several conversations going on at once; bedside vigils are a sort of social occasion and family reunion for people who may not have had a reason to be in the same room in a while. I notice that there are also a lot of spontaneous group prayers. It is a Catholic hospital where political correctness doesn't apply—if you don't want crucifixes in the hallway and a rosary placed by your bedside, go somewhere else. Here even the nurses mouth the words to an Ave María or Padre Nuestro if they have to change an IV during a prayer session, and they always offer a blessing to the patient before they leave the room, *Dios la bendiga*. As the woman in the bed on the other side of the curtain is being prayed for, Ángel and I wait for the *amén* before moving or speaking. The prayer leader, who turns out to be an evangelical preacher of another faith, falls silent at the end of his impassioned impromptu sermon to allow the Catholics in the group to conclude with the Act of Faith, the

Credo. *Creo, creo, creo.* I believe, I believe, I believe. He comes over to offer my mother a blessing. We bow our heads to him, offering my mother's situation to Providence, unless Dios feels she has a greater duty to us on earth. I have an impulse to wake her so I can remind her that she certainly does have a duty yet to fulfill, one of many, but one that is very important to my daughter and me: we want her to meet her *biznieto*, Tanya's little boy, given a name that both sides of the family, Spanish- and English-speaking, could pronounce—Elías—so that Mamá Fanny, as Tanya calls her, could say her great-grandson's name with ease. John and I chose "Tanya" for the same reason. My father, just learning English when I was born, had insisted on naming me Judith. It comes out "Joodit" on the Island, or even "Hudit," the *th* sound simply not well managed by Spanish speakers' tongues. Elias will come to see you next year, Mami, or we will send for you and Ángel, a vacation in Georgia at our home in the country. You love John's cooking, southern meals made from vegetables grown on our own piece of red soil. And you will fill our home with the smells of your guisados. We will have to go to Augusta to find the right kind of rice and the can of Goya beans—the best we can do for Island foods in Georgia even though they taste of homesickness, of exilio. As you cook on one side of the kitchen, John and Tanya will be making peach something-or-other for dessert. I'll be trying to help with the menial tasks, and everyone will be teasing me as usual, warning me to stay out of the kitchen since, as the noncook, I have nothing to contribute to the culinary chaos except unsolicited advice.

The temperature continues to drop. I huddle in my hard chair, knees to my chest, arms wrapped around them. Ángel tucks the pink blanket around my mother's thin body. I can see the violent rise and fall of her chest, each intake followed by a slight gasp. I look up to see what he's doing as he begins to perform what looks like a familiar ritual. At first I think he is applying medicine to her forehead, but then I see a sticker with a Catholic cross on the little jar he is holding. He dips his thumb in the jar and draws a cross on her forehead while whispering something close to her ear. I see now that he is anointing her with holy water. I don't know why this makes me break down, but I run into the restroom to cry so as not to frighten her or him. I hear her say, "Ángel." And him, "Sí, Fanny, sí."

Her hairbrush, her toothbrush, and a jar of Pond's cold cream are neatly arranged on a shelf in the bathroom. My aunts told me that she had insisted on being helped up to wash and use the toilet a couple of days ago, struggling to walk the few feet from her bed. "I could hear that pitito, a little whistle sound like wind through the trees, as she breathed," one aunt said. I did not inquire further about the *pitito*. I know what my tía was telling me. My mother's lungs are like a sieve now. I cannot bear to dwell on the painful image.

She had been upset by the insertion of a catheter. She knew it meant that she would not be getting up. I am grateful for the fact that she was already only semiconscious by the time they placed the pad, universally called *el pamper* here, under her body. What am I saying? I would be grateful to hear her rage against this humiliation. She was always exquisitely private about her body's functions; I'd hear her turning up the radio in the apartment in Paterson and later in her little house on the Island before she went into the bathroom, ironically announcing what she wanted to conceal. The smell of deodorizers permeated the house. One of the last complaints she'll have, whispered so that only I can hear, is "Tengo que evacuar. Pero no puedo." *Evacuar*, evacuate—a delicate euphemism, a cognate. She has to but can't. She is not eating, so there is nothing in her stomach or bowels. It is only as a last measure, during an impending disaster, that one evacuates. Is she punning? I think not, but she loves language, her language, and making a joke or pun out of life's small miseries is one of her best survival techniques.

Ángel has produced a bedroll and placed it on my chair. He has also put an extra chair borrowed from an empty room in front of mine so I can stretch out. He sits up all night. The next day I begin requesting a sleep chair for him, again and again, of nurses who nod and say, "sí, sí, sí," meaning nothing. I ask until I become what I will be for the next week, that relative *de afuera*, the daughter from outside, who will not follow the unspoken rule that if someone says, "sí, sí, sí," OK, OK, OK, repeatedly to a request, it means maybe, and if you keep asking, we'll make sure it doesn't happen at all. The sleep chair appears eventually. He insists that we take turns on it. I get it most of the time.

"Ay, Fanny," Ángel occasionally says, a lament followed by a deep, dramatic Puerto Rican sigh. I have heard him speak this phrase in different tones many times. The main mode of their marriage has been that she is acknowledged "La Jefa," and he, her bemused and always good-humored lieutenant. Of course it's their show, but it goes deeper. Everyone can tell that he has really enjoyed her take-charge attitude, and his scrambling to do her bidding has been rewarded by the good life she choreographed for them both. Duty followed by pleasure; hard work during the week followed by trips, dancing, and family gatherings on weekends. She'll order him to do something in a mock-military tone, and he'll usually look at her with a big smile and say, "Ay, Fanny," as if to imply that she is asking for too much, but because he is her Ángel, he will do it. It is their marital script. Now his "Ay, Fanny" is painful to hear. Entering the room late at night, I hear him say, "Ay, Fanny, ¿por qué me haces esto?" Why are you doing this to me?

Ángel and I do not talk about her situation, for she can still hear and is struggling to respond. When I said buenas noches and kissed her, she raised her face up and spoke through her oxygen mask, nearly inaudibly. She asked about my brother. I told her he'd be flying in tomorrow. I asked her if she heard me and she answered in the weakest voice I had ever heard coming from my mother, "Sí, Hija." Then she added, between hard breaths, "Tell him to drive carefully. These roads are dangerous." I promised her that I would text him immediately. "Hay peligro," she repeated. There is danger. Even in her direst hours, she remains the concerned, protective mother, Mami. Whenever we travel to visit her she always reminds us of the dangers she thinks we can no longer perceive as "hijos de afuera," children living outside the Island. Never mind that both of us are seasoned travelers; she still worries about the cultural signals peculiar to her *Isla* that we could miss. The roles have reversed and she has become the interpreter of language and culture—my role during her exilio. On her Island, in her native tongue, she is the guide.

I spend the night reading through *Cancer Caregiving A-to-Z*, published by the American Cancer Society in easy dictionary format for the uninitiated, in preparation for my new role as advocate for my sick mother. Knowledge, facts, books, mastery of words—these have always been my weapons and my tools, from my role as child interpreter in an immigrant family to my career as a teacher and writer. "I own English," I would tell myself when in doubt. "Puedo defenderme"—"I can defend myself," the idiomatic phrase used in answer to the question "Do you speak English?" I thrive in what has become my first language, English; now I have to find a way to empower myself in Spanish so that I can talk to the doctors and nurses without falling into the inferior category my mother felt she was placed in when she tried to "defenderse en inglés." She could not defend herself in English because, she claimed, as soon as she opened her mouth, people judged her as "ignorante." Through writing and by watching her successful return to a life in Spanish, I have tried to grasp how much she had given up when she had to make her native tongue secondary. I never thought much about her struggles with language while I was growing up; I thought of my role as her personal translator as another immigrant chore, child labor that set me apart from other kids, who were lucky enough to live exclusively in English.

The first entry in *Cancer Caregiving A-to-Z* is "Anxiety," *ansiedad*. Anxiety is the last diagnosis my mother was given by the specialists, who could not find anything physically wrong with her and suggested she start taking Xanax. As I practice my vocabulary so that I can ask her doctors the right questions tomorrow, I feel the ansiedad, and I understand that a word is not truly yours until it makes its way into your body. I desperately need my Spanish-English dictionary and a Xanax. Suddenly, the first of many alarms I will hear sounds on one of my mother's monitors, and it goes on and on. Ángel has learned to wait for a nurse to come in to replace the IV—he has learned which alarms are really alarms and which signals will be ignored at the nurse's station as not urgent. But my nerves are already rattled, and I decide to practice my emergency Spanish.

Assuming a modest demeanor, I go to the nurses' station, where the night shift is looking pretty worn out, and I address the oldest, kindest-looking *enfermera* in a polite voice: "Por favor," I say, "¿Puede venir al cuatro dieciséis?" Please come to 416? She does not look up from the chart she is reading, and I am silent as I dig around in my brain for the translation of "I think my mother's IV bag is empty" or "Her morphine drip needs replacing." The kind-looking nurse finally lifts her eyes, and I am relieved to see that there is sympathy in them.

She looks closely at me. "¿Eres de afuera, verdad?" She enunciates each word. You are from outside, right? I feel exactly as I did that day when the third grade teacher at P.S. 11 brought me into the classroom and said to the class: "This is your new classmate. She doesn't speak English, so speak slowly and clearly to her. *E-nun-ci-ate* your words so she will understand."

I say, "Sí." I say, "Gracias." I keep myself humble as she follows me back to my mother's room to check all the plastic bags hanging like macabre Christmas tree ornaments from several racks around the bed.

She pats my mother's hand and calls her "Mama," a term of endearment used by many of the staff when addressing older female patients. "Sueña con los angelitos," she whispers to my mother. May you dream of little angels—the familiar use of the diminutive brings images of cherubs to mind. What is in my mother's brain at that moment? Not angels. She moans a little, and I don't know if it's in response to the nurse's attentions or to the renewed drip of medications coursing through her veins.

I say "Gracias" again as the nurse leaves; I go back to practicing my vocabulary.

In the kingdom of the sick, as in the kingdom of the healthy, the official language of survival is whatever those in power speak.

In the last hours of that first night I grow so cold that I feel a need to cocoon myself deep into the sleeping bag, almost in a fetal position. I fall into a stupor; I would not call it sleep. It is like I am in the suspended animation of a deep freeze. I awake when I feel that someone is standing next to me. I think I say, "¿Mami?" but it's Ángel offering me a cup of hot chocolate. He says, "Hija, tienes frío, te traje chocolate."

It may be machine-made chocolate, but it tastes like ambrosia. It is heaven-sent. I feel it going down my throat and into my stomach, restoring feeling in my toes and fingers. It warms me from the inside out, and I am able to sit up to face the day. A tiny figure in white appears at the door. In a whispery voice inflected with a Castilian accent, a very old, tiny nun announces that it is a beautiful day that she will offer to the glory of Papá Dios. She approaches my mother's bed, takes her hand, and asks if she may say morning prayers for *la señora*.

Ángel and I nod our assent, and she begins reciting the Hail Mary and the Lord's Prayer while still holding my mother's wrist. I notice that she is taking my mother's pulse while she prays.

After she makes the sign of the cross over my mother, she comes over to Ángel and me.

"Tenemos que prepararla," she whispers. "Has she had the sacrament yet?"

With a jolt that makes me collapse back into the chair, I realize that the sacrament she is referring to is Extreme Unction, the final blessing the Church will offer a living being.

Ángel says, "Todavía no." He looks down as if ashamed to admit that he has not made this decision for her yet.

I had come to get my mother treatment, to take her home if it meant getting her a private nurse. I was not ready to hear that she needed to be prepared to die.

The nun leaves and the hospital begins to come to life. One of the nurses is singing; they often do that here. There seems to be no rule about singing and laughing outside my mother's room. But there should be. Unable to bear their cheerfulness, I sink deep into my bedroll so I can be alone with my fear.

In the light of day I look closely at my mother's face. I see a look I have recently learned to recognize as the face of a dying person. Her jaw seems to be pulling her face downward, revealing the bones of her skull. I readjust her oxygen mask and try to gently close her mouth. She moans a little. I stroke her head. "Estoy aquí, Mami."

5   *A circuitous journey*

Thirty-six days before I arrived at my mother's hospital bed, John and I had been at our condo in Athens, Georgia, going through the annual rite of belated spring cleaning and childproofing in anticipation of a visit from our daughter, Tanya, her husband, Dory, and their son, Eli. In a few days, we would do the same procedure at "the farm"— our home a few hours away in Louisville, Georgia, where John, his parents, and several of his siblings had built homes on land that had once been the working family farm. We planned to spend most of the summer there, restoring ourselves from the long academic year and watching Eli run around unfettered. Last summer, John had had eight tons of fine sand delivered to the edge of our large pond so that we could surprise our grandson with his own beach. Eli's Beach was a great hit, and we were looking forward to watching him dig and sculpt his construction sites and race tracks again this summer. Also, we had spent all year planning a trip to Disney World with him. At four, Eli is at the ideal age to enjoy the Magic Kingdom, and we were hoping to replicate for him—and ourselves—the delight of Tanya's first Disney experience when she was around the same age.

The phone rang just after the Salvation Army truck had pulled away bearing the previous year's discards, the baby toys Eli would no longer want, the playpen he would no longer need. We needed to come back to the farm, John's sister said. "Daddy has taken a turn for the worse."

C. H., as everyone who didn't call him "Daddy" called him, had been fighting a second bout of bone cancer for several years, and lately his once-razor-sharp scientific mind (he was a health physicist at a nuclear plant before retiring) had begun to fail him. Alzheimer's, we'd learned, perhaps triggered by the many radiation treatments and chemotherapy. The family had made a decision to stop the treatments and bring him home to hospice care. In less than two weeks he'd stopped getting out of bed, but we were hopeful that he'd regain his strength after adjusting to the new palliative treatments. We were educating ourselves in how to deal with his dementia. We had discussed with Tanya how important it was for them to come spend time with Eli's great-granddaddy this summer.

We dropped everything at the condo and drove the two hours back to the farm. We walked into the living room where C. H.'s hospital bed had been set up. It had been placed in front of the large-screen TV where he had enjoyed so many football games, cheering for the Georgia Bulldogs at the top of his baritone voice. We were shocked to find him wearing the face of imminent death. He was breathing through his mouth, his jaw pulled down to reveal his bottom teeth. John and I sat with him for a long time. John spoke softly to him and at one point put his big hand on top of his father's. The two hands were almost identical. I stepped outside to look at the endless field that had once sustained this family. Now it is green grass all the way to the road. Crepe myrtles line the driveway; the house and lot are almost suburban in appearance, although the farm is deep in what we jokingly call the piney woods. But if you look beyond the crepe myrtles, you will see a large, lush vegetable garden. It is a small garden. It can be encompassed in one glance. But you can easily imagine it spreading for hundreds of acres, as it once must have. It is a small plot, but it still supplies all of us with corn, cantaloupes, tomatoes, squash, peas, onions, and the biggest sunflowers I have ever seen. And more, much more bounty than I could have ever imagined a little rectangle of land could yield. You can also find shards of Creek Indian pottery and arrowheads buried in the rich, red soil, reminding us that we are not the only ones to have reaped what we sowed on this land that cannot ever really belong to anyone forever: we are only the caretakers. I have come to love this generous red clay the way my parents loved their inner-city bodegas.

This Georgia landscape—I have described it in my work as "Martian"—is as different from my native Island as any two places can be, but I am now more at home in these woods than I am anywhere else. It has been a long circuitous journey from Puerto Rico to Paterson, New Jersey, to this Georgia farm. A long way home.

C. H. lived through the night. The next day we got the second call, identified by our caller ID as "Dad": "Come now." The farm is big, over seven hundred acres, but it's only a three- or four-minute ride from our house to John's parents' house. He was already gone when we arrived. I could feel the different kind of silence as we entered through the kitchen. It was the silence of a house already in mourning. There in the silence was my mother-in-law, Nita, now mostly blind from macular degeneration but otherwise healthy and clear-headed, seated next to his hospice bed, her hand over his. I saw his daughters dabbing his face with a washcloth and touching him in ways I recognized as the necessary and eternal anointing of the body of the loved one, doing it naturally, lovingly, not as in a practiced ritual. They needed to groom and prepare him to leave the house for the last time. John and I sat on chairs brought silently to us on either side of this big man, and we waited for his hospice nurse to arrive and "pronounce" him. Much hushed activity began behind us. There were relatives to call, the funeral home would need to send a hearse; all these sad tasks were done by the daughters. All I had to do was sit with my husband, who I know was looking intently at his father for all their resemblances, and perhaps because we must confront the death of a parent so we can begin to imagine our own.

After C. H.'s funeral, we went to the church's fellowship hall to eat lunch. We were led in a long prayer of gratitude for his life, and the preacher exhorted all to pray for the bereaved family, and for the family to pray for peace of mind and acceptance. We shared a huge southern-style meal prepared by the church's women. A slideshow of photos the family had chosen ran continuously on the wall in front of us. C. H. as a young husband fishing at the lake with his lovely young bride; C. H. as a young father holding his two sons; a family photo of him and Nita camping with their two sons and two daughters; C. H. in his business suit as a community leader; as church elder; and finally, toward the end, as a gaunt but still-handsome old man, his face showing the stress of years of cancer treatment, smiling with obvious pride at the great-grandson whose thick, curly head of hair must have reminded him of his own. This is an orderly and satisfying timeline. But as a writer I see it more like Virginia Woolf saw it: "I dream; I make up pictures of a summer's afternoon. . . . This how I shape it; and how I see myself."

6 *Black hills, black lakes, la esperanza*

My mother's breath grows more labored. I ask the morning shift nurse when the doctor will come. She shrugs her shoulders expressively as she checks my mother's vital signs and feels the IV bags and tubes. "El doctor will come when he comes. No tiene hora de llegada." Her smile tells me that, like God's will, doctors' schedules are not within her province to predict. But, perhaps noting my anxiety— I feel myself tensing up, I am getting angry, preparing to fight the tropical passivity I know could defeat me if I let it—she adds, "Her doctor is usually good about coming in the mornings. Él sabe que está muy malita." There. It has been spoken by a professional. I heard her say the strange phrase, speak the code, for my mother's condition. *Muy malita*. Suddenly the diminution, the diminishment by word, seems insidious to me. *Say she's gravely ill*, I want to shout. She is not a child, and she, we, deserve grave words at this grave hour.

Instead I remain silent: a sudden knot has closed off my throat. La ansiedad rising. My mother's breakfast tray is brought in by someone who also calls her Mama, entreating her to eat a little. I move between them, letting the orderly know I will take over. *She is not your mother*, I want to say but don't. I depend on these people's goodwill for my mother's sake. I take my mother's oxygen mask off carefully and try to feed her some of the watery oatmeal. "No quiero. No." I plead, "Por favor, Mami, come un poco." But it is obvious that she cannot swallow and breathe at the same time. One of my aunts arrives, the one who has the most experience feeding recalcitrant eaters, as she managed an elementary school cafeteria for years, and she tries to help. She manages to get a little juice into her, but no more. The manual said that the patient would lose her appetite due to the effects of medication, or if the disease had spread to any part of her gastro-intestinal tract.

When my brother arrives, he has to make his way through the relatives already surrounding the beds of both patients in the room. I tell her that he is here, and she says, "Lo sé." I know it. Her agonizing rise from the semicomatose state she is rapidly descending into is hard for me to see. The effort is evident in her drawn face and her hands clutching the bed as she struggles to open her eyes. My brother kisses her forehead. "Estoy aquí, Mami," he says. And she flutters her eyelids halfway open, the most response she can offer. My brother says to me, "Her temperature is good. She is warm." It is the most he can manage to say after seeing in our mother's face what I saw: the cold is coming. She has always hated the cold. Winters in the United States had always depressed her and made her homesick. I remember her looking out our Paterson, New Jersey, apartment windows on many gray snow days, sighing deeply and repeating her mantra of those years: "Si tuviera alas." We knew the ritual. Look out at the sunless day, sigh, repeat: If she had wings, she would fly home to her Island and her familia. For many years, when my father left on his long tours of duty with the navy, Pan Am wings would fly us home, away from the cold, back to her mamá's house for months at a time. She lived for that time in the sun, among young versions of the same people who are now keeping vigil around her bed.

All those bodies help bring the temperature in the room back up to a bearable level for me. The doctor finally shows up when Ángel has gone home to shower and rest a little and has taken my brother with him. The others have reconvened for coffee somewhere else. I believe my oldest uncle has let them know that I need a little time alone with her now that I am beginning to understand the gravity of her illness.

The doctor's youth startles me, perhaps because my mother is seventy-five, but I expected her to have an older physician. He is friendly, almost affectionate in a fraternal way. He tells me my mother was one of his first patients when he took over a practice from an old doctor. He had arrived in our pueblo fresh out of medical school nearly twenty years ago. That would make him younger than me by at least a decade, but not young enough to be my son. I find this calculation oddly reassuring. I won't have to put on my maternal authority cap with him; perhaps we can reason as fellow professionals. He says, "Venga conmigo, señora." Come with me, using the respectful *usted* in addressing me. We are negotiating for mutual respect here. He is leading me toward the room where we will view my mother's X-rays. I feel myself slowing down, my feet turning into the cliché of "lead weights." He says, "Your mother told me about the books you have written. She brought me a copy of your novel. She is very proud of you." Despite his generous chitchat, I am in the fog of dread. The X-rays are hanging in front of the light screen. They look like the etchings of an old edition of Dante's *Inferno*. Black hills, black lakes. The doctor prompts me with a light touch to come closer.

I cannot quote his next words exactly, but they include "fast spreading," one of two types of lung cancer, most likely small-cell. When I hear the word "small," I express the hope that this means less deadly, perhaps treatable. No, small-cell is the cancer most often caused by cigarette smoking and known to spread to places like the liver, quickly. There are clear indications, the doctor said, that this fast-spreading *fuego* in my mother's body has reached her liver. Spreading like fire. He sits down in front of a computer and offers me a chair. I am glad to anchor myself to the cold, hard plastic.

I drag out my basic medical Spanish and ask him about treatment options, *tratamientos, quimioterapia*. In my confusion, I have failed to note that he speaks English, as most doctors have studied in the United States. What can we do next? He stares at the X-rays for several seconds too long. Her condition is grave. He repeats it in Spanish, with more emphasis: *Su condición es muy grave*—two cognates, I note, my brain irrationally turning to the revelations of language at a moment of dread and confusion—he informs me in a more professional tone, leaning back in his chair, perhaps hoping to avoid a possible emotional breakdown on my part. "Señora, I recommend that you speak to the pulmonologist, who will decide if we can safely do a bronchoscopy." His tone is strictly professional now, discouraging doubts or questions. "We cannot determine exactly the type of cancer she has until her lungs are biopsied, but it is a risky procedure, as it involves anesthesia, and she is not strong enough to breathe on her own. You should also talk to la doctora." I do not get her name, but my heart lifts a little—hope, a female doctor in the midst of the male-dominated medical staff here. It'd be good to talk to a powerful woman at the hospital dedicated to Mary, Queen of Heaven, but run by men. The doctor, placing hands on the back of a chair in a gesture of finality, then asks me if I want to tell my mother that she has cancer or wait until the other doctors have determined whether to do the procedure that would confirm which kind. He has been telling her that he suspects it is a serious case of pneumonia. It is up to her husband, my brother, and me whether to tell her the truth, as her doctor believes the news may send her into unnecessary emotional distress in her final hours.

"When can I see these doctors?"

But my mother's doctor is already on his feet, on his way to his next patient. It is a nurse who answers me. "The doctors don't have a set schedule for their rounds. But la doctora is usually here in the evenings, sometimes as late as nine o'clock."

"She works at nights?"

"Yes, la doctora is a busy woman, with practices in several towns."

Back in the room I find my mother's three sisters, her older brother, Ángel, and my brother. I motion for them to come out to the hallway, where I tell them about my meeting with the doctor. It is her older brother who suggests that we wait to tell her about the cancer until she gets the confirmation from the doctors. We will have to explain the bronchoscopy.

"Let us not deprive her of hope." He has been fighting prostate cancer for several years and tells me how receiving the news, hearing the word *el cáncer*, had made him so sick he'd had to stay in bed for days.

My brother is less sure that this is the right decision. Always a pragmatist, he says, "Even lung cancer patients have a chance of survival." Like me, he has been on the Internet, looking up statistics, words he can repeat to my mother at the proper time. "In some cases up to five years."

We take an informal vote and decide in favor of *la esperanza*, hope.

Back in the room, I see that my mother seems agitated. She asks for me. "¿Qué dijo el doctor?" She somehow knows I have met with her doctor. *Pulmonía*. I tell her that lie with as much conviction in my voice as I can manage. But she shakes her head. Leaning close to her, I hear her say "vacuna." I ask her to repeat it. Ángel explains what she is trying to say.

"Your mother knows that she had the pneumonia vaccination not too long ago."

I feel *la esperanza* leave the room like a doctor trying to avoid questions, like the hope-announcing angel called to another bedside. My mother has reversed roles on me again. She is insisting on reason even as I weave a fantasy around her, trying to swaddle her in it, to keep her safe and warm for as long as I can. It is not just for her; even as I speak words to her that include future plans of what we will do when she is well, I feel a lifting of my spirits that must be similar to what the devout feel after intense prayer. It is a sort of self-hypnosis. You must say *I believe* again and again, until you do.

7   *The way my mother walked*

No one can grasp the suffering of another. I tell myself that as a writer I should know this. As a chronicler of my family's life, I am inventing as much as recollecting. My early poems are an attempt to experience my mother's loneliness as a young woman in a strange country, to make a metaphor that will transmit her emotions.

> Alleys
> Made her grasp my hand teaching me
> the braille of her anxiety.

When I was a child I was aware that her dark beauty made others look at us in a way that frightened her.

> She was the gypsy queen of Market Street,
> shuttling her caramel-candy body past
> the blind window of the Jewish tailor
> who did not lift his gaze . . .

Her exotic allure would embarrass me as a teenager, when I cut my wild black hair short and sprayed it close to my skull so as not to resemble her.

The wire contains its energy, but it is not the electricity. My images for what she represented to me grew more complex with time as I kept trying to keep pace with her personal evolution. But as geographical and cultural distance separated us more and more over the years, and because I could not truly tap into her mysterious inner life through my words and imagination, for many years I failed to see my mother as a whole, complex being and idealized her as both Mother and Homeland in my mind and in my work.

Now, as I watch her leaving me, I make a commitment to try to meet the demands of her/my culture as a form of penitence for my failings. It is true that I have given her things, have helped her financially, and that I love her, but somehow I failed to prove to her that she could trust me with the truth about her illness. Apparently she thought she had to hide what she knew would disturb and hurt me. Even days before I arrived, my cousin told me that my mother, already in the hospital for almost a week, had begged them not to alarm me. "She is a busy woman. She will be uncomfortable here. You know how it is with children who grow up afuera. She will hate it that I'm not in a private room." And it hurt me when I heard these things. My mother had believed that I had become so used to American luxuries and American ways that I would not "adjust" to suffering in my native land. And so I have resolved to learn to suffer in Spanish.

I know, and have been made aware in indirect ways by family, that my place is by her side either all night or all day, preferably all day, to greet her visitors respectfully and to let them see that she has a dutiful daughter. This is not spoken but is offered as a question: "Who is staying here tonight? Ángel, she calls out for you in the night, maybe it should be you?" (In my paranoia I consider whether she wondered that in the case of emergency my Spanish would fail me. I forgive you, Mami. I wonder that too.) And, "I believe some members of La Legión Americana will be dropping by tomorrow. Certainly they would like to meet you. Your mother gave her compañeros many of your books."

I greet the old ones who knew my father in times so distant that the scenarios they describe seem made-up, but I listen hungrily even as new wounds open when they tell me that my father—the psychically and emotionally wounded warrior, the distant and unknowable, mostly absent Papi, now dead for thirty-five years—was once a promising athlete, president of his high school class, so articulate and intelligent he had been considered a natural for a public life. Why couldn't I have known that golden boy? I remember my father as a man hurt and almost defeated by a life in the military that had ultimately sapped him of any joy he may have once had, and by lost dreams; he is the painful absence in my life and my work. I both rejoice in and am hurt by each memory. I let the images of my mother as a beautiful young girl and my father as a promising young man overtake me, filling in for my as-yet-unformed grief.

8   A field of azucenas

A *comadre* of my mother's, my brother's godmother, comes to visit on a day when I am looking at the old photos I put on my iPad. One of them is my parents' wedding picture. I have written about this photo, as it intrigues me. They both look like children playing "wedding." My mother is not quite sixteen, and my father is eighteen and wearing his graduation suit. My mother has a petulant expression, her mouth in an obvious pout.

> The tiara is crooked on her thick black curls because she has bumped her head coming out of the car. At her side stands my father. . . . He is holding her elbow as the photographer has instructed him to do: he looks myopically straight ahead since he is not wearing his wire-frame glasses. They are posing reluctantly.

I pass the photo around, and a round-robin of tales about the wedding day makes the room come alive. Most of the stories I have heard and written about. But the comadre adds her narrative. Everyone cooperated so my mother could have a nice wedding, although money was scarce, she tells me. La comadre had led a group of girls to a field of *azucenas*, lilies that grew wild on a pasture owned by the American director of the local sugar refinery. They had gathered enough to make a beautiful bouquet for my mother. She points at the flowers woven together and trailing beautifully like a musical scale from my mother's hands. "It took us hours to link them together!" I had not known many details about the day but had dared to write the essay anyway, blending my mother's memories with my imagination. This is the nature of time to me and, I think, to anyone obsessed with narrative: one image fills the hours, expands, becomes a poem, a story, a novel.

As I listen to the constant Spanish chatter around her in the hospital, I think about the bubble of silence my mother inhabited in her *exilio*—how she craved Spanish and insisted we speak it at home. At least in Paterson there were others in the barrio she could talk to on the rare occasions that she left our apartment. (Father, who had become more and more vigilant as his depression deepened, had curtailed her outings to walking us to and from school, plus a few hours of grocery shopping on weekends while escorted by a family member.) There was the bodega, the "Spanish" beauty salon, and Sunday Mass delivered in Spanish by the Chinese priest who had been assigned the barrio as his foreign mission, his version of castellano, Castilian Spanish, as hard to understand as the Latin. There was a growing community, and that must have given her hope.

9   *No se habla español*

When I was between the ages of two and fifteen, my family shuttled back and forth between Paterson, New Jersey, and Puerto Rico. Our annual migration followed the patterns of my father's tours of duty with the navy. When he reported for overseas duty at Brooklyn Yard, we boarded the airbus for San Juan, where relatives would be waiting at the airport to drive us to our pueblo of Hormigueros, all the way across the island. I did not think of my mother's loneliness much in those days. I was busy negotiating a difficult life between two cultures and two worlds myself, totally involved in my own childish concerns. I hated always being the new kid in class. I was the Puerto Rican kid in the Paterson schools and the gringa on the Island. It was not a multicultural America in those years; it was black-and-white America. We were called "Spanish people," not Hispanics or Latinos. We were all lumped together as Spanish speakers, no matter our country of origin. Not white and not black, we were not counted in the struggle for civil rights. And because we didn't officially count, especially economically, we were not acknowledged in a variety of crucial ways. It was difficult for my parents even to get the foods they wanted—no ethnic sections in the supermarket. It was almost impossible to get Spanish-speaking professionals to help us at hospitals and law offices. *No se habla español* was the unspoken message. Everything was hard, hard. For my mother, even the simple pleasures, such as hearing her own language on television, were denied. I think about this when I flip through the three hundred cable channels now and note the large number of stations dedicated to the explosive Latino demographic; even the tiny Georgia town where we live has several Mexican restaurants, and the drugstore carries Spanish-language magazines.

My father's brother and his family lived in Paterson, and we socialized a little with them. But my strongest memory of my mother in those years is of her reading the romance novels she sent me to buy at the drugstore, while listening to Daniel Santos's heartbreaking boleros on her suitcase-sized portable record player.

When we moved to Augusta, Georgia, in 1968, her isolation became almost complete. The "Spanish" community there consisted mainly of a few Puerto Rican soldiers and their families, stationed at Fort Gordon, and my two uncles, also military, who had relocated with their wives and children. Papi had brought us to Augusta at his brother's prompting when riots and civil unrest were threatening to overtake Paterson, as they had Newark. The move, which was supposed to be temporary, was a traumatic shift for us. To me, it felt like moving from Earth to Mars—and I was an English-speaking teenager by then. How must it have been for my mother—more like a move to another galaxy?

We watched the moon landing in our living room in Augusta, and I remember her shaking her head in disbelief, or sympathy. I didn't ask. Was she thinking about the desolation of being so far from home, perhaps seeing her island as distant as the little blue marble above the silent, colorless landscape? I didn't ask. I had my own problems as the foreign girl, the dark child with a New Jersey–Puerto Rican accent, starting my sophomore year at a school where the all-white population was about to be forced to accept black as an alternate human color. But what was I? I stood outside both tight circles, feeling invisible. That first year in Georgia, I began to understand my mother's loneliness.

My favorite reading for pleasure is popular brain science and medical histories. I am not scientifically trained, but I want to understand how the mind and the body work or fail to work, as specifically as possible. As a sort of substitute for faith, I have stockpiled scientific facts about how we perceive the world, how we navigate our bodies like ships in a rough sea at night, trusting the compass of our synapses and senses—which of course sometimes backfire and sometimes break beyond repair. During my childhood the explanation of life's mysteries was God's will. "Si Dios quiere," God willing, is a phrase I constantly heard as an automatic reply to statements of potential or possibility. If a person of faith declares a wish or plan without adding the disclaimer "Si Dios quiere," the closest available believer will say it for her, thus saving the dreamer from offending God.

Recently I saw a documentary on time perception and time distortion. The sense that time speeds up or slows down according to our engagement with it is real only in our minds, but what is real in your mind is strictly your reality. For me, the following week in the hospital next to my mother is made up of two distinct experiences of time: first, that the days feel more like weeks, and each hour passing is an entire cycle, each image examined so thoroughly that I seem to be reliving the experience rather than just hearing words; and second, that I am being cheated out of time with my mother. I desperately want a few more weeks so I can make up for wasted or lost days with her, so I can hear her voice again, beginning a new story or a different version of an old story.

At her bedside, I have learned that story assuages grief, and it also grants the chaos of our emotions some shape and order. As much as it hurts me to listen to the stories of my parents as young people full of vigor and potential while seeing my mother lapsing deeper into unconsciousness, I accept the bottom line of my own life as a writer: that story is as necessary to my survival of these anguishing days as language was to my survival as an immigrant child. Even as I watch my mother become more and more distant from the lives around her—eyes turned inward, the synapses in her brain firing less frequently, and, I imagine, the memory banks in her brain slowly erasing themselves—I am doing what I have been preparing all my life to do: listening again to the old stories and committing them to memory in order to preserve them. I am still doing my work in terms of what I have come to believe defines immortality. Being remembered.

I don't know how I came to English. One day I didn't speak it, and then I did. In my mind it came to be a confluence of need and fear—the forces that drove us in those early years when we could not enter the mainstream without fear of drowning—and my brain took possession of my language of survival. The butterfly effect in chaos theory, from what I understand of the concept, seems to me a good metaphor for what must have happened. In a poem I try to make sense of the mystery of a time when

> I could not speak English
> and so was totally alone.
> Words in the new language
> were simmering in my head
> like bees trying to communicate
> salvation through dance.
> My life was chaos
> shaped by chance, biology,
> and either *el destino*
> or circumstance. I did not know
> or care then
> that I carried the coded message
> to make language from pure need.

10 *Like God's own thunder*

At C. H.'s deathbed, Nita called him "my sweetie" and began telling us, in a low voice and in the tone of a prayer, about the romance that had started over half a century earlier when they were both teenagers. He had pursued the tall, green-eyed Irish girl—a Lauren Bacall look-alike, she had been told many times—and "pestered" her by sitting at a table in the hotel café where she waitressed until it became obvious that unless she agreed to go out with him, he'd drink that bottomless cup of coffee during all her shifts day in and day out. She talked in a low voice about how simple their wedding had been, the honeymoon in Savannah (I had seen the pictures of the movie-star-beautiful couple, he tall and dark with curly black hair, and she a long-legged, radiant strawberry blonde), and how impatient C. H. had been for a baby.

"Honey, we were so young and naive, we thought I'd get pregnant the first time, you know . . ." She smiled, leaning across her husband's body toward John, the much-desired first baby. "We didn't have to wait for long."

She told the story of her long marriage and the births of each of her four babies as though it were the first time and to a new audience. I knew that this long marriage, like any other passionate relationship, had had its shares of troubles and woes, and I was enthralled by how a final leave-taking can blow away the storm clouds and leave us with a sunny day. I wondered whether this need for total amnesty was also a function of our aging brains, the mellowing one hears about. I sat at my father-in-law's side watching the power of story wrap this family like a blanket. No one interrupted the narrative until the hospice nurse arrived, all business, with her black bag to check pulse, heart, respiration. My youngest sister-in law told her what time she believed he had stopped breathing.

The nurse stated formally, "We will accept this as time of death," and logged it in her black book. As simple as that, this big man—whose brain contained eighty years of information, of knowledge and experience, and in whose face so like John's I measured the gradual progression of time and saw how my husband might look in twenty years, in forty, in sixty, and in whose lap my daughter and

my grandson had snuggled—the loving and attentive "G
would say, pausing before finally uttering "Granddaddy
nounced" by a near stranger, gone away from us forever

Someone called the preacher. A young man caugh..
work in jeans and a T-shirt who had to be asked by my sister-in-law
to please remove his muddy work boots at the door, he was visibly
shaken by the news. He sat down, and after a prayer and a blessing
over C. H., he told the story of how C. H. had made a prophecy for
his life one day after church services. C. H. had waited for the young
man outside to tell him that it was obvious he had a calling, for he
exuded a love of God and his fellow man. C. H. said he should consider answering the call. "Until that day when I heard this man speak
to me in that deep voice, like God's own thunder, I had heard the
calling but had not felt worthy of answering it," the preacher said. The
two men had become companions in charity work, running the food
pantry and helping the needy. They had sung together in the choir,
and eventually the younger man had entered seminary with C. H.'s
help and had become a preacher.

"Here I am today because of Charlie Cofer and our Savior." The
preacher stayed until the hearse arrived. The children, the wife, and
the little foreign girl whose "Spanish" accent had always amused
her towering father-in-law were there to say good-bye. The foreign
woman was now part of this southern family by osmosis. The men
from the funeral home, sweltering in their black suits, asked the
preacher if he wanted to lead a prayer. We said the Our Father holding hands around the deathbed, and then we each kissed C. H.'s face.
The older of the two men asked us to please leave the room while they
loaded him into the hearse. Prayer, protocol, ritual. It was all obvious
to the believers. The Book of Life was one I had not read in years.

"For thine is the kingdom, and the power, and the glory, forever
and ever. Amen." These are words added by King Henry VIII to dis-
tinguish the reformed Lord's Prayer from the Catholic version. In
John's Methodist and Baptist family, they were always part of the
prayer. But I had automatically stopped where I had been told to stop
by the nuns at my Catholic school, where we had always stopped

in Mass. No matter how long I am away from my country and my native tongue, I carry the signs, the symbols, and the grammar within me. *Por los siglos de los siglos.* Forever and ever. Amen.

II   *Dream of los angelitos*

One morning at La Concepción, the little nun catches me weeping and offers me what she has: "¿Un Rosario para tu madre?" Would I like her to say a Rosary for my mother? I am reminded of the official definition of a Catholic Rosary: a long series of repetitions, ten Hail Marys, called decades, followed by Our Fathers, interspersed with *alabanzas*, Glory Bes, and credos. I remember saying them as part of penitence in my teenage years; they were given as punishment by the priest on hearing about all the black spots I had put on my soul in any given week between confessions. But before I can say, "No, gracias," my aunts arrive and need no prompting to dig out their rosaries from purses and lower their heads. *La hermanita* begins the prayer while holding my mother's hand with her left hand and counting the beads with her right. I look at the little sister as she chants in a hypnotizing Castilian-inflected Spanish, observing her as she leads the prayers: a plain woman, not ugly, just plain as a rubric, a sketch where the lips are two thin lines, the eyes lively but small, the eyebrows etched lightly, almost invisible. She is perhaps in her seventies or older. She sways a little on her rubber nurse's shoes, and at least twice she has to pause to breathe deeply. I try to imagine this woman's life and how she can do this all day, every day, in the name of a God that sent so many into darkness and despair, seeing the evidence of his work in these rooms. In my mind, I see a shy little girl in a Spanish village full of pious people, a little nondescript girl who was loved for her kind spirit but was never called pretty. Perhaps this *niña* learned early that goodness and service could replace the attention she would never receive for her looks. But this thought is too ungenerous of me. This little woman, who makes me feel tall and robust although I am only five feet tall and labeled "petite" by those who do not want to call me very short and small, has an energy that I can attribute only to her sense of being a tiller in God's fields. Maybe I can no longer grasp how identity may be forged out of faith and piety, how it happens—this total yielding of ego in the service of something greater. I will later embrace the *hermanita*, a fragile bird in my arms, and tell her how much she has helped me get through the agony of this week.

I find myself swaying a little, too, after the prayers begin to lull me; although I fight it, this false sense of calm induced by chanting the repetitions makes me feel like an infant being sung a lullaby again and again until her mind goes blank and she begins to "soñar con los angelitos."

12 *The Ouija board answers*

Later that day, when I am urged to take a break, I take my iPad to the hospital lobby, where I can tap into the Wi-Fi, and I look up "lung cancer" on WebMD. I read through the stages of what I understand to be my mother's diagnosis of Small Cell Lung Cancer (SCLC). I read, with a sinking heart, how we may have already gotten past all the treatment stages to the one they call "watchful waiting." Nothing left to do except palliative care. But still, we could do something.

For comfort I turn back to *Cancer Caregiving A-to-Z* and use my iPad like a Ouija board, letting my finger tap on any entry while looking away. I get G, Grooming and Appearance. To the patient: "Caring for your appearance can help you feel better about yourself. . . . Looking your best can help you feel more confident and in control." To the caregiver: "Help the patient keep a supply of favorite toiletries, lotions, and grooming supplies on hand."

Later that day, I am told that the oncologist is making rounds. I post myself near the door. A nurse points out a young woman with long dark hair coming down the hall: "la doctora." La doctora looks about Tanya's age, which is old enough to have made it through medical school and a residency, but not much more. I go up to her, bold enough to block her path. I ask her if my mother is one of her patients.

"I have reviewed your mother's files." She does not offer any more. There is that silence that means "Don't you know? Do you really want me to say it?"

I embarrass myself by choking on a sob before I pose my question. "What can be done?"

"I do not recommend any radical intervention at this point. I spoke with the pulmonologist. He agrees that a bronchoscopy might do more harm than good. It would just confirm what is becoming more obvious by the day. Metastasis. The cancer seems to be spreading to her liver."

"How long?"

"It can be days, weeks, or months. I do not think it will be months. She may go into respiratory failure anytime. Her husband and you will have to decide if you want to take measures."

"Take measures?"

"Intubate. Resuscitate. It is a family decision unless she has a living will."

I must look sick because she takes my elbow and leads me to a chair outside the room.

"Do you need anything?"

"No, gracias." Why would I need anything other than for this to be a scene in a sentimental novel? I would turn the page, skip these tear-jerking parts, maybe put it down altogether. I hate sentimental books. I hate the trite. I hate how I am turning into a blubbering fool in front of this serious young woman. I have always disdained pity, the kind of self-pity I am now wallowing in.

After washing my face in a hallway bathroom, I go back to the room and call Ángel, my brother, and my oldest uncle out of the room.

"It can happen anytime. We have to decide whether we want to sign a DNR order or whether Ángel has other ideas." Ángel begins trembling so hard that my uncle puts an arm around his waist. My uncle whispers something to Ángel. I make out the word "entubarla."

Ángel finally speaks in a pained voice, "I will not let her suffer if there is no hope." He looks at me for confirmation.

"No hay esperanza de recuperación." As I enunciate the foreign sounds, I feel as if I am pronouncing her dead. I feel a series of locks clicking shut inside me. I am checking my emotions into compartments, making ready for the realities I will soon face. From the corner of my eye I see the white habit of the little nun pass by and not enter my mother's room. Esperanza, leaving.

13 Listen

The last time my mother visited our home in Georgia was for Tanya's wedding in 2005. Tanya wanted a "country" wedding. I jokingly explained to her that I'd have to import our Puerto Rican relatives, and soon found out that I was right—no easy task to get people from the Caribbean, Washington, D.C., Chicago, and elsewhere to the piney woods of Georgia. I asked my mother to bring a sister along so she'd have at least one other person besides me to talk to. She and my aunt arrived in Atlanta and visited us at our little condo in Athens before traveling down to the farm. It had been so long since my mother had been back that she was surprised by the obvious presence of Latinos in the area. We showed her the many Latino businesses and restaurants. She loved watching the telenovelas in Spanish on Telemundo, one of several Spanish-language channels I could offer her. I asked her what she had watched all those years ago when we lived in Augusta.

"Pues, Hija, I watched el *General Hospital* and *The Guiding Light*. I could understand what was happening even if I did not always know what they were saying. People suffer the same in any language." I ventured that she learned some survival English from those soaps. When I say this, she smiles. It is her maybe so, her *quizás* smile. That look. *Listen*, it means, *listen*. And

The words come to me in rhythmic gasps
that mimic passion . . .
el amor, la vida, la tristeza.

She and my aunt admired the campus of the University of Georgia, especially the giant magnolia trees and beautiful landscaping. I felt a sense of pride showing them the place where I came to work every day.

Although a hurricane passed through on the day of the wedding and all the guests had to be walked under umbrellas from their cars to the lodge, it was a wonderful day. My mother looked healthy and vital. She danced with the young people and was pleased when the band switched from "Play That Funky Music" to a salsa number.

During the week she and my aunt spent at our home, John cooked her favorite southern dishes, and we sat for hours on the front porch and took walks on the land. We looked at hundreds of old photos and recalled our early days, both the bad and the good, in Paterson and Augusta. She said she was glad to be a tourist in los Estados Unidos now. The only bad memory I have from those few days after the wedding is of the distinctive smell of cigarettes early in the morning, when she'd go to the porch alone to have that first smoke of the day.

From my mother's perspective, the United States seemed to have transformed, but those changes are, of course, neither unilateral nor abiding from generation to generation. The country has not been declared officially "multicultural." Instead, it is like a beach in the morning—each day it is a new place, new offerings on the sand, from perfectly articulated shells to broken pieces of glass. Some will be declared treasure, others detritus; and sometimes even the discards are declared treasure or at least collectable for their potential future value. I allow myself this objectification of the immigrant because I see it in news reports and images all around me. There's the commercial featuring a Latina college grad who overcame much adversity and has now been grabbed by Procter & Gamble for its labs—a shiny copper penny, a true twenty-first-century American dream. Never any advertisements featuring the parents, slightly darker, smaller versions of their children, their clothes not quite right. No one who looks like my mother in her late thirties, wearing a matronly housedress outside our house in Augusta, watering her plants; no one who looks like my father under the hood of the Rambler station wagon on which he performed the equivalent of organ transplants to keep it going year after year—so upsetting to me, my parents in full view of any of my high school friends who might drive by! The little house, the first they had owned, was transformed into una casa en la Isla on the inside: crucifix on the wall, a print from Woolworth's of Da Vinci's *Last Supper*, knickknacks (*miniaturas*) my mother collected with every trip to Puerto Rico, and the turntable always playing what I considered sappy love songs in Spanish. I never brought friends home. After school I hid in my bedroom, which I had tried to decorate with pages clipped from teen magazines and posters of the Doors and of places I wanted to visit someday: Madrid, Paris. I'd stay in my room and study so that I would not be like them. And I did become the immigrant poster child. I got the scholarships and grants and degrees, and one day I woke up to realize that it had all been because they had allowed me to reject them as models and to objectify their lives. This is how the immigrant story goes. I turned the page, and it was all written in English. I could read and understand the stage directions, and I knew my lines, but my mother could not. Her script had been written in Spanish and she was bound to follow it.

Belonging is a choice. I think it is a subcategory of the now clichéd term "assimilation." Assimilation does not interest the parent who is serving her children. She does not need to belong in a foreign land; she needs only to nurture her children into a different life. This is not an outdated concept. Only a couple of years ago, we got to know the Chinese owner of one of our favorite restaurants in Athens. Her daughter waited on our table and recognized me as a professor at the university where she was getting a business degree. The mother wanted to meet us and the daughter timidly brought her over. In her halting English the older woman told us about how she and her husband had moved to Athens and bought the restaurant, and how they were staying until their daughter graduated. They had spent five years in a place so foreign to them that she had kept a poster of the UGA mascot, Uga the bulldog, decorated with a green derby for St. Patrick's Day, hanging on the wall all year, along with a Christmas wreath of lights. They were, she thought, the symbols her customers wanted to see. John and I always tried to sit at the Christmas booth. It was our designated spot to meet. When we saw a "for sale" sign on the restaurant we asked her why they were selling. Joyously she told us that her daughter had finished school and they were moving back to Taiwan. They had given their brilliant girl an education, allowed her to choose the culture she wanted for her life, and were now returning to a place where they would not have to struggle to belong. This is a different kind of American dream, and not many get to live it.

I relished the days my mother spent in the new Georgia. We took her around to see the "multicultural" sights but did not ask her to move back, although I missed her and wanted more than the few weeks each summer we spent together. Even though I could have helped her enjoy a much higher standard of living than she had on the Island, her quality of life here could not compete with her life there, surrounded as she was by family and friends, living in a place that she could easily navigate, where she did not have to apologize for her strange ways. By dislocating her to a "better" situation, I would have been dooming her to the "not belonging" status again. I did not ask her because I was afraid she would agree, for me.

Many aspects of the immigrant's life have without a doubt improved, but not all. An article in the *Atlanta Journal-Constitution* on the subject of pedestrian deaths in Atlanta haunted me for months until I wrote a poem about it. The article claimed that it was mostly "Hispanics" who were struck by cars while attempting to cross major highways. The statistics showed this to be the case in many southern states experiencing a huge surge in their immigrant populations—because immigrants either could not get driver's licenses or were too poor to own cars. The article told about a Mexican woman who was crossing the highway in Norcross with a toddler by the hand and a baby on her hip when they were struck by oncoming traffic. One of the boys was killed. The young woman had been trying to get to a pay phone to call her mother in Mexico.

In recent years I convinced my mother to get a cell phone, for me, so I could reach her anytime, anywhere. When I was a child, she could reach no one, nowhere. Eventually we got a phone in our apartment, but long-distance calls were reserved for announcements of serious illness or death, or to tell her mamá to expect our arrival. But soon after we moved to Georgia, my father had received a medical early retirement from the navy, and the time between our trips home to Puerto Rico grew to years. Her sojourn in Augusta was, I believe, the loneliest time in my mother's life.

14 *Cálmate*

I called her soon after C. H. was pronounced dead. It took many rings before she answered, and her voice sounded weaker than I'd ever heard it. I heard her labored breathing. I asked her if she was all right, and this time she didn't claim that she was. The tremors and *la taquicardia* were bothering her the most, she said, but she could tell by my voice that I was upset so she asked me if something was wrong. I told her that we were waiting for the hearse, and she spoke her usual mother-language, "Cálmate, Hija." She spoke words of condolence to give to John and his family and told me that I must be strong for Tanya, whom I would call next. This was the last real conversation I would have with my mother. The next time I called her, only a few days later, she would be in real distress. I would hear the wheezing and would demand that she go straight to the emergency room. She would never walk out of that hospital where I had sent her.

15 My mother is sinking deeper into a semicomatose state. She occasionally raises a hand in the direction of her oxygen mask, and I jump up to adjust it, although it doesn't need adjustment. I start fantasizing that my mother is trying to tell me something, and I hold her fingers in case she wants to signal me. I look for any signs of wakefulness. The last full sentence she will utter, "I have to evacuate," sends me into a frenzy of activity. I clear the room of relatives. "She needs privacy," I tell them. I send Ángel for a nurse. "Please give her something so she can empty her bowels," I plead. The nurse shakes her head. My mother has not eaten anything solid in days, has nothing to "evacuate." But the nurse agrees to a suppository. I step outside while she turns my mother over like an infant, avoiding the sight of my proud mother, naked under her thin gown, exposed and vulnerable. As I wait, I read the Buddhist website on death with

dignity that I bookmarked but have been avoiding. It details the signs of approaching death, explaining how the muscle spasms of the dying person are one of the first stages toward the shutdown of the body's systems. I read about the gradual falling into a deeper sleep, and the apnea that will signal the final moment. It is called Cheyne-Stokes respiration. I am surprised it has a name. I regret it has a name that I will now sit for hours next to my mother repeating—*not-yet-Cheyne-Stokes, please let it not be Cheyne-Stokes todavía no*—like a spell against death as I watch her chest rise and fall more and more violently. There will be an increase in the rate of breaths taken toward the end. Final breathing will involve the rib cage. I will begin to feel dizzy as I fall distractedly into rhythm with her breathing. I will place my hand on her chest as I did on my child's when she was agitated in her sleep, trying to convey calm by my touch.

The Buddhist site recommends a calm presence by the side of the loved one. I have never been a calm person. I channel calm by hearing her last entreaty to me when I called to tell her about my father-in-law's death: "Cálmate, Hija." I will listen to my memory for that voice again and again in the painful weeks ahead. "Cálmate, Hija."

The priest comes by on the third day when I'm in the lobby taking a break, looking up strategies for achieving inner peace, and so I miss the rite of Extreme Unction. While my mother's soul is being prepared for departure, I am looking at more old photos of my parents, and specifically at a poignant one of my mother at sixteen, holding three-day-old me in her arms. Her father hovers behind her, watchful, as if fearing his young daughter might drop the baby. Still pudgy from her pregnancy, she holds me like a package she is offering someone—perhaps her husband stationed in Panama, a stranger by now who was not present for the birth of his daughter, whom she knows he wants to name "Judith."

In another photograph my brother is a toddler in my father's arms. My mother looks beautiful and elegant in a feminine dress and ankle-strap high heels. She holds my hand. I am looking away, outside the frame. My foot is turned outward and I have my fingers in my mouth; I am obviously missing being the center of attention. My father looks happy. He is smiling. This is unusual. But it is a time of new beginnings. He has left the army and will soon join the navy when he sees that there are no real prospects for him on the Island. But for now, he is planning a future, maybe even one that will not involve an exilio. This would account for my mother's look of contentment. My brother was born in that rare interval of hope.

I can count the few times I saw my father smile a real smile, not the social smile he put on for others. He smiled when I got accepted to college. I remember the day clearly. He stood almost at attention as I read the letter of acceptance. He smiled and nodded. Yes, this is what he wanted for us. I know I must have made him proud at times or disappointed him in many ways over the years. I don't really know, because he and I never talked like my mother and I talked. We had polite exchanges.

I never asked him about his other life in the navy, nor about his medical early retirement, although I knew it had something to do with his nervous breakdowns, the last big one resulting in months spent at St. Albans hospital in New York. He didn't let my mother go see him or take us to see him. On visiting days, his brother went and reported back to her. She seemed to accept it as she accepted his long tours of duty. Always, "Your father is away. He will be back in a few months." I must have known it was an unusual situation, but the arrogance of youth is such that whatever did not immediately involve me, I simply accepted. I did what she told me to do by rote, unquestioning. I followed orders. I did the errands I was sent on. In those days of my father's decline, at an age as young as maybe ten, I was sent to the "candy store" for a package of L&M cigarettes at least once a day. I remember paying twenty-five cents for a pack. She'd give me a dime to get myself some Little Debbie chocolate cupcakes or chewing gum. I didn't mind the trips to the candy store.

Our father always purchased copies of our schoolbooks when we had to move back to the Island for longer than a couple of months. He'd have us read to him and he helped us with homework. This I remember well. He was good at science and math. In the navy he had been a boiler engineer, working the day shift in the dark underbelly of the USS *Chilton*, an old warship. My first poem about him contains the image of him rising out of the dark:

> and only flesh and blood when he rose from below
> the waterline where he kept watch over the engines
> and dials making sure the ship parted the waters
> on a straight course.

It was the loss of the light of day, the life underwater in the dark, that brought on what my mother always called his "tristeza." An immense sadness, a loss of his vitality, his hopes for himself. He was also a victim of the genes passed down to him by an alcoholic father. Many things outside my limited perception of him shaped my father into the great absence in my life. I walked outside his dark aura, afraid of being sucked into the black hole, in fear of the contagion of *la tristeza*. I did not want to know about his life because I was young and selfishly involved in my own. Later, I saw how much of him there is in me: the darkness like a tumor inside me waiting for any calamity to trigger it to multiply like a cancer and consume my joy of life as it had his. But while I was young and healthy and happy, I did not honor his illness; his lifelong depression was an affront to me. I saw my childhood opportunities for carefree enjoyment as having been sacrificed to his tristeza. How could we laugh when he sat silent and distant in a chair, sometimes for entire nights, waiting—for what? For the wolf in his head to stop howling? He was as distant and cold as a marble statue when he went inside himself. Now, sitting at my mother's bedside, I understand his need for solitude and silence because I am in need of it myself. I have always retreated to regroup, just like my father. But as a child, I tried not to think about his strange ways, and after I graduated from high school in Augusta, when they told me that he had a job offer back in Paterson, I actually felt relieved. I could pretend to be a normal college freshman without my parents dragging me down with their neuroses and their constant struggles. *La lucha*, Puerto Ricans call their life's challenges. I wanted to be free of the sight of their *luchas*.

What I didn't know then and didn't ask was that he had taken the job to help with my college expenses, and that it would finally push him into total darkness. He became the night watchman at a dismal warehouse for a denim factory. In a failed story I tried to redeem myself by claiming for the narrator something I did not have the chance to do: to value his humble work because he was doing it for us. He led a

life of graveyard shifts as a security guard in cavernous warehouses, guarding gargantuan bolts of blue denim cloth no one man could lift . . . meaningless labor, he liked to say. But in the future his daughter would assure him that he had been the keeper of the cloth that would become the symbol for legions of New Americans parading in their blue denim uniforms of change.

During the two years he worked the night shift in that unheated, dismal place, he sent my brother and me a significant portion of his small paycheck by telegraph. Every week I went to the Augusta Western Union, and there it was, not much, but enough so that I could buy food and more while I attended my first year of college. I did not know that his mental health was deteriorating all the while, and I didn't ask. Eventually, I had to do the only thing I know to do as a writer: try to imagine my father's life of service, try to forgive myself for wanting to live free of the burdens of obligation that had shortened my childhood as the eldest child of immigrants. I felt entitled to enjoy the beginning of my American life as an adult.

16 *A continuous thread*

C. H. was taken to the small funeral home in town. The family and their preacher greeted the sedate line of visitors. Tanya, Dory, and Eli arrived in time to meet many diverse people whose lives had been touched by C. H. Eli asked why Great-granddaddy was sleeping in a box. John carefully explained that Great-granddaddy had been very sick. But Eli had been sick before, and the doctors had "fixed" him. Dory and John took him aside to talk about how old people sometimes get too sick to be fixed. Eli started crying and asking for his mommy and daddy. He wanted both his parents to hold his hands. Eventually he said he did not want them to get sick. Long talks followed about what "old" and "too sick to be fixed" meant. I sit here now, in the cruel country, helpless as a child, watching the tumult in my own mother's chest, and I understand how unfair this must have felt to Eli, how frightening.

C. H.'s viewing was a tableau of different levels and styles of grief. John and his siblings were sad but had expected this loss, so there was a sense of acceptance that I felt as I stood next to John in the receiving line. The line led to Nita, sitting by the head of the coffin where her "sweetie" of sixty years lay, peaceful, as if asleep. She did not weep openly but graciously thanked each person for attending, listened to their remembrances of her husband, and nodded her head. She smiled at the stories of her Charlie, who had loved life and had touched many lives in that small community. Any rancor in their long marriage, any lingering dissonance, all was now to be buried with him. She spoke of him now in a tone she must have used in the first years of their romance. In a side alcove, the grandchildren, all adults, gathered with their children. From there sobs could be heard, as well as the squealing of the little ones playing on the floor. The grandchildren were not in a mode of acceptance. Granddad had been there for them, always. Visits to the farm were to them symbolic of Christmas and summers. Tanya and her cousins were disconsolate, and we all took turns sitting with them, doing what we could to comfort those to whom this death meant the end of childhood. Losing a grandparent is like learning there is no Santa Claus—the part of us that wants to hold on to the symbols of a carefree time in our lives is suddenly faced with the end of innocence.

At the funeral, on a white-hot summer morning in Georgia, C. H.'s casket was lowered into the red clay he so loved. Eli asked, "Why are they putting Great-granddaddy into the ground? Where is he going?" which made Dory, who was a pallbearer separated from Eli by the casket, look at his son with such dismay and sadness that it brought me to tears. John was holding Eli, and I heard John whisper, while gently patting Eli's chest, "Great-granddaddy is going here. He's in your heart now." I saw my smart but still literal-minded grandson frown a bit, the metaphor hovering just a bit beyond his grasp. I could almost hear him posing the next question, "How is Great-granddaddy going to fit there?" But he didn't ask the question. He watched with a worried expression on his face as his father, along with other relatives, helped maneuver the oldest person he had known during his three years on earth, so old that doctors could not fix him when he got too sick, into the ground.

In the days that followed the burial, we grieved, but we also worked hard at the task of restoring life to a more normal course. Eli kept us busy. Every morning he'd run around the house getting ready for play at "Eli's beach." His antics gave us a reason to smile, but his preoccupation with Great-granddaddy's fate worried us a bit. He'd occasionally stop his play—which he took as seriously as a job, usually a messy construction job, building roads on his sand hill—to ask, "Why did they put him in the ground?" Either he finally got the idea of "He is in your heart," or he got tired of us repeating it. But then, out of nowhere, he began to ask, "Are Mommy and Daddy going to be put in the ground?" We decided that it would be good to follow a plan we had made earlier in the year and take Eli to Disney World. It would distract him and us. His sense of wonder at everything was a hook for me and John—we wanted to feel this surge of wonder again, a feeling we had once experienced through Tanya.

We planned to go in July. We had the tickets and the hotel reservations, but only days after the funeral, I took the call from Puerto Rico. "Está malita" was said several times in a portentous tone, meaning, *Come quickly, she may be dying.*

17   *The reluctant quinceañera*

"A woman writing thinks back through her mothers," wrote Virginia Woolf. I have used that quote as an epigraph to various pieces I have written about my grandmother and my mother, and I have mentally added my own words to it: "and forward through her daughters."

The news that my mother was critically ill devastated my daughter. My parents had taken care of Tanya from birth to age two and a half.

After my father's death and my mother's return to the Island, we had sent Tanya to stay with my mother for weeks at a time, to experience the culture and learn the language. Tanya had bonded with her, although now it had been years since they had seen each other, as Tanya had been busy with her new marriage, new job, and new baby. My daughter's was an angry sorrow—she hated herself for postponing the trip to see her abuela, and now it was too late to introduce her to Eli. Tanya is a mathematician; empirical evidence, the facts, are as crucial to her as words are to me as a writer. She immediately wanted to know what had caused the cancer, why it had not been diagnosed earlier, and what her treatment options would be. I had to tell her that I suspected cigarette smoking as the cause, and I did not know yet what options we had.

"How could Mamá Fanny do this to us?" Tanya felt betrayed by my mother's smoking. She used words in English to ask the same question I would hear Ángel ask my mother. "¿Por qué me haces esto?"

All I could do was hold my daughter that night when I had reopened the wound of her grief. I consoled her as best as I could while at the same time asking myself the same question about my mother. If you knew that you were poisoning yourself, would you still choose that cigarette over breath, your life, and a future? Addiction to the nonaddict seems like a choice, a vice to be overcome. To this day, I have no way of knowing the power of it. I continue to try to understand.

I have been writing and thinking back through my mother all of my adult life. As much as my father sacrificed his own dreams for us, I have never been able to imagine myself as him nor fully empathize with him. This is unfair, and perhaps it is as simple as gender, but I think that the truth lies in my fear of becoming like him. I have always known that I have a propensity for depression, that pessimism is my natural mode. I pass for a vivacious Latina. The darkness is known only to those closest to me, and I am fortunate that my family understands and sustains me. I am lucky they are not as afraid of my dark side as I was of my father's. After I emerged from the years of adolescence when I wanted to be nothing like either my mother or father, and particularly after the birth of my daughter, which was also when I began to write poetry, I started to see and envy my mother's resilience, her ability to inhabit the moment.

She and I have talked about her years as the middle daughter in a family of eight, how she loved volleyball and hated becoming a *quinceañera*, which in those days meant announcing your status as a potential wife—nothing like the social extravaganzas of today's young Latinas, but a serious passage into adulthood. My mother said that when she turned fifteen, she began her training in domestic functions such as childcare and cooking, which didn't interest her, and she was not allowed to play ball again.

> My dolls have been put away
> like dead children, in a chest
> I will carry with me when I marry. . . .
> I am wound like the guts of a clock,
> Waiting for each hour to release me.

18 Omens

Everything in my mother's house, in which I wander as if it is the living museum of her, seems ominous and deeply symbolic to me late at night as I begin to say *adiós* to her. I find an unopened Amazon box with the latest books I had ordered for her, a biography of the Kennedys and the life of Eva Perón. My mother transformed herself into a fiercely political person on her return to the Island, working at polls, sometimes all night, during elections, and actively recruiting members for her organization, *Mujeres Progresistas*. Progressive women. But she was also totally immersed in the Kennedy romance, as were many Puerto Ricans of her generation—the great Catholic president who had been martyred. On her desk, she still kept the store-bought framed photo of President Kennedy in front of which she had placed candles and a rosary at the time of his assassination.

I think that I might bring the books with me to the hospital so I can read to her and practice my Spanish at the same time. But there are always others around, and reading has always been so private an activity for her that she often went to her bedroom to read. I remember seeing her reclining luxuriously in her pillows while totally immersed in a book. Now if only she could just hear me stumble through the Spanish. For the first time ever, I want her to correct my pronunciation. I can hear her laughter in my head, the chuckle she reserved for my verbal gaffes. *Far-MA-cia*, she would correct me, not *FAR-ma-cia*.

How I wish reading had been her worst addiction. In *The Emperor of All Maladies*, Siddhartha Mukherjee details the shockingly difficult process of establishing a cause and effect between tobacco and lung cancer. Because smoking was so prevalent and widespread among all classes of people, even medical researchers were reluctant to give up their smokes. The joint commission appointed by President Kennedy and his surgeon general to establish the link between smoking and lung cancer was described as "split exactly five to five among non-smokers and smokers—men whose addiction was so deep that it could not be shaken even when deliberating the carcinogenesis of smoke." There were always ashtrays filled with cigarette butts on the tables where they met. And these were the best-respected men in their fields; the best minds could not shake their need to inhale the very poison they were defining and identifying.

There is one ashtray in my mother's house. It is the one she carried with her to have her cigarettes. I realize, with a painful jab in my chest, how she must have hidden it. In our early homes both on the Island and in the United States there had been many ashtrays. Both parents smoked, our infrequent visitors smoked: no need for stealth.

My mother's only area of denial and secrecy has been her smoking habit. We could talk about almost anything, except her smoking. We could even discuss subjects as contentious as the virgin birth and the mysteries of the sacraments and the resurrection—endlessly, until I gave up, my last word as I exited the room, *superstition* (another cognate). We could talk about almost anything, but a mere allusion to her smoking would make her clam up or, at best, offer her "Ya casi no fumo." I have almost quit smoking. I know Ángel treaded carefully around the subject, as her ire could be devastating. I am guilty of failing to pursue the subject. I justified it by the fact that I had so little time with her during the year, and she did not smoke heavily when I was there to see it—or maybe she just hid it very well.

Her doctor told my oldest uncle that he could not have revealed to the family what he had repeated to her year after year because of confidentiality laws, and he never saw Ángel with her on the occasions of her yearly physical. Ángel admits that she would tell him to wait outside or send him on an errand, although on all other medical appointments she expected him by her side. The doctor said that in the last years he had detected "áreas sospechosas" in her lungs, suspicious areas that usually indicated precancerous tumors, and had informed her. She had responded, "Pero si ya casi no fumo." But I have almost quit. I know that my mother can guard secrets and memories like a dragon sitting on its gold. I also know that Ángel would not have insisted or probed: her smoking was foremost among the topics that elicited her ire; disagreement with her political views came second, and Catholicism third.

My mother lived her early adulthood, the years when she was most energetic and most beautiful, in a bubble of silence and solitude, yearning for her home and her language. To bear her exilio, she turned to her two private pleasures: reading and smoking. One of them would keep her mentally alive, full of ideas, hopes, and dreams; the other would turn her insides black, slowly spreading like mortal sin, spotting her organs like those outlines of three hearts the nuns once gave us in catechism class. The sisters had told us to leave one of the three hearts blank, for that was a pure heart, the heart of a person with faith; in the second heart we were to draw many black spots, one for each sin we thought we were still carrying inside us, not yet confessed or absolved; the last heart was to be all black, the heart of a person whose soul was riddled with sin. I do not want to have this image return to me. I do not want to think of my mother's lungs turning black. I turn to my books to read about the black tide rising within my mother so that I can understand this wrong she committed against her own body. Was it worth the hours of comfort it must have afforded her during her darker days? It wasn't a crime or a sin; it was her guilty pleasure, something she did for herself and to herself. Who am I to judge her?

By the third day, Ángel and I have agreed on shifts at the hospital. During my time away from the hospital, I struggle to sleep and instead spend hours wandering around the rooms of her house. I begin identifying the objects I remember from my early life, the days when I was growing new skin so I could rush out of my nest in the sand and plunge into the bountiful American sea. I see the store-bought, massively reproduced (seen in countless Puerto Rican homes) print of a handsome young Jesus knocking on a door. It is now on her bedroom wall, though in New Jersey and Augusta it used to hang somewhere more prominent. I see the painted conch shell from Capri that my father sent her during one of his tours. I am dismayed to see that there is a little ash in it—a late-night cigarette in bed? There are ceramic dogs with gold chains on their necks and an elephant with raised trunk (for good luck); there is a Madama, a black woman cloth doll, no doubt a gift from a Santera—my mother saw no contradiction in keeping these symbols of other religious practices and her Catholic faith. In the extra bedroom she used as an office, library, and catch-all are a worn Bible and other religious books on a little desk, and there is a bookshelf with a collection of my books and several scrapbooks of family accomplishments from birth announcements to graduation programs and wedding invitations. In her backyard is a plaster statuette of Mary that had been a permanent fixture in her mother's yard. It was moved to her garden from her mother's patio after my abuela's death. Year after year I have watched it sink into the soft earth that my mother watered constantly for the sake of her many plants. The badly deteriorated statuette is now in the middle of some home repairs. Ángel has spray-painted her mantle blue and her robe white, but her face is discolored and chipped, and she is missing some digits. "Tenemos que salvar a la Santa Madre," my mother had joked last year—we have to try to save the Holy Mother. I now see Mary-in-repair as symbolic of my mother's reinvention, not as the Holy Mother, for she was anything but a saint, but as the fragile woman with a steel frame who rose above the pull of others' designs and expectations, and who managed to find her true self once she was back on her own soil. Over many long months she oversaw the transformation of her little plot of land into her dream of home. How could any of us know that a clock was already ticking? I wrote about her in a lyric piece I called "The Aging María."

The Queen of Heaven is aging on a Caribbean island, sustained only by the collective memory of her one year of living dangerously, and the still popular assumption that glory clings to her presence. Her new smile may be the irony created by loss, the real revelation: she is beyond repair. Yet year after year a tiny crèche is placed before her in December, as if her arms could still hold a child, although it is plain to see that her fragile fingers are chipped at the tips and broken at the joints. In fact, all that is unsustained by cast or mold has begun to fall away. Still, year after year, she stands firm in my mother's garden. In crepuscular light, her still regal form acquires a certain luster, the yellow patina of age briefly turning to a luminous gold, as though she were lit, as she is, from within.

I see the note by her telephone, the phone number of a funeral costs insurance company, and I hang on to it as if it is an important clue left for me to find. When I ask Ángel about it he says that it is something she had been paying into for many years, and she was in the habit of making notes about everything she needed to do. This is something I do too. My students and family laugh at the number of sticky notes I have all over my office, on the covers of books, the dashboard of my car, my dresser mirror. But I am living by omens and symbols by now, so these little scraps of paper begin to take on immense weight. Why are her shoes lined up in front of her closet, and why is everything folded so neatly on her shelves? She has never been a domestic goddess. She insists on cleanliness but is not a slave to neatness. Ángel says that in the last months she had wanted a big purging of closets and storage, but this was not unusual. Over the years I had gotten into the habit of sending her at least one package of clothes, shoes, and other gifts almost monthly, and more for her birthday and Christmas. I knew she loved dressing well, and it was my pleasure to buy things I thought "looked" like her. I wanted her to have clothes and shoes people would notice. I knew she liked to say, "Mi hija me los envió." And her house is small, so every year she had a great giveaway to female relatives and made donations to her church. I liked knowing that she could now do this, be generous with others, for during our Paterson and Augusta days clothing money usually was spent frugally on my brother and me—although she and I always did a lot of window-shopping, even in the early, lean days.

I have memories of our walks in downtown Paterson, especially at Christmas, and of her love of beautiful clothes and shoes. We always got new clothes at Christmas and Easter, so the shopping excursions preceding these special holidays involved many hours of comparison shopping. She loved the days when she had a legitimate reason to look slowly through the racks and for both of us to try on outfits. The final selections would be modest in appearance and price, but those days taught me how a woman living through a gray winter may dream in color, and how it is style rather than cost that finally matters. I loved the fashion shows she put on for me, loved seeing her in fancy party dresses she did not intend to buy and extra-tall high heels she knew would be completely out of the question. She was a beautiful woman, and her fantasy choices were Puerto Rican extravagant to enhance her dark looks, her curves. But they were a fantasy, and even as a child I understood that we were just playing dress-up. I recall our postshopping celebrations of chili dogs at the Woolworth's counter, followed by a chocolate malted for me and coffee and a cigarette for her.

We didn't live in poverty; we lived cautiously on the outer edge of lower-middle-class status. We had doctors when we needed them, and we could pay our rent, even if not always on time. But extras were a rare privilege. For instance, my mother and I could not both buy new dresses on the same shopping trip, and while I never thought this meant we were poor, I know it's why I have indulged her in clothes over the years. As I take inventory of my mother's life, her closet reveals to me that she no longer lacked for beautiful clothes. Her closet is like one of those department store racks she so loved to go through, replete with outfits in the tropical colors that looked best on her *café con leche* skin. I count thirty-seven pairs of size five shoes, all in a neat row, like troops waiting to be inspected or deployed.

In her elegy for her husband, *The Year of Magical Thinking*, Joan Didion writes, "Survivors look back and see omens, messages they missed. . . . They live by symbols." In my mother's house, I see more and more signs that she has been preparing to leave. Or perhaps I am imagining this in retrospect. She has arranged her bookshelves so that all the mementos of my brother's and my lives are organized, almost as if she expects us to be picking them up soon. She has our report cards, yearbooks, and a scrapbook for each of us containing newspaper clippings, reviews of my books and of the plays my brother acted in, of every little accomplishment or event worthy of being recorded in print. Every notice or clipping I have sent her over the years is taped to a page and dated. She has separate albums for pictures of my family and my brother's. She has my books on one shelf, all signed to "Mi querida madre," several of them dedicated to her and Tanya.

Yes, I believe Virginia Woolf is right, a woman writing may think back through her mothers. Between my tiny mother and my tall daughter there is a vast distance; yet the daughter with a Ph.D. in mathematics and the grandmother with a minimal education were still so tightly bonded that the last time we talked, when she told me to be calm and strong for Tanya, my mother called her "mi nena," my baby girl. And Tanya showed her affection in areas where the vast chasm of worldviews between them seemed cosmic. I remember a conversation when Tanya was a student in physics and mathematics. My mother was telling her about my father, who she said had come to her after his death. This topic, deeply felt by my mother, that the dead are nearby and accessible, inculcated into her by her Espiritista parents from childhood and as important to her as her Catholic faith, always caused rifts between her and me. I feared that Tanya would eventually be driven away by my mother's superstitious beliefs. Instead, I heard my daughter say gently to my mother, "I wish I had known him," and soon they were laughing together over memories of Tanya's control over my father as a toddler. He became totally malleable in her little hands. But by the time she was two and a half, he was gone. I have discovered that Tanya is much more tolerant of the strangeness of superstition because it is eerily familiar to her as a scientist in an area of mathematics—a field so abstract that it comes to resemble the supernatural realm, at least to the mathematically challenged like me; even in hard science there is a theory of time travel. And in theory, the past and the future exist, working in the same way as the present. I heard a physicist say that the future is already there, and we are merely stepping forward in time to meet it. Ghosts and wormholes. I get to witness my mother and my daughter meeting in a special dimension, beyond time and space. I live in the wormhole between them. I do not believe in ghosts, and I do not understand quantum mechanics, but they, my mother and daughter, represent the *was* and *will be* of my timeline.

19   I am looking for a way to connect what Eudora Welty called "the continuous thread of revelation" of my mother's life in every word I read, every object I see or remember, every photograph that has even the most minimal remnant of a memory of my mother. I am trying to inhabit my grief fully so that when she is gone, I will eventually think of her without an overwhelming sense of loss. I know I am still aboard an avioneta on my way to the cruel country that Barthes claims is the state of mourning. I know I haven't even arrived yet. My mother's presence feels insistent in all her things in her house, yet across town she is slipping away. I must find a way to comprehend that fact. I must learn how to manage my pain and make good on what she has left me—not these things, but that insistent energy.

    I look for that continuous thread and know I must not get lost in the frayed loose ends, the sequence of misfortunes that rattled and shook our family from the start and that have recently fallen upon us like cluster bombs. Instead I have to find the one golden thread that, through my mother, holds our tapestry together: her ability to hope is the quality I want to have inherited. I want to know how she maintained "la esperanza," how she knew that one day the winter of her exile would end and that she would lead the life for which she saw herself destined. For she was no hopeless dreamer. She was a persistent, sometimes angry dreamer. When my father argued with her about how our erratic travels to and from the Island were unnecessary and harmful to our education and sense of stability, she remained undeterred and packed our bags the minute she heard he was to go on a tour of duty. Despite our tantrums over saying good-bye to the always-new friends and once again clearing out our lockers, this was the deal at the heart of their marriage: She would stay in Paterson while he was working in Brooklyn Yard and able to come home on weekends, but once the absences extended longer than a month or two, she had the right to take us back to her mamá's house. This arrangement was fine, and better than fine, while I was still too young to have forged the emotional ties of adolescence, but it drove a wedge between my mother and me later on. Only when I began to write about the days of back-and-forth travel did I begin to understand that her ability to cope with life in a country she would never accept as her own depended on these periods of diving back into her Island culture like a new convert at a baptism. She kept the hope alive that when our father retired, they would go back together to the Island. And with this hope, she was able to remain at my father's side even as his pervasive despair cast a black shadow over her insistent light.

20 *The albums*

One of the old photos I have on my iPad is of a group of my Island playmates posing in the middle of what looks like a park, with a hill rising above us and with palm trees in the distance. Standing close together in a sort of cluster are eight children between five and eight years of age, including my mother's youngest siblings—an aunt who is only two years older than I am, and my uncle, one year older—my brother, and three neighbor girls, one of whom was my closest friend. The youngest in the picture, I'll call her M, will visit my mother in the hospital. Now a dignified matron, she is still easily recognizable as the pretty girl in the picture, with a wide smile and lively eyes. She was the girly-girl in our group. In the picture she is wearing a frilly dress with crinolines and white shoes and socks; I don't remember ever seeing her in the usual play clothes of the day—"pedal-pusher" pants, a T-shirt, and sneakers. When I show her the picture, she smiles, agreeing to my assessment of her as the princess. Then she points to her older sister, my best friend in those days.

"You know she died of breast cancer," M says. I have a vague memory of this. My childhood friends and I lost touch a lifetime ago. My mother surely mentioned it, but the words *cancer* and *death* did not resonate with me then as they do now. I express my sadness to M at hearing this but shut down my electronic photo album. I do not want to talk about death in front of my mother. Later I will ask M for the whole story; later I will be hungry for stories of inexplicable illness, needy for the parallel narratives that will comfort me in my misery. I will then open myself up to the company and the tales of fellow sufferers so that I can stop myself from asking, "Why her, why now, why me?" I will nod my head and pretend I understand the constant reliance on blind faith. I will hear again and again about a God who takes and takes: *God took my sister at fifty-two, my daughter at twenty-three, my son when he was a teenager.* . . . It is always *lo que él quiera*—his will, his right. I will have to swallow this placebo and hope it will work on me as it obviously has on so many.

As I look at this picture of us in that field, a series of associations come to me that may seem paradoxical but are really an alchemical compound made up equally of lead and gold. The "field" where we played was really a fenced-off pasture that belonged to the American sugar processing company. At the top of the hill stood a large white house where the American company manager and his family lived behind a grove of palm trees. *La casa grande* was fenced in and screened in. Many sugar-mill towns had a big house where an American family lived, usually the manager of the plantation and refinery, called the *centrales*; at that time only those houses had mosquito screens. We hung mosquito nets over our beds but lived with windows and doors thrown wide open, as if in the belief that mosquitoes waited until nightfall to strike natives. I never questioned it, but as children *de afuera*, my brother and I learned to live with a layer of calamine lotion over the exposed parts of our bodies because mosquitoes, our playmates told us, mocking our fake-pink faces and arms, liked the fresh meat of gringos best and could identify us by our foreign paleness and the smell of insect repellent.

The pasture was accessible from my grandmother's house through a dense area of plants, trees, and vines, where guavas and banana plants grew wild. Making our way through the vegetation, we often stepped on a magical kind of grass called morivivi—its scientific name, I learned recently, is *Neptunia plena*—that folded into itself when you touched it and then came back after a while. Resurrected. At the top of the hill was a gigantic mango tree with limbs as thick as most trees' trunks. It had huge knots at its base where the women sat to embroider, have coffee from a Thermos, and watch us play.

We called the tree *el barco*, the ship, and we managed to lower a huge limb down over the hill so some of us could sit on it while others made it sway—a feeling that, to this day, I find beyond compare. It was not a carnival ride; it had not been constructed by adults. It was the pure product of childhood imagination and effort. We were allowed to tumble and roll down the grassy hill, and to gather wild guavas and ripe bananas from the unfenced section, but we were forbidden to go near the Americans' house, especially since a huge white horse had occasionally been spotted grazing nearby. But I could see fruit trees growing near the house, and I just knew that whatever was growing there would be like nothing I had tasted before. So one day, when all the children had been sent to the bedrooms to take an afternoon siesta, I snuck out wearing only my underwear (my mother ensured that we would not get out of the house by insisting that we take off our clothes before a nap), and I ran through the woods, past our ship, and up the hillside. All I remember after that is the sight of the horse galloping toward me, and my dash to the nearest exit from the pasture, which happened to be a barbed-wire fence—which I dove through. The gash in the lumbar region of my back sent my mother into hysteria. I was rushed to the nearest neighbor who had a car, and then to the hospital for a tetanus shot. The next day I got a premium spanking from my mother, and I was ordered to sit down at the table and write a letter to my father. My mother wanted me to tell him exactly what had happened. She always feared his anger when something bad happened to us, as he constantly reminded her that her main obligation while she was at her mother's house was our health and safety. I don't remember my exact words to him. But this was my first written story, and I must have made it a contrite one, because a couple of weeks later I received a pair of dolls from Greece, both wearing skirts, so my entire family sat around puzzling out whether they were both females. They arrived in the same package in which my mother received her painted shell from Capri—the same shell in which, fifty years in the future, I would find cigarette ashes.

Back home, I note that near the painted shell on her dresser are several framed pictures of my brother and me as awkward teenagers. One is a picture of me I have always hated. I look like an impostor. I am wearing a zebra-striped shirtdress and ugly pointy shoes, and I'm sporting my new Twiggy haircut. It was taken on the day we boarded the Pan Am airbus for my first trip back to Puerto Rico as a teenager, and on that day I hated my parents. I hated my mother most of all for putting her nostalgic need for her casa and familia ahead of *my* need for a normal life. It will be a bad interlude for us. I will be in full rebellion. I've dressed as outrageously as possible, especially for the flight there, so I can make an entrance at my grandmother's. Once there, I will refuse to follow her rules, refuse to visit relatives with her, refuse to attend Sunday Mass. During an argument over an unchaperoned trip I desperately want to go on—to the beach in the nearby town of Cabo Rojo with friends—I will tell her that she is everything I do not want to grow up to be. I will tell her in front of her mother and sisters that she is a relic and an embarrassment to me; I'll tell her that I hate the Island and the crowded house we live in with her many loud relatives. I'll swear to her that when I'm on my own I will never return.

I remember her tears, her escape into her mother's bedroom, and the hushed women's voices. I knew they were advising her about dealing with me. I remember them trying hard to make peace between my mother and me. I disdained them, ignoring their attempts to talk to me by hiding my face behind a book. I wanted nothing more than to get back to *my* world. I had friends in Paterson, where I was beginning to find my way out of the barrio. All I wanted to do was get back to my almost-American life.

There is an old Polaroid of her taken that year, which in stories I have termed *The Year of Our Revolution*, with thick black hair down to her waist. It's clear that showing its lushness and length was the point of taking the picture. And there is another photo taken later that same year of her in a fashionable new haircut. She kept them side-by-side in her photo album. I am not sure why she cut her hair, and why she did so behind my father's back. I didn't ask her. I know that it caused a loud argument between my parents. Over the years, in retrospect, I've come to find her act symbolic and have tried to discover meaning where there may be none. All I know is that she never wore her hair long again, and a year later I started to let mine grow long and wild, and my brother did the same. It was the sixties, and the Beatles had invaded America. Shaggy was in; my father's crew cut was offensive in my eyes, a sign of his subjugation.

For the next couple of years, I plugged myself into my transistor radio and stopped talking about anything of consequence with my parents. The same neighbor that took the instant photo of my mother's long hair also took one of me. In a poem I tried to use the photograph to reconnect with the fifteen-year-old who, like my mother as a quinceañera, was wound like the guts of a clock, waiting for each hour to release her, although it is only now, at the moment that I write these words, that I connect my mother to me at around the same age. Writing transforms. And on the page, it is always *now*.

I am skinny and brash, thirteen or fourteen,
aware of my bones, of the angles and curves
reforming my skin. I am challenging gravity
My parents are outside the frame, waiting
. . . .
to see if the present moment can really
be captured on film.
—from "Here Is a Picture of Me"

I claim no expertise in photography, but I can feel its strong kinship to writing: developing a moment on the page through the carefully chosen image. Images in a frame, on paper, in the brain, at the moment of death. We live and die with a slideshow in our minds. We don't just *think* of ourselves during our moments of being, we *see* ourselves.

The events in our lives happen in a sequence in time, but time itself is a human construct, an invented artifice, a scaffold to sustain the illusion of order in the chaos. Childhood years, teenage years, early adulthood, and so on seem to fall neatly into a timeline, but as I watch my mother come to the end of her days, memories come to me more like photos in my randomly ordered electronic album. There are pictures of my grandson at birth interspersed with pictures of Tanya as a baby and then as a young bride, and then more of Eli, dozens of Eli, and then the old photos of my brother and me on tricycles in front of our first suburban house in San Juan during the two years my father was stationed on the Island's navy base, probably happy years for my mother, as we lived only hours from her mamá's house. Photos unlock time, they transport: I remember vividly the crazy car trips during the 1950s and early 1960s on treacherous, narrow mountain roads before the American engineers blasted through the Cordillera Central to create the interstate that joined east and west. Photos transport you to places you've never been or can't remember: my parents' wedding picture and the one of my mother holding me as a newborn, followed by a series of new pictures John and Tanya just e-mailed to me from home—Eli on the beach by our pond, Eli and Tanya on the fishing trip John arranged and where Eli learned the fine points of freshwater fishing. Another where they are eating breakfast on our front porch. These are pictures I would have printed and sent to my mother. I fight an impulse to show them to her now, to try to get her to open her eyes, eyes that by now show only a gray milkiness on the rare occasions when she flutters them halfway open. This is how we've overcome space and time for so many years—through photos. In Barthes's book on

photography as memorial, *Camera Lucida*, I recognize my
to keep looking at these recent photographs. I am trying to
family as they experience these days of our separation. Bart
not analyze the photos he writes about; he does the opposi__
to discover the essence of the moment caught in time. What is it that
evades analysis in a photo, that makes one respond as if to an image
lingering from a dream? Barthes looked for the ineffable something
that made his mother her own unique and irreproducible self, and
he found it finally in a photo of her at five years of age. That ineffable
something was, of course, beyond words—a way of remembering
her that would mean nothing to you or me. In fact, the photo does
not appear in the book. Barthes writes, "It exists only for me. For
you, it would be nothing but an indifferent picture." I look and keep
looking at these photos, out of sequence, out of any order in time,
but representing my past, present, and future. I wonder whether her
slideshow has begun, the one all those near-death-experience survivors claim happens as a sort of prelude to the tunnel of light. Which
photos have you chosen, Mami? Please, not the one of me in that
hideous zebra-striped dress, a Puerto Rican Twiggy with an attitude,
ready to use words to hurt you.

At her house I find an album dedicated to photos of Tanya. There
is one of Mami with Tanya at around age five posing in one of Disney
World's improbably perfect flower gardens. She is a young grandmother, still beautiful. Tanya wraps her two little hands around one
of Mamá Fanny's hands. There are also many photos of Tanya in my
mother's modest garden on the Island, learning how to water and
care for the orchids, the hibiscus, and the ornamental palms. Before I
go to bed, I sit in an old wrought-iron rocker that my mother inherited from her mother and now keeps in her pink-tiled carport, and I
inhale the scent of the flowers that she and Ángel cultivate with so
much dedication. There is a white hibiscus plant that is now as tall
as the roof. Ángel tells me that she will not allow him to prune it.
She wants it to grow as tall as it will. It is one I bought for her when
she finally built her little house. It is Judith's hibiscus—*la amapola de
Judit*, this is what she calls it.

21   The next morning—the day before she will die—I see a huge yellow caterpillar making its slow, meandering way from the front yard by way of the carport. It seems to be heading drunkenly toward me. Before I leave for the hospital, I note its progress—only one third of the way to the grass in her garden. I imagine the world from his perspective: a hard surface, vast distance, threatening dark shadow (me) lurking above. Danger. Danger. I make sure not to step on him as I rush out. That night, when I sit on my mother's rocker to sort through the day's fears before trying to sleep, I look around for the caterpillar. I finally locate him at the bottom of *la amapola de Judit*. I hope it will be enough refuge for him.

22   "Her memory depends entirely on me." Barthes made this note in the journal he kept after his mother's death. My mother did not keep a journal except of finances and appointments, and so I do not know how she wants to be remembered. Her memory depends on my efforts now, and I will use the skills I learned not only as translator of language but as interpreter of culture for her, to try to shape her life in my own words and to rearrange words I have already written about her into a narrative of a meaningful life. I have to do this, even if her ordinary life, as Barthes said of his mother, is nothing but an indifferent picture to others, even if "it exists only for me."

23   *A hunger for words*

Life in a large city helps immigrants hide and minimizes the differences, and may even standardize the strangeness in which they live by encircling them with a microcosm of familiar faces and familiar structures. Think Chinatown, Little Italy, Loisaida in Manhattan, Little Havana in Miami, Little Haiti, Washington Heights. Some people live within the circle of alikeness all their lives, never confronting the mainstream or learning English beyond the few phrases they absolutely need to survive. It is especially true for Puerto Ricans, who, having been granted U.S. citizenship at birth, can hop on a plane at any time and go home, even if briefly, to reconnect with their native language and customs. My mother chose to keep and protect her

Puertoricanness and enveloped us in the circle of impermeability she created in our homes. It was easier to maintain in Paterson, where the smell of rice and beans, heavily spiced meats, and plantains cooking, the sound of loud salsa music emanating from apartment windows, and the shouted conversations in Spanish from the fire escapes that became porches in the summer were a cover for even the extreme oddness of my family's life.

We lived according to my father's strict rules of silence and discretion, keeping mostly to ourselves. He went so far as to rent an apartment in the next block, outside the imaginary borders of the Puerto Rican barrio, to keep us at a safe distance from its negative influence. In order to live there my father must have signed a special contract, because we saw no other Puerto Ricans in that block. The apartment building was owned by two brothers who were also the proprietors of a Jewish deli on the ground floor. We had to walk in our socks so as not to disturb one of the landlords, who lived in the apartment below; my mother's record player was to be turned low and not played after dark (a rule she violated as soon as our father left the house for more than a day). Father bought a table fan, which was kept on in the kitchen to dissipate the pungent aromas of adobo and sofrito. We lived as if we were in danger of being caught and punished for violating all the rules of mainstream society. I remember my father's anger after my mother's high heels had made tiny punctures on the linoleum when she forgot to remove them at the door, and how he had replaced the entire living room floor in a fit of anger. We learned to keep secrets then, to trust no outsider with revelations about our private lives. The visits from relatives were strictly scheduled so that the noise level, which admittedly does seem to rise exponentially when Puerto Ricans gather, was kept to a minimum. My father justified our separation from the barrio—one block and a world away—by claiming that it was for our protection, as drunken fights were likelier to erupt in front of "el bildin," the tenement, which I have called a "vertical barrio" in my stories, that was almost exclusively populated by Puerto Rican families. The tenement was like one giant boombox, always tuned to the loud soundtracks of the soap-opera lives of its residents.

Despite my father's concerns, I know that most of the people there were hardworking and law-abiding. They were the people we saw at the bodega or at church. My mother would have been less lonely in that company. But my father wanted to come home to a quiet, orderly home in a quiet building. He wanted solitude, and he did want us to be safe. But I perceived that something was really wrong with him when his normally suspicious nature escalated to the point where he would stand on the street corner to watch us walk the few blocks to school, and he would be there again in the afternoon. He interrogated us constantly about our activities and whereabouts. During his long absences, he wrote letters to my mother that made her frown, and sometimes cry, as she read them. The list of rules for us to follow grew until my only permitted outings were to the Paterson Public Library, to buy groceries, and an occasional shopping trip downtown with my mother. And though my father imposed the rules, it was my mother who received the brunt of my anger during my years of teenage rebellion.

But it was not always like that; I remember the noisy parties we attended at my uncle's house, which was full of teenage cousins who loved to dance and who used me as "cover" for secret meetings with boys downtown. I would ask to be taken for a hamburger at White Castle, and then my older cousin—she must have been a junior in high school—would call her boyfriend from the public phone, and they would hang out just beyond my vision while I was bought off and kept entertained with a burger and a new Wonder Woman comic book. I could always be bribed with comic books, which provided me with an active fantasy life in those days. In my daydreams, I was Wonder Woman instead of the skinny, bucktoothed, bespectacled "Spanish" girl the boys called Bugs Bunny. I envied my two girl cousins their curves and their boldness. But I knew my parameters. Their father danced and sang out loud; mine didn't. Their mother let them wear makeup and lent them her party clothes; I had to pass my father's inspection to leave the house. They had a level of freedom I could only imagine. My parents dealt with our incipient adolescent madness by enrolling us at St. Joseph's Catholic School, where, along with a good education, we got lessons in good grooming. The day I was sent to the principal's office, where Sister Olive took out her plastic ruler to measure the half-inch of bare skin above my knee I had laboriously achieved by rolling up my uniform's waistband, was an agonizing ordeal for my mother. She was called in and lectured to by a nun who treated her as if she were a deaf-mute, acting out her words, pointing to my skirt with the ruler, so that my mother would not fail to understand that I was certainly a Jezebel in the making. I was humiliated along with my mother and swore to myself that no one would ever treat me that way again.

So I rolled my long wild hair into a tight bun, kept my hem at my knees, and waited out my time, trying hard not to be overwhelmed by all the knowledge that was being placed in front of me like platters at a banquet: the nuns were the best teachers I ever had. I hated to admit this to my parents. My resistance was useless; I was a nerdy kid trying to be cool. It was at St. Joe's that I began my long romance with language, and I owe it to one nun who broke the mold, who saw my word-hunger and fed it. With her help, I became a serious reader. Through her I learned that I would never have to be lonely again. In English class and in the after-school Confirmation preparation class, Sister Marietta introduced us not just to the usual texts, but to classical music and contemporary music. She talked about lyrics by the Beatles as poetry and let us compare them to the works of Shakespeare, by asking us what the words made us *feel*. It was then that I began to focus on the one area I knew would save me from life in the bubble: literature. I learned that language, specifically the English language, was my medium. Later I would memorialize my first mentor in an essay as "Sister Rosetta." And she *was* my Rosetta Stone, teaching me to decipher the foreign tongue, showing me how to assert my dominance over the language that I needed to make mine by giving me books to read, books she checked out of the forbidden adult section of the Paterson Public library, and by challenging me to go beyond what was expected of me as the Puerto Rican scholarship kid in a mostly white school. I give her credit for recognizing my need and for feeding my hungry mind. By helping me not be invisible and silent, she helped me change my *destino* forever. I became a book addict then, consuming words without restraint. Never again hungry for words.

24 Word-hunger. This is what my mother must have felt all those years. It is what I feel when I corner her primary care physician after seeing him trying to walk past my mother's room without stopping. I know he is avoiding my questions because it is late, too late for questions, too late for explanations.

With studied patience, he once again tells me that there are no more "recursos" left. That if we want to "entubarla" when she goes into the respiratory failure—which "Sí, te lo aseguro," he says he can assure me is inevitable, considering the struggle to breathe she is undergoing—we needed to let the staff know now. What else do I need to know?

I need to know what she is feeling right now. Are there images in her head? Is her life playing out behind her closed lids continuously like a slideshow? Why do images flood my brain when I hold her fingers, by now unresponsive to my touch, but so familiar, so familiar to me. A friend will say to me, "Whatever life force was in her she passed on to you." This is figurative language, I know, words of comfort to reassure me that she will live on in my memories, *está en mi corazón*. But when I hold her right hand, so small and fragile, I cannot help but relive the times it slapped my bottom smartly to teach me some crucial lessons, and the times it caressed my feverish head and combed and braided my hair. This is also the hand that did not dare to touch my head during those years when I chopped off my hair and sprayed it into a hard black helmet, and when I let it grow long so it would fall around my face like a curtain to hide behind—the curtain that she would not risk parting when I hid behind it, trying to escape those Spanish words she used when she knew I was angry or afraid: *Hija, Hija. Cálmate.*

25 Orar: Teach me to pray

Ora, Hija. Everyone tells me that I should pray. But what is prayer to me now? I still reflexively turn to it in times of stress or sorrow as I was trained to do. And so my lips move when the nun comes to my mother's bedside, feels for a pulse, and tells us we must now pray for her, as she is getting ready to meet Papá Dios. But she does not address the Father; it is a Hail Mary that she says. Ave María. I grew up with the invoked Holy Mother hovering over our days and nights, and I feel the intensity of what sociologists call Marianismo even now. This goddess worship—a term that would cause outrage here if I spoke it aloud—shaped my imagination, as I spent part of my formative years in a town that was formed around the supposed apparition of the dark-skinned Virgin of Monserrate. The shrine, later a basilica, was built in 1590 in the dead center of the pueblo and has been the site for generations of baptisms, weddings, and funerals. Pilgrims come from all over the Island to visit the sacred place of the apparition. The marble statue of the Virgen Morena has her own alcove in the church, an ornate room of intricate carvings and gilded, framed depictions of the dark lady from many epochs. The focal point is an enthroned brown Madonna with the white Child on her lap, dressed in luxurious robes, handmade by devotees. During my childhood, I saw how my mother, her mother and sisters, and most of the other women I knew paid tribute to Nuestra Señora and made "promesas" to her, usually for the safe return of sons, husbands, and fathers. The "promesas" often involved wearing nunlike habits for months or years, or in the case of my paternal grandmother and some of her contemporaries, climbing the rough-hewn steps to the church on their knees during the wars in which their sons were combatants. These women wore the scars on their knees as badges of honor if their loved ones returned from war, or as down payments toward their heavenly rewards if they did not. "Mira," I heard a very old woman say, tapping her knobby kneecap, "my son is sitting next to Jesus and his dear mother, waiting for me."

"Santa María, Madre de Dios, ruega por nosotros, ahora y en la hora de nuestra muerte. Amén." Pray for us Mary, now and at the hour of our death.

I have become a cynic about conversions at the last hour. John and I love true-crime shows and compete to guess who did it. Once the murderer is caught, especially if the murderer receives the death sentence, he or she will most likely find Jesus. Jesus can be found in Death Row, but Mary haunts the rooms of the Catholic faithful. She is the mother who intercedes. Surely her busy son, handling all those calls from repentant sinners, will take the time to listen to his mother's entreaties for the life or the afterlife of one ordinary woman? I want to believe like my mother believed. I would give anything to feel that her life force is not simply draining out into the indifferent universe, following the laws of physics rather than some divine imperative.

I recently saw a documentary on television about scientists who have run experiments to prove or disprove the existence of the soul. Some studies placed a deathbed on a large scale to see if it weighed less after the patient expired, and others positioned high-definition cameras above a dying person's bed to confirm near-death visions as the "soul" or the conscious part of the person hovered above the physical self in a flight to . . . where?

I admit to feeling like the death-row inmate, wanting something beyond the scientific facts.

A resident comes into the room and spends a long time examining my mother. He takes notes; he seems excited. He is young and has an American name. I follow him out of the room in hopes that he has seen something the others have missed. John Charles is his name. I introduce myself. He tells me that my mother's doctor has told him who I am. He is familiar with my university and partied in Athens, Georgia, when he was a student in the United States. To establish rapport, even though my "other" life as a teacher and writer is not my present reality, I talk to him about the Georgia Bulldogs, Athens, and my job. Then I ask him about my mother.

"Did you find anything interesting?" I try to make my voice sound calm, my question seem casual, although I am trembling with the force of my need to hear that it has all been a mistake, that this brilliant future doctor will get credit for discovering errors made by his distracted seniors.

"It's an interesting case," he says to me in a heavily accented English (his name, I found out early in our conversation, was "Americanized" from Juan Carlos by his parents, who hoped that he would attend medical school in the United States just as his father had). "I am hoping to specialize in pulmonology, and this is an unusual presentation of very rapid metastasis."

I don't know what my face shows, but he quickly says, "Lo siento," and bolts away toward the nurses' station. His enthusiasm had been for my mother's case. My mother presented an interesting *case*. I go to the farthest visitor's bathroom I can find and get on my knees. I try to pray, but I can only think of a few lines from the Dylan Thomas poem "Do Not Go Gentle into That Good Night," which I have assigned to my classes many times over the years as an exercise in form. I repeat the passionate words until I feel them as Thomas must have intended, in my bones, until my knees start throbbing with a pain I can feel outside my chest.

> Do not go gentle into that good night.
> Rage, rage against the dying of the light.

26 *Fighting demons*

I wanted my mother to fight for her life. As she always had. I've immersed myself in the language of the war against cancer, and I've concocted a spell against death out of the demonic words that are attacking her: adenocarcinoma, bronchoalveolar cell carcinoma. Begone from her trachea. Begone from her supraclavicular lymph nodes, her hilar lymph nodes, her upper mediastinal lymph nodes, her bronchial lymph nodes. Vanish from her bronchi. Do not enter her body. Metastasize not. Get thee behind us, Cancer. I repeat my chant on my feet with my hand on my mother's head. Any passerby in this pious place who saw me would have thought I was praying, but I was not calling on ángeles; I was summoning her duende, her fuego, whatever its name, whatever its shape, to give her back her will to fight.

To be on your knees is to relinquish your power, to allow someone to stand above you, to bare your neck to the world or the wolf's teeth. It is the position of the victim, the oppressed, the soon-to-be-executed, and early in my life I resisted even the symbolic knee bending required of the faithful. I stopped attending Mass regularly as soon as my mother was out of the picture, when I started college. It was 1970 and the zeitgeist was still infused with the mystical: poetry as religion. Khalil Gibran was discussed seriously around the "hippie" table at the local college I attended. But it was Joseph Campbell's work, and later Robert Graves's, that would affect me the most; although I can barely recollect most of it now, it seemed to be generative to my incipient feminist leanings. The womb, the goddess. Marianismo in a different guise, although I did not connect the two then. I would not have thought of my mother's and her mother's devotion to Mary as similar in any way to my attraction to the mind-bending concept of the all-powerful female that these powerful white male intellectuals were sanctioning. The irony escaped me then. These women who depended on one another for comfort and protection, and when all else failed prayed to Mary, offering her bargains to get them through the worst times in their lives, seemed to me in my sophomoric haze to be passive victims of circumstances they could change through self-empowerment, assertiveness, and willpower. The religion I would practice would be literature, poetry as prayer, and the goddess was in me. I once made my mother weep in frustration by challenging her belief in the Virgin Birth. "Sex," I insisted. "She had sex with Joseph or another man, and the charismatic leader known as Jesus was the result." The more she argued about "la fe," the blind faith that had helped keep her sane through the years and through many personal tragedies, the more I quoted the biological facts of life to her. I sealed my case by bringing in all the powerful minds whose works I had read in my Introduction to the Humanities course, from Socrates to Freud. She rarely let words defeat her, but this one time I had felled her by attacking with the full force of the one thing I would always have that she lacked: a formal, advanced education. It was years later, too long afterward, that I looked closely at my mother's ways of making meaning in her life and recognized my advantage of book knowledge as something I would have to subsume to become an artist. To practice poetry, not merely to quote it, would require a letting go of the artifice of intellectualization and objectification. I had to become more like her to be a poet.

27 *Fighting the restless spirits*

At El Hospital de La Concepción, the name of María, Jesus' long-suffering mother and everyone's liaison, is constantly invoked. But during a visit by one of my mother's friends, I am reminded of the spiritual backup system that many people still practice: Espiritismo, the commonly held belief that the spirit world is entangled with the world of the living in immediate ways. This woman claims that an Espiritista de Mesa Blanca, a medium my mother knew and had visited, had a vision of my mother reunited with her parents, and that she had not told my mother because she had heard my mother was "malita" and did not want to frighten her. I do not encourage this thread of conversation in my mother's room, but it does bring to mind strong memories of my abuelo, the gentle soul whom everyone consulted in times of crisis as one of our pueblo's most trusted and beloved Espiritistas de Mesa Blanca. His "consultations" always took place at a little *mesa blanca*, a table covered in a white cloth where he kept the artifacts of his vocation: a Bible, a crucifix, a bottle of holy water, and a hollowed-out, gold-tipped wooden stick he had carved himself with mysterious words and filled with dirt from his birthplace. It was his most important symbol of power, and no one else was allowed to touch it. Even I, the eternally curious grandchild who dared to look through dresser drawers and wardrobes and borrow his books without asking for permission, even I did not dare to touch his wand. It was what he used as a conduit of calm with grieving women and anguished men, and what he used to draw forth the *espíritus intranquilos*, restless spirits that often entered people who had been made vulnerable by illness or suffering. Papá Basi, as he was known to his children and grandchildren and the many people who came to him for spiritual sustenance, did not boast about his powers. He gave all the credit to God—that is, the benevolent version of the Heavenly Father that Papá believed in. The Mesa Blanca did not involve any Santería rituals such as animal sacrifice (which some Spiritists had adopted); rather, his "trances" were gentle, a simple closing of his eyes as he prayed for guidance and peace for the sufferers. He took no money but graciously accepted gifts of produce and homemade treats, which he shared with the whole barrio. Growing up with this daily exposure to Espiritismo meant that I did not find it strange to overhear discussions about ghosts visiting someone or about restless spirits causing trouble for a neighbor; as a rebellious teenager, however, I was infuriated to hear my actions discussed in terms of the restless spirit that was my constant companion.

But it was Papá Basi who told me something I have never forgotten and now choose to believe affected my developing sense of self. I recall the occasion vividly. One evening when my mother and I had been arguing, Papá had tried to change the mood of the house by putting a record in the old Victrola. He was still a musician then, a player of the cuatro, and he liked to play along with the scratchy recordings. He put on a waltz and came over to me. I had my nose in a book in an attempt to ignore my mother. He bowed and formally asked me for a dance. I was reluctant to show any signs of reconciliation, but I saw that my grandmother and several other relatives had come out to hear the music. I could not embarrass Papá by refusing. He led me around the room, and at some point he said softly to me, "Sé tu secreto." I know your secret. "I have no secrets," I answered, assuming that he knew about what I had done to have so infuriated my mother—I had lied about going for a ride with my young uncle on his bicycle, had actually involved him in a plan to meet a boy I liked. We had been ratted on by my youngest cousin, who was always left out of our best adventures and had become the snitch in retaliation. But my grandfather said, "Tú tienes facultades, Hija." You have the gift.

"Facultades," in the parlance of Espiritismo, means the incipient or latent ability for clairvoyance. If you develop your *facultades*, you will be able to talk to the dead and access the other dimension, invisible to normal people. The waltz ended, and I decided not to pursue the conversation. I did not want to talk to most living adults that year, much less to dead ones.

The last I remember about the influence of Spiritism in our lives was when my father, given a medical early retirement by the navy, came home to suffer a series of psychological crises. His depressions deepened, his paranoia grew, and he haunted our home, sleepless all night, wandering the rooms like a restless ghost. My mother began to light special candles, the kind you find in botánicas and bodegas that come with different prayers and images of saints. I overheard her talking to someone about Papá's instructions for ridding my father of the espíritus intranquilos that had taken hold of his mind. Strangely, my father did not object to these rituals, although he was usually a harsh critic of "superstitious nonsense," as he called the séances famously conducted in the Paterson barrio by mediums who took cash for their services. Their séances were usually staged affairs in Santería costumes and included cigar smoking and dramatic trances. But he loved Papá and may have even hoped that his despair could be exorcised. I do not know. I did not ask.

The candles and the prayers did not keep my father from self-destruction. And I did not think about my grandfather's words to me, about my gift, until after my father's death, when I discovered that writing poems was as close as I would come to having a relationship with the dead; it would lead me back to a sort of faith, toward becoming a believer in incantation and the power of words to transform the ordinary.

I want to believe that my grandfather was not so much a clairvoyant medium as he was a sensitive, perceptive man—a poet. Perhaps what he a saw in his book-obsessed granddaughter was potential, and so he took on the guise of the seer to grant me permission to see myself as a potential seer too. I understand that this is interpretation made in hindsight. In my medium, I can grant myself the right to find, in the significant moments of my life, *the continuous thread of revelation.*

28 *Pruebas*

"Es una prueba." I often heard these words spoken by people around me, but particularly by my mother. Life's trials, or pruebas, are a test of one's faith and character. This is one of the dogmas in Espiritismo — the human spirit must go through a series of trials toward perfection. Pruebas measure our spiritual fitness. The greatest prueba in our lives was my father's illness. To my mother, the added factor of facing her pruebas without the support of her familia made her more determined than ever to prove herself worthy of the only reward she desired: to return home.

The test included the children, too, and as the older child I was the designated defending champion of my mother's causes. She seemed to believe that her faith in my abilities and the purity of her intentions would keep me safe. I remember my father's first major breakdown and how both she and I fought against the reality of what it meant. He was in such despair that he wanted to die, but saying such a thing out loud, *he wants to die*, was forbidden, self-murder being the greatest of mortal sins. She would not allow herself or her children to harbor the thought that he had lost his faith to such an extent.

One evening during my first year of college, I came home to a frantic phone call from my mother telling me that my father had fallen from a building and had been hospitalized with almost every bone in his body broken. I flew to New Jersey, to an empty apartment, as she was staying at his bedside. I had to walk the unfamiliar streets of their new neighborhood to find a bus. I have never felt such paralyzing fear. Fear of the dark alleys, fear of the figures I saw or imagined congregating ominously on street corners, and mostly fear of facing my parents; he broken physically and mentally, and she deep in mourning, *La Dolorosa en luto*, the mother at the bottom of the cross. I was only able to exorcise these fears from my unconscious by writing about them many years later.

> *Había una vez*, there was a girl, who one night learns the power of fear, of el terror. Her father has fallen or jumped from the roof of *un edificio*. . . . *En el hospital* they only speak in questions: Insurance? Do you? Don't you?

Preguntas del seguro. Her father *habla inglés*, but he is wrapped in bandages and *en el silencio.* Her mother *no habla inglés*, and her father, *silenciado* by a false or true step from the roof of a building where no one he knows lives, lies broken and silent on a hospital bed. It is dark and cold and the streets *son muy peligrosas.* . . . she confronts the shadows with her avenging angel eyes, her cara de loca face. *Miedo, terror.* The power she has conjured out of her own fear is a fire in her heart that lights her way through *la noche oscura.* This night she is invulnerable. . . . Fear and anger propel her through the dark. She must get there to translate her mother's angustia, and to help name her father's pain.

29 In the throes of the Puerto Rican Syndrome

In the throes of the so-called Puerto Rican Syndrome, Puerto Rican soldiers would fall into fits or seizures that were like a combination of epilepsy and demonic possession. American psychiatrists assessing the troops during the Korean War believed it to be a form of malingering. A book I read some time ago tries to deconstruct the Puerto Rican tendency to sublimate aggression, to protest against the reality that was being forced upon them in situations they could not understand or control. As the author states, anger and social unpleasantness in general are discouraged by the culture (an arguable point in my opinion). The book cites another expert's claims that much of the violence within the Puerto Rican culture, whether it's erotic or simply a dark impulse, is acted out on the dance floor. I find this hypothesis irresistible: Make dance, not war. My mother did not dance much (except on rare occasions and by herself) during her twenty-five-year exilio, but she became the "spinning top" of her social circle when she returned to the Island. One of the few times she persuaded me to go dancing with her and her friends, she pointed out that rock and roll had ruined my style. "You take up too much room." She drew a large frame in the air around my body. "You have to remember that it is all in the hips. Subtle, small movements that fit within one tile." I had been ruined by rock and roll, and she had become the salsa queen, expressing what emotions? Suppressed desires, anger, rebellion against the inevitable slowing of her body, the arthritis that would eventually force her to retire from dancing the night away with her Ángel?

Both my mother and my father suffered from displacement and loneliness, and yet my mother's psyche survived. It was as if she practiced a sort of psychological martial art, for I saw how tenaciously she defended her idea of home and her dream of returning to her Island and family against the ever-diminishing odds of life with a man whose main impulse as time went on was toward death. Yet to watch them living out their days between pruebas, you would have seen a nice immigrant couple, quieter than most of the other Latinos. He was so hard-working and she was obviously the light of his life. You'd be right. For many years, as he became progressively more distant and reclusive, she was the only source of light in our home.

I have researched and read hundreds of articles and casebooks that try to explain people like us. I have tried all my life to understand the mystery of my father's mind in particular. How did his descent into *la tristeza* begin?

When I went back to New Jersey after my father's accident, I told my mother for the first time about John, a boy I had met that first year in college in a course called "Courtship and Marriage: A Survey." I came to believe that the course was created to feed the professor's research interests. We were to read articles on marriage in America, divorce rates, and the factors involved in the choosing or leaving of partners and compare them to the practices of marriage and divorce in other cultures. The sociology professor gave us a questionnaire to fill out, on which John and I had failed every compatibility issue. I was Catholic, and he was Methodist; he was a white southerner, and I was a nonnative English speaker of mixed racial heritage; and so on. The statistics the professor quoted mattered not at all to us at that time: our ethnic, religious, and other differences did not matter in view of how close we became during a time of my growing anxiety over my father. We wanted to be together to face what lay ahead. With each phone call I got, my mother sounded more and more frantic, and

John and I suspected that a crisis was looming. We were married soon after my return from New Jersey.

Not long after I was back in Georgia, before we had decided on a wedding date, my mother called to tell me that the hospital claimed that my father's insurance coverage had run out and wanted to send him to a veterans' hospital in New York. She didn't know how to drive then, and I knew she would not be able to maneuver through the maze of public transportation, let alone find a place to stay in the city. When I told John, he suggested that we go get my father and bring him back to Fort Gordon Army Base, where as a veteran he would qualify for government-subsidized care. Get him? He was in a full-body plaster cast. I do not know how at nineteen years of age both of us saw this plan as possible. One of my uncles rented a large station wagon for us. We discharged my father from the hospital, and without ever having had a conversation with my father, John transported him from Paterson, New Jersey, to Augusta, Georgia. We drove through the night—my father lying flat in the back of that old vehicle, my mother hunched over next to him, and me in the front seat helping keep John awake by playing music on the radio. Mainly what I remember of that nightmare journey was that the song "American Pie" played again and again, on every station I could find, so that the words have stayed with me: "This will be the day that I die. This will be the day that I die." Even today, as soon as I hear the first notes of this song, I smell plaster. I smell my mother's fear. I think of two kids entering a marriage with such heavy baggage.

30 *La limpieza, prayer, and poetry*

It is July 4, and no one is speaking of celebrations or of American independence. In better times, my mother would have attended a party with her political friends. She is one of those red-letter-day Islanders who celebrate all federal, local, and religious holidays, following the celebratory schedule that lists Puerto Rico among the ten happiest nations in the world; the Island has more holidays than ordinary work days on the calendar. She is an *Estadista*, an ardent prostatehood party member, and not just in thought but in deed.

To anyone who questioned her loyalty to her Island or culture, she would tell the *Reader's Digest* version of the story of her exile, minus the parts about her pruebas, her loneliness, my father's illness, or her devotion to the Kennedys. She would talk of my father's military service and how we had lived a good life because of U.S. "beneficios." My brother and I were living proof of what an American education could do. And when it was pointed out to her that she had returned to the Island and become, as converts often are, more *Puertorriqueña* than the ones who had never left, she would reply that her dream had also come true because of the dues she and my father had paid in their years on the mainland. Her return was made possible only because, upon his death, she had received a small navy pension that had allowed her to start anew. But the force of her desire for a return had propelled her back more than anything else to a place that had changed so much in the twenty-five years of her exilio that she must have felt like Rip Van Winkle, waking from a decades-long dream to a changed world.

This July 4 she is drawing her last breaths, surrounded by family and friends I barely know but who are connected to my mother through the intricate weave, the universal thread of a common language, faith, and blood. My mother has achieved something few of us ever will. She reinvented her world—as she had known it before my father, her children, her *exilio*—and how many of us can do this? I can't. I am de afuera, now and forever. I cannot subsume what I have become and will myself to be woven into this fabric the way my mother is. I love and respect my blood relatives, but I have grown very different from them over the miles and years. I think of the way my mother transformed the needlework she had learned as a recalcitrant quinceañera from a task to a prayer for meditating, dreaming of home. Somehow she found how to keep a thread moving through time, connecting her back to her origins. Not that her homecoming was easy. On her return to her mamá's house, where she lived until she found a little house of her own, she had to learn how to be independent, and that would mean, even when she was a widow in her forties, cutting off the same apron strings that had drawn her back year after year—apron strings that were parachute-cord strong.

The attending physician looks and acts harried. Everyone else has taken the day off, and he is running from room to room. He does not have time for diplomacy. He informs us that we have to prepare ourselves, as her vitals are erratic. He will have the DNR form available for Ángel at the nurses' station.

"When?" I want to be here with her in the end, although I am exhausted, hungry.

But the doctor will not commit. It could happen today, tomorrow, in a week. He has to go.

As the room fills up with visitors, and after my brother and I are assured by several of them that we will get a phone call should anything change, we go back to the museum of my mother's things. I cannot rest, so I decide to do what she called *la limpieza*. The term means "the cleaning," or more specifically "the cleansing," and to believers in Espiritismo it refers to a spiritual cleansing, a ritual often prescribed for ones who have troubled minds or have been "diagnosed" by the Espiritista as carrying within themselves a restless spirit. A restless spirit may attach itself to a living person through love—an attachment they are unwilling to surrender in death—or because they failed to fulfill their potential in life. These spirits are seeking light; they are seeking release. Their host can help these tormented souls by performing certain rites: one can light candles or "*darles luz*," pray, and offer them the scent of flowers. Scenting your home is an important part of the ritual, but first you must purify your home and yourself. "La limpieza espiritual" was much like the thorough housecleaning my mother conducted every week but with the addition of candles, plain white ones for Mary and ones with *oraciones* on their tall jars for the sundry spirits that might have been hanging around. As a teenager I knew that my bath had to be scheduled before the candles were placed in the tub. In her Island house my mother kept a little altar in her dining room. Here she didn't have to hide her devotional practices. Here she was not an odd Other.

These hours that I spend in her house while practicing what the Buddhist site calls our "watchful waiting," I feel a need to clean and to somehow make order, so that Ángel will not arrive from his watch to find unmade beds or no freshly washed clothes. At home, I normally practice minimalist domesticity. In partnership with John and a wonderful woman who runs a housecleaning business, we manage to keep our home clean and orderly enough to suit us. At home, I am grateful for my dishwasher and clothes drier, neither of which my mother owned or wanted to own. When I asked her if I could buy her a drier, she retorted that God had given the Island more sunny days than any other place she could think of, and her laundry dried on the line in no time. Her clothes, she claimed, smelled like sunlight and like her roses, as her laundry rack, an upside-down umbrella-like apparatus, was planted smack in the middle of her backyard garden. It had been only in the last few months, Ángel told me, that he'd had to hang the clothes because she became fatigued so easily. Another thing she didn't tell me. When visiting, I've always carried the tub of clothes for her as she turned the carousel rack around and hung them. She would make fun of the fact that I had to lather on sunblock to spend fifteen minutes out in the full blast of that very effective natural clothes drier. The fact that I sunburn and that mosquitoes eat at me as if I am a smorgasbord makes her declare me fully Americanized.

She's always loved going outside to her tiny square of green grass with its profusion of trees and flowers during the hottest part of the day to hose everything down as part of her routine after lunch. "¡Qué delicia!" she would say. "How good it is to feel cool water on your skin!" Afterward she would sit down and light a cigarette at the little ceramic-tiled table I had bought for her on one of my visits. She considered her life good, although she raged against the ravages of aging, particularly the bone pain she said was el artritis. The pain that got so intense toward the end that it kept her from getting to the phone when I called, so that I was finally able to talk her into getting a cell phone. Pain that for a while now may have been a part of the metastasis, but that I had wanted to believe was just a natural part of getting older.

I do the wash, put on my sunblock and repellent, and go out in the burning sun to hang clothes. I feel strange doing this without her telling me yet again how important it is to leave space for the sun to shine in between garments, and to hang the heavier ones in alternate rows. We would laugh at her belated attempts to teach me the domestic skills I had bypassed long ago. I find some of her bras and panties among the clothes, and I take them back to her laundry room, where she has a small version of the umbrella hanger set up for her "cosas personales," her intimate apparel. I hang them to dry in private, although I know that she will not be needing these things again. I then dust around her many knickknacks, these miniaturas that seem to be necessary to so many women on the Island. Collecting these objects is a widespread practice among the older ones, a type of obsession that is sanctioned by the culture. It seems to be related to class, age, and educational level, as I see less clutter in the houses of my younger relatives, but even among the college-educated, better-off people, it seems that every surface has to be filled with figurines, porcelain favors from numerous baptisms, weddings, anniversaries, and souvenirs from every trip. I have to be careful not to knock anything onto the ceramic tile floor, as it would smash hard and possibly break—something I learned the hard way, tumbling around my familia's houses on the Island as a child. I love tile to this day because nothing looks as clean when mopped. I use the pine-scented cleaner Mami has always preferred. It is a part of my sensory memory of our homes. I mop the tiled car porch too. It is good to feel the cool surface under my feet.

As I go through these timeless, ordinary motions, I am not thinking in metaphor or symbol. I am not telling myself that there is significance beyond the activity of making order. I do not grandly label what I'm doing *a spiritual cleansing*, although all of it is connected to what I remember her doing. It is mimesis. These are her objects; they are markers in the narrative of her life. There's a little trolley, a souvenir we sent her after a trip to San Francisco, a city about which she said, "Me fascina." California, Hollywood especially, fascinated her, since she was an HBO en español subscriber and watched a movie every night before going to bed, even if she'd seen it before. She was addicted to storytelling in all its forms. I had offered her a trip to California many times but had failed, for one reason or another, to make it happen. There are clay pots from Alaska, where my brother went often to visit his son. And there is her most beloved object, a small head carved by her father from a piece of mahogany. It resembles the Easter Island heads and other primitive carvings I have seen in museums. I have one of Papá's carvings at the farm too. He gave them to us as guardians for our homes, watchful presences with vigilant eyes, on the lookout for evil influences.

As I go about my humble tasks, which I have seen her do all of my life, I do not think I am performing the rituals of *riego* and *sahumerio*, the purification and scenting that would appease the restless spirits. I am just falling into my survival mode. It's the same as attaching these letters to the blank page, making words and then sentences. I impose the order of syntax and grammar onto them and hope they yield meaning. My survival mode is more than symbolic, however. My early life made me wary; it made me subject to a mindset that has a specific name in the Puerto Rican idiom, *por si acaso*. Just in case. Since my father was so often absent, our homes were outfitted to the hilt with por si acaso preparations and supplies. Flashlights, canned goods, plans to fill tubs with water, lists of emergency addresses and phone numbers. My mother lectured us endlessly on possible emergency scenarios. And, of course, we dealt with the scenario we could not discuss openly, my father's long spells of depression, his increasing despair, and, ultimately, his loss of will to live. And although for many years now I have enjoyed a relatively normal life, I am as over-prepared as anyone I know. It is a joke in my family that I could probably perform an emergency tracheotomy if necessary, as I have a collection of emergency preparedness books and have now downloaded many survival manuals to my iPhone. To humor me, Tanya once gave me the *Worst-Case Scenario Handbook* for Christmas. If I ever find myself lost in the wilderness, threatened by a mountain lion, I will know what to do: I'll make myself look bigger than I am by spreading my arms, and I will bare my teeth and look fierce. Earlier in my life,

I did not have to read a manual to know what to do when attacked by a large opponent. I learned the basic steps to follow in the face of catastrophe through experience: One, think of events in a sequence, make a plan, believe in it, and then follow it no matter what the optimists say. I know that imposing order on a chaotic situation allows your brain to think clearly. Two, have a mantra ready to use, a mental exercise to keep focused, such as "I am not afraid. I can get through this." Sometimes I have fallen into the old habit of saying the Hail Mary in Spanish again and again when I am afraid, not because I am a believer, but because it has been deeply ingrained since childhood. On the flight to Puerto Rico, the Ave María repeated in my head dozens of times; it kept me from falling into an anxious state before seeing my mother. And last, deny denial. Go into the emergency fully aware of the consequences. It was in this final step that I missed with my mother. I not only slipped in and out of the hope-against-hope all survival guides warn you against, I denied her the terrifying truth of her situation.

I have been warned by my aunts that it rains without fail at 4:00 every afternoon during the month of July. A tropical downpour that drops in, lets it all out, and then leaves just as suddenly. I set my cell phone alarm for 3:30. My mother would hate it if I let the clothes get drenched. She loved these afternoon rain showers because of the clean smell of ozone they left behind, "un mundo limpio," a fresh, clean world.

31 I have my mother's long nose and her sensitivity to smells. When I return to her hospital room, the first thing that assaults me, making my eyes sting and water, is the smell of a powerful disinfectant. I notice the smell before I enter, and then I see that the second bed has been removed. The patient, along with her bed and her myriad visitors, has been relocated. My mother's roommate was an old woman, I'd guess in her late eighties, who held court from her bed. It was obvious that she was full of life, used to being the center of her boisterous extended family's attention, present ailment notwithstanding. But in

her last day in the shared room, there had been an uneasy silence on her side of the curtain. Her family must have known my mother was near the end, and they must have requested that their lively mother, grandmother, possibly great-grandmother, as women of her generation married and bore children at a very young age, be moved away from sadness, mourning, and the contagion of la tristeza on our side. Her half of the room has been thoroughly cleaned and sanitized with strong chemicals. I can't help but suspect that my mother, even as she gasped into her oxygen mask, must have inhaled that irritating odor that permeates hospitals, where the air is thick with the reminders of our susceptibility to illness, and the spirit becomes uneasy as we breathe in knowledge of our own mortality.

32 *Death by la tristeza*

Knowledge of my own mortality was something I did not possess on the day I came home from the university where I had been working on a paper, possibly my master's thesis—I have developed a sort of amnesia about this time in my life—to hear that my father was dead. It had started out as a normal day. John had gone to his job, my father had gone to run errands, and my mother was playing with Tanya in her backyard swing. Before I left for school, I had stopped to listen to Tanya singing a made-up song in Spanish and English. She often spoke in a version of Spanglish she had invented to communicate with all of us. Later in the day, when I called home from a pay phone, my mother told me that my father had been gone all day and had not called her as he usually did. She revealed that he'd had one of his bad nights—wandering sleepless and obviously depressed. I called John, and we agreed to meet at my parents' place. He'd go look in places my father was likely to be, such as the Western Auto store or Radio Shack.

When I pulled up there were police officers at the door. John rushed to meet me holding Tanya. I don't remember the exact words, but he told me that there had been an accident. A bad accident involving a head-on collision between my father's Volkswagen and an embankment wall. He had not survived it. I am not sure of the sequence of events that followed. John with Tanya in his arms, my collapse—did I pass out? The officers helping me to the sofa. Someone called my mother out of the bedroom, where she had gone to change clothes and get her purse, as she had heard only "accident, hospital." I don't know how we told her. I don't know whether we held each other and wept. We must have. It's all lost except for the barest details.

John took care of everything. He identified my father's body in the morgue. He decided on a closed casket, which he chose, he told me later, because my mother and I had dissolved into an amorphous mass of weeping and paralysis. I do not remember how we let my father's brothers and their families know; I do not remember how my mother's oldest sister learned the news and arrived with her husband and daughter. My brother came home from college. John must have made all the calls, including notifying military authorities, because there was a gun salute and the ceremonial playing of taps, followed by the presentation of a flag to my mother. I remember that for some reason I could not get Tanya's shoes buckled that morning, and one of my uncles said, "All this commotion and now we will be late to his burial because you can't get her shoes on." Why would I remember this and not any words that may have been spoken by a priest? Why don't I remember more about his accident and his funeral? Denial. I believe now that I was in denial out of guilt for not giving my father my full attention while he lived, for not responding when he said, after I showed my parents my first published poems, "Maybe you can write my story." I did not want to know his story. His story frightened me. I was afraid I would end up like him, already having experienced my own dark days and nights of inexplicable sadness by then. And now, no one could explain how an expert and inordinately careful driver had run head on at high speed into an embankment wall he had passed on a familiar road dozens if not hundreds of times. No, I did not want to know. In an essay I wrote recently, "Word Hunger," after visiting my mother during her previous illness, while she was still able to have long talks with me, I try to fathom the mystery of his death.

I ask [my mother] many difficult questions about my father's battle with depression, about the horrors I suspected he had experienced in the military, which I had only heard about in snatches and rumors, and more significant to my understanding and acceptance of his early death in a car accident during one of his worst bouts with what she has always referred to as la tristeza. I had always respected her reticence, and had tried to piece together his story through other channels. Here was my chance to ask the source, the keeper of our shared memories of my childhood. And I knew what the questions were, but they had to be phrased exactly right. We were both emotional, and I could not run out of the room to find a dictionary, or turn to my laptop and "Google" the translation. [She] not knowing what to say, and [I] not knowing how to ask her, I was left stuck in my silence, and the moment passed, the window closed. I had felt the pangs, the spiritual hunger, but I had been unable to make the right sentences out of the wordless pain. Now it would have to wait some more.

33 There are hundreds of pictures in my mother's albums and in my closets and digital files, but only a precious few of my father. I have a sepia photo of him as a very young soldier stationed in Panama the year I was born, one of him in his U.S. Navy dress blues, and another of him posing next to a palm tree in Guantánamo, looking like he's been out on the town, wearing a wry grin and a cap at a jaunty angle. And there is the scratched and obviously much-handled one that shows the four of us, each child holding one parent's hand. This photo is the only one that survives of the family as a unit. These rare photographs were collected from my grandmother and aunts after my father's death. I also have a few of him with Tanya taken during the two years he knew her. The reason there are no more early photos of us with him is that in one of his bouts of despair, he took the album my mother carried with her on all our trips back and forth from the Island, and he cut himself out of every picture. I remember the horror on my mother's face when she found the desecrated photos. I remember the decapitations, and it is something that stayed with me, leaving a smoldering resentment that would linger for years, like

an acrid taste in my mouth. She must have thrown out the pieces of those pictures she had cherished. I never saw them after he mutilated them. Maybe she buried them. She cried hard enough on that day that it seemed she was mourning a death.

34 *Too late to ask*

Barthes calls a photograph a look at death in life: whatever or whoever is in the frame no longer exists in that moment, but the photo contains an essential truth beyond the image. What did my father see in those pictures that filled him with despair? I do not know. I did not ask. I was a young girl who saw only rampant, inexplicable bouts of anger. I thought that he hated us and did not want to be a part of our family. Simple act, simple interpretation, lasting misunderstanding and unfounded rancor. "Every photograph is a certificate of presence," claims Barthes, and all these years later those words resonate with me as a clue to my father's existential despair. Taking the words out of the context of the author's intent, I ask myself whether it's possible that my father wanted no certificate of his presence left behind, that he was already visualizing his self-erasure. Excising himself. Was it a cry for help? What did it mean? I do not know. And it is too late to ask.

I know that he loved his little granddaughter and that she gave him a reason for play. His tender attention toward Tanya was always in evidence. He held her, fed her, bathed her, and rocked her to sleep. Not usual practices for him. I have old Instamatic prints of him on the floor with her, arranging her toys according to her very explicit demands, and another of him holding her at her second birthday party: she has cake frosting smeared over her face, and he looks at her with an expression of wonder. I know now, as a grandparent, the shock of recognition in witnessing the development of new life that somehow contains mine, and Tanya does resemble him, with the same facial structure and big, expressive eyes. Her second would be the last of her birthdays he'd see. Six months later he'd be on a table at the morgue. He was forty-two years old.

35 *El respeto*

In my scattered reading in brain science I have come across the theory that even a planned death is somehow hard-wired into a person's brain—that death comes to us or is summoned by us at a time and place that is part of our biological blueprint. And so perhaps my father was fated to die in his early forties in an inexplicable motor accident, alone on an American highway, and my mother was destined to gasp for breath for a week and half at the age of seventy-five, surrounded by her children, family, and friends but still alone, as we all are when we enter that place where no one, not even the neuroscientists and the MRI machines, can follow.

In the penultimate day before my mother's predetermined journey toward oblivion, or the day before the day she enters her version of an afterlife, the little nun comes into the room, dressed in white from her coiffed head to her orthopedic shoes, and offers to say the Rosary, focusing this day on the mysteries of Christ's suffering, death, and resurrection. My mother's numbers on the flashing monitors are falling, ever so subtly, and the alarms connected to all the tubes going in and out of her child-sized body go off more often. The nun prays right through them, giving the machines a glance now and then without pausing in the repetitious chants of Hail Marys and Our Fathers. Every time she starts an Ave María, I am reminded of how often this phrase is used in different tones throughout any given day here—to express surprise, anger, and even just plain irritation with a world where faucets leak, ¡Ave María! Where little girls fall on hard tiles and put bumps and bruises on their fragile bodies, ¡Ave María! "¡Ave María, Hija, por favor. Come here! How am I going to explain another scar on your leg to your Papi?" Where one can live to have a great-grandson who has curly black hair and big brown eyes! "Ave María, ¡qué chulo!" Ave María, and she never got to hold him. Ave María, my mother is dying, and I will never again hear her rejoice, complain, or rage against this cutting off of all that might have been that was predetermined either by her DNA or by the Papá Dios this nun keeps calling forth as if he were a distracted host who is not sure when the guest is going to arrive. I commend her soul, the nun says, announcing my mother's imminent departure for that mansion of gold. ¡Ave María! I say it in my mind as a curse, in anger, as I have heard my mother scream it on occasions when something so outrageous has happened that calling on Mary to come see, come help, seemed the only thing to do.

On the penultimate day, I begin to have doubts about the decision not to tell her she has an advanced, inoperable cancer, or as the medical articles refer to it, a *medically futile* condition. By this time, she is in a deepening semicomatose state, and I cannot reach her. She does not respond when I call her name; all of her energies seem to be focused on that violent breath intake and release that makes her clavicle and breastbone jump up like a separate living thing. But should I have told her, as had been the plan? The doctor wanted to wait until at least one of her children was present to tell her the diagnosis, and the diagnosis could only be confirmed by an invasive bronchoscopy. But the surgery never happened: the pulmonologist told the oncologist, who told her doctor, that it was too late for radical treatments. I had felt a sense of the rightness of the decision to spare her the cruel truth, with my oldest uncle's and Ángel's assent. But now, as I see her numbers falling, I begin the phase of my mourning that is a sort of obsession, or at least a nagging suspicion, that I have failed her.

I have always fought against being patronized for being an immigrant, raged against being catered to because I am a woman, pushed away any efforts to sugarcoat or deny me any truth, cruel or not, that I feel is my right to hear, my right to know. Yet I denied my mother the truth about her condition, falling into the easy, familiar route that she herself had shown us when she refused to discuss my father's mental illness as anything more than a bout of la tristeza, a sadness brought on by circumstance, or by the restless spirits she appeased by giving them light, by praying to María. To her credit, in the last years, after his "accidental" fall from the roof and our "this will be the day that I die" trip to Augusta, she took action in getting him the psychiatric help that the navy had once imposed on him and that he was no longer capable of getting himself. But I remain ignorant of what she must have endured in silence in order to save us from the cruel truth during our childhoods. I now know that culture is a force that motivates some of us more than others, and the customs and traditions that defined home early in life remain imprinted, no matter how far behind we leave them.

As a professional woman living in the United States, I have a strong sense of my own power of volition. But as soon as I entered the world of my mother's culture, as she lived it, with its deep ties to tradition, I fell into the traditional role of dutiful daughter. I feel driven by a prime imperative vibrating all around me to honor my mother by doing whatever it takes, no matter how foreign it seems to me as the woman de afuera. Each day since I arrived, one of my aunts tells me, "Dios te bendiga, Hija," followed by "Ya sabes, Mija, si hay algo que no entiendes, pregunta." If in doubt, just ask. I think my aunts are telling me that I am in charge of how the world will remember my mother, that I should do the right thing. And the right thing is often counterintuitive to me. I follow the hierarchy of family decision making as observed by the aunts and uncles: oldest uncle as nominal patriarch, and then the other siblings according to their age. Fortunately my uncle is the embodiment of gentleness, and I recognize how much he is hurting, seeing his little sister on her deathbed—but it was to him that I naturally and without hesitation turned in deciding whether to tell my mother that she was dying. I unthinkingly followed the rule of *el respeto* I had so often been lectured about. Why do I have to sit quietly and listen to a boring conversation by adults? *Por el respeto.* Why do I have to ask for a blessing from every older relative? *Por el respeto.*

36 My way of making meaning has always involved research and factual confirmation. Can I look this up? Is there any evidence, any proof? It is the obverse of living by faith and trust, and I recognize it as a defense mechanism. This is a great time in technological history for the slightly paranoid, the cynic, and the nonbeliever. As a child in Paterson I had to risk walking through enemy territories to get to the public library—that was a time when African American kids and Puerto Rican kids were fighting their parents' turf wars on the

streets—and I was often threatened if not actually beaten up. The name "Lorraine" will always remind me of my school rival—her hair pulling and kicks to my bony rear. And in spite of the negative association with those unpleasant walks, I love libraries—where facts rule rather than Papá Dios's willful decrees, restless spirits, or the "that's the way we do things" dictum of my early life. Now, I can stay home and look up anything online. Nowadays, for better or worse, my searches for truth and beauty often begin with Google. So to ease these dark hours, I once more turn to research. I look up the cultural practices of my native land and try to grasp the reasoning behind them. I look up "el respeto" in Puerto Rican culture and come upon a site called *Minority Nurse* where nurses discuss their experiences caring for "people of color":

> When working with bereaved Hispanic patients and their families, nurses must understand the concept of el respeto (rules guiding social relation-ships—literally, "respect"). In many Hispanic cultures, the entire family is involved in making important life decisions, and there is a strict fam-ily hierarchy that must be honored. Traditionally, status is usually ordered from the older to the younger family members and from males to females.

I am always relieved to have my suspicions confirmed. In our Paterson and Augusta years, while my father was still alive and the unquestioned maker of rules, I felt sure that no one lived like us, and in many ways, because of his need for secretiveness and his suspicion of almost everything outside our home, this was true. We were not part of a cult or secret society, but we were different. I was aware of this difference and did everything I could to hide the seams. I tried to learn as much as I could about the way "normal" people lived so I could blend in with that world. I still feel that need today. Whenever I'm returning to Puerto Rico, I prepare myself through reading and research, almost like an anthropologist going out in the field. I'm always the one carrying the *Frommer's* guide and the maps and the traveler's Spanish-English dictionary in my large purse. In going home, more than to any other place I have traveled, I need to get it right.

Long ago I discovered something shocking after a trip to the Mayan ruins in Mexico. As the gullible student-*turista*, I was fascinated by the clay figurines and pottery still being made by the descendants of that glorious pre-Columbian civilization. I blew my small budget on pots and statuettes of Chac-Mool and several animal gods. Some years later, I came across a photograph in *National Geographic* of modern Mayan artisans studying an earlier issue of *National Geographic* that featured early Mayan pottery. The artisans were tracing and copying the photos of the artifacts once created by their ancestors. I reeled in the time-warping vortex, the bizarre reversal. I felt a bit cheated. I had bought Mayan copies of Mayan artifacts made by Mayan descendants who had forgotten their cultural heritage and had to rely on an American magazine to make the knickknacks gullible turistas would take home as cultural objects. Now, as the daughter de afuera, the parallels seem a bit too close. I *feel* my connection to my birth culture and language deeply, but I have to look it up in order to make sure; cultural uncertainty is my default state of being.

37   When I mention to my oldest aunt, with apparently some disdain in my tone of voice, that the elderly señora who occupied the other half of my mother's room and her retinue of talkative relatives have been relocated so they can continue their socializing in a more congenial environment, my tía gently points out that it was done out of respeto for us. The quietness necessary in the death chamber is being imposed. Even the nurses and technicians walk in and out on quieted feet; they address me in softer voices and occasionally even touch me as they pass by to minister to my mother. As she grows weaker, alarms go off more often. My older relatives are now taking turns sitting with me in her room. My aunt finally offers me the words I need to hear: "No te preocupes, no vas a estar sola." You will not be alone. She says this to me several times. I sit and watch the monitors and wait.

38   *Sola means alone*
The next morning, my brother and I get up early to prepare for another day at the hospital. We stop at the local Walgreens to pick up

a few things. I have developed a painful sore throat, and he suggests a big bottle of hydrogen peroxide with which to gargle. He buys a folding beach chair, as lately he has had to give up one of the two chairs in our mother's room to elders. Being a practical man and a professional traveler, he knows how to outfit himself for the duration. I have my Thermos of coffee in my arms, my bag of cough drops, and my iPad, and he has a green canvas chair ready to go, when we get the call from Ángel. "Vengan," come now. "Es la hora," it is time. How strange that a call of imminent death sets people in motion in much the same way as a call about imminent birth. My brother's knuckles are white on the wheel, and we are nearly sideswiped by a tractor trailer. I feel that my heart could not pound any harder without me passing out.

My aunt, the one who has assured me that I will not be alone, meets us at the entrance. My uncle holds my elbow as we ride the elevator to the fourth floor. My mother's three sisters stand around her bed. My brother and I stand on either side of her. I kiss her forehead and she emits a soft sound, a questioning sound, like someone makes in their sleep when you touch them. I tell her, "Estoy aquí, Mami." I say it many times as I alternately watch her labored breathing and the dropping numbers on her monitor.

Ángel puts his hand over hers. In his posture, head bowed, shoulders hunched, so unlike his normal athlete's bearing, I read a total surrender to sadness. "¿Ay, Fanny, por qué me haces esto?" I imagine him thinking. I know that this loss is unimaginable to him. He will be the one to miss her on a constant, daily basis. He will be the one truly left alone.

The little nun and a nurse arrive. The nun holds my mother's wrist between her thumb and index finger, counting, while the nurse takes notes. The nun says in a respectful whisper, "Todavía hay vida," addressing me. There is still life. She repeats it several times as my mother slides deeper into herself. I look closely at her face as she takes deeper breaths followed by longer and longer pauses. I have read about this final phase, the "agonal" phase. The resonant word, *agonal*, from the Greek *agon*, meaning a struggle, unlike most of the other medical jargon I've been immersed in, seems right as a name for the final moments of life. My mother's agonal moments were an agony for me, but her struggles are minimal. She engages in the only "rage against the dying of the light" she is capable of. The body in its agonal phase, Dr. Nuland says in *How We Die*, can be seen as a "raging against the too-hasty departure of the spirit; no matter its preparation by even months of antecedent illness, the body often seems reluctant to agree to the divorce."

Although I have been preparing for this moment, and though I am aware of the futility of fighting against the end of the light, I still want her to surprise us all by opening her eyes and stating in her assertive manner, "Todo está bien." All is good. It is what she would say when I called her every week. "Gracias a Dios, todo está bien."

My mother takes one last breath and exhales. It is a long Puerto Rican sigh, an expiration that lifts her chest up as if she were going to rise out of the bed, and then she lies back still and flat. The nun says, "Está con Dios." The nurse pronounces the time of death: 9:59 a.m. I see it on the monitor, the lines undulating, slowing, but it is as if through a film. The numbers fall, fall, and then lie down, a flat line. I see the anguish descend over my brother's face. I hear one of my aunts say, "Fue mi compañera de la vida," she was my companion in life, and begin quietly sobbing. I stand by my mother as each of her close relatives files past and kisses her. Then the protocols of death begin. They go out to the hallway to give me time alone with her. I keep watch over her while I wait for whatever comes next.

What comes next I have not prepared for. The nun (I wish I had learned her name) comes in carrying a clear plastic package, which she puts down on the bed. As she struggles to remove the gown from my mother's body, I help by turning her on the side, and it is at this moment that I truly feel the full force of what dead means. My petite, warm, utterly familiar mother has become literally a dead weight. Her skin, which I have described as café con leche in color, is now a dull gray, her partially open eyes reveal a glassy surface of milky gray, and her lips are stretched out over her teeth. But it is how she feels to the touch that makes me feel weak—more than weak, defeated by this mystery no amount of reading can ever prepare you for. She feels empty yet heavy. My mother is not there, and how can this be? I can't bear to see and feel any more of what is rightly called the remains. I make myself busy by opening the bag for the little nun, who is still working hard to undress my mother. I pull out the label: Adult Shroud Kit, 54" × 108", Small, Adult.

I put the label in my purse. I don't know exactly why I have this impulse, but it is like the need to bite down on the tooth that's hurting. A shroud, a bag to put my mother's remains in, is something I will need to ponder later. I decide to get a nurse to come help us. The nurse gently reprimands the nun, "You know you are supposed to ask for help in the shrouding." To me, "Señora, please step out of the room."

The little nun speaks to the nurse gently but firmly in the distinctive Castilian accent, which by now I have come to associate with a generosity of spirit I have rarely encountered, "But, Hija, how am I going to do God's work and improve myself if I am always running for help?"

Before I leave the room, I embrace this infinitely godly woman and thank her for all she has done for my mother and our family.

"I am at the service of anyone who needs me. Do not forget your hermanita in your prayers, Hija. Your madre is with the Holy Mother and her Blessed Son now." She hands me the rosary she always placed on my mother's bedside table. "Put it in her hands, Hija. Send it with her."

The nurse gives me a look that indicates her discomfort at my being there. I exit the room where my mother said her last words, breathed her last breaths, and will now be shrouded. It is not the glorified death chamber I had envisioned, the air heavy with the sanctity of the passage into the afterlife. We have all seen the lithographs—heavy velvet curtains, men with hats in hand, black armbands, women in black veils and swathed in yards of black crepe, silk handkerchiefs to their faces. No, this cold room was full of tropical sunlight gleaming off the metal of IV stands, white tile floor gleaming, the air redolent not with the scent of flowers but with a strong disinfectant, the last earthly scent my mother had inhaled before she expired. She who loved, who lived for, the smell of her roses.

As I walk out of her room for the last time, I desperately hope that my mother is either *tranquila*, asleep forever, or in the good company to which she has been recommended by so many for so long. I know one thing with absolute certainty. She is not on that bed. She will not be zippered into that shroud. What I am leaving behind is not my mother. She is not in that room.

I felt *sola, sola, sola*. Alone like I have never felt in my life. This is what grief must be, an utter desolation, if desolation means to be deprived of comfort in any form. Bereavement, says a hospice guide to grief, is the natural second stage of grief. I know it is the purgatory you enter alone, where you will suffer in a way designed by you for you. In my purgatory there will be hurricane winds that will toss me around without warning, and if there are moments of peace, it will mean only that the eye of the storm is hovering above me. An image from Dante comes to mind: Paolo and Francesca blown around within sight of one another, never to touch. *Bereavement.* The word sounds like a euphemism for severing.

I send John a text, "She is gone."

"Oh. Oh no! I am so sorry. Wish I could be there with you."

In a few hours he will call in tears to tell me that he had to take Tanya to a doctor, as she was inconsolable.

In the hospital hallway, the protocols are already being put in place even as words of comfort are passed around, blessings offered and accepted. Perhaps because Ángel is so obviously in distress, and I am the oldest child, all the decisions are run past me, as if I am the foreman at a construction site where the workers already know what they are supposed to do.

"Your uncle and Ángel will call the funeral home to have them pick her up."

"Está bien."

"You, your brother, and Ángel should choose a casket as soon as possible. You do want the funeral to take place soon? Es la costumbre aquí. Sometimes families have to wait for people de afuera to arrive. Will we have to wait?"

John is still grieving for his father and concerned about his mother's frail condition, and now he is taking care of Tanya and Eli. I cannot ask him to drop his obligations. The first obligation is always to our children.

No, I do not see any need to wait for the funeral. I have given myself over totally to *la costumbre aquí*, the way we do things here, por el respeto, to whatever it takes to set my mother's spirit free according to the customs she observed, and I will do it how she must have expected it; she will be remembered by her people by the ways she had reshaped her life. I will give her the right Virginia Woolf claimed for herself and for anyone who makes and creates: "This is how I shape it."

"You and Ángel will have to check on the gravesite. You will have to pay a cemetery worker to drain it, if necessary—and with all these rains . . . You will have to pay him to mow the grass and to wash the surface of the tumba."

"Está bien."

"And there is matter of el velorio, how many days do you want to sit with her? And the novenas. She belonged to a group that says the Rosaries for the dead. I'm sure she told you about this. I can talk to Doña L or Doña M, if you agree. But we can help you with that. No vas a estar sola, Hija."

"Está bien." I will have to familiarize myself with these Catholic rituals. The velorio is the viewing and wake, but held for longer periods of time here; after the velorio there will be a funeral service and then the novenas, which will take place over nine nights and will require contacting the *rezadoras*, the women who will lead the prayers—so much to plan when all I want to do is sit still.

I want to be by myself, which is not the same as sola. I have never felt more sola. Desolate, disconsolate, isolated, all stemming from the same etymology, all versions of *alone*.

A sweaty, corpulent man wearing a black tie, black pants, and starched white shirt arrives from the funeral home with a clipboard and speaks my mother's name, "Fanny Morot, verdad?" as if he's taking roll, dropping my father's last name, Ortiz, which she still used but only on documents and other official business, even after marrying Ángel, as is the custom here. Morot, her birth name, was the name she used in her daily life. It is la costumbre here to give the birth name preference, always acknowledging blood relations first.

"Sí." Ángel steps up and shakes the man's hand, pointing to the room where the little nun is still standing by the bed praying.

I take Ángel's arm as we leave the cold, antiseptic castle of La Concepción, the capital of the kingdom of the sick, whose border I had crossed only days ago. As I exit its automatic doors, just past the mural of the Holy Family, I enter the cruel country of mourning.

"A cruel country where *I am no longer afraid.*"

39 *Verde: the color of hope*

My mother died, and the only way I can forestall the wave of grief threatening to knock me down is to tell myself that I no longer have to wake up fearing her death. It is a turning back to myself that I fear now. I want to continue focusing on what has to be done for her and postponing what I know will be like the contractions of childbirth, but in reverse. I will have to end my pain by accepting an end, not a beginning.

My uncle drives Ángel and me home so we can discuss the funeral arrangements before meeting with the funeral home director about a casket. My youngest aunt, the one who accompanied my mother to Tanya's wedding, meets us there. She offers to help me select a burial outfit. She knows my mother loved to dress well and has taken the initiative. She pulls out several of the more formal dresses. I stare at these clothes, half listening as my aunt recounts the occasions to which my mother had worn them. "Mira, you sent her this one. She wore it to a birthday party where tu prima added up the ages of all of us old ones and came up with fifteen hundred years!" I remember calling her the day after that party and joking with her about her family's cumulative age. She had laughed, saying that no one should live past one hundred—one had to make room in the world for the next generation.

There was a story for every dress. But it is not the story as much as the new way of talking about my mother that interests and saddens me. As she begins to pair the outfits with matching shoes, my aunt says, "Tú sabes como tu mamá era." You know how she was. The present-tense version of this phrase is one I had often heard when discussing my mother with family members. She was known as the stubborn one, the one who was unmovable in certain matters such as politics and fashion. She called what young women wore these days, the torn jeans and tops with gaps and holes, "trapos," rags. There were clothes and there were rags, and the distinction had little to do with how much money they cost. Some celebrities, in her opinion, dressed in rags.

"Mira," my aunt says, "she was so fastidious that she hanged on each dress the shawl or bolero top that she planned to wear with it." She always covered her shoulders and upper arms. Another thing my mother hated was older women displaying their "cueros." *Cuero* is the word used to designate animal flesh, rough leather—the ugly or flabby parts of your body. But like many women in the culture, she had no qualms about displaying her good parts. She was proud of her strong, smooth legs and showed them off in high heels. She knew she had a lovely bustline and joked that I was a late bloomer in that department, as well as in the hip and bottom, which had been the source of a joke in recent years—"You and Jennifer López are not from the same mold of Puerto Rican woman." She liked for me to wear clothes that showed off my best qualities. She would point out that I dressed like a Jehovah's Witness and said I would scare people away when I arrived at their door. I knew that it was her way of encouraging me to relax my self-imposed professional restraints, my need not to appear like the overdressed Latina, the loud Latina, the always-late Latina. I tended to overcompensate in my efforts to defy stereotypes, and in her view, I was becoming an oxymoron: a boring Latina. She and I exchanged clothes and roles often. I would go through her closets and point out the ways in which she was becoming another contradiction in terms: a conservative Latina, covering her arms and wearing more practical shoes (but never flats) year by year. I didn't want her to change. I wanted a mother who was slightly more alive, more outrageous, and funnier than I. She was my Puerto Rican alter ego, my conduit to a way of living that I loved yet was constitutionally unable to imitate.

Tú sabes como era. You know how she *was*. The past tense. Her clothes and her scent emanating from her things undo me. I have to go to my room for a few minutes to do the hard crying I have not done yet. It is the past tense that hurts me. I hear my aunts talking softly. I smell the coffee they are making in her kitchen. I hear my brother and Ángel saying that the director is ready to meet us.

I go back to my mother's room and pick up a light green silk dress with a matching bolero jacket she had worn to a new family member's baptism recently. I choose a pair of tan sandals. I find the pearl earrings that Ángel had given her for her birthday, and I put it all in a bag along with the rosary the little nun had given me. I had recently asked my mother on the phone, while I was out shopping for a gift for her, about a green dress I was considering. She had said, "Verde, sí, verde. It is a good color. Es el color de la esperanza." Every color had a meaning for her, every flower was symbolic, and everything around her had a story. She collected stories. Green was a favorite color. It was the color of hope. As I start out of the room, I think that I need to discuss my choices with her. *Tú sabes como es.* I have not absorbed the past tense yet. It is the crucial first step I will have to take if I am to survive in the cruel country. I have to start thinking of my mother in terms of that most difficult of Spanish grammar constructions, the irregular verb "to be" with its special counterintuitive forms in the past tense: *Era. Fue.*

40 There was always, from the moment she rose and all through the day, the smell of coffee brewing in my mother's house. Today someone else has made a pot of coffee in her house, and even this small intrusion into her personal space makes me sad and a little angry. But it is an act of goodwill, a show of familial affection by my youngest aunt, who hands me a cup of café con leche and tells me that we will soon be

going to *la funeraria* to select the casket with my oldest uncle and his wife. *No vas a estar sola.*

I know I have to be careful in making these final decisions. I want Ángel to know that I am not usurping his place as nearest of kin, although everyone seems to be deferring to me. I decide that in the matter of funeral arrangements I will pass every question on to him and stand by him, literally, as a stand-in for the woman whom he jokingly referred to as his boss. I can see that he is as unsteady as a listing ship or a building that has lost part of its foundation. I am hoping to do something I have a hard time with in most aspects of my life, give up control, especially when I feel my own foundation shaking under me. My impulse is to pour in the cement, to start building a scaffold to sustain me. Ángel will need some instruction in this. He was her lieutenant, her dance partner, her Ángel, and he is not comfortable, even now, making decisions for her. After enduring an early life of poverty, a cruel divorce, and then years of loneliness as a struggling bachelor, Ángel had welcomed my mother's reinvention of their lives as a civically and socially active couple. She had devised and executed a life plan for them. I have marveled as how successfully she constructed a completely different way of being for them both. It was the opposite of the way she had lived for twenty-five years of her life as the mostly accepting, if not submissive, wife of a domineering man who had dictated everything down to what types of clothes she should wear. I have always had to watch my mother closely in order to understand why she allowed herself to be controlled by my father. Perhaps she understood that it was not mere machismo that drove him; his authoritarian stance may have been rooted in his fear that if he did not control every aspect of his and our lives, they would all fall apart. I think I absorbed too much of his fear and not enough of my mother's formula of mediation and compromise, which apparently involved having her decisions be or become necessary and desirable to others. My mother, the benevolent dictator. One way or another, she got what she wanted.

She had even told Ángel and other family members that she wanted to be taken to a specific funeral home that had served most of the pueblo's families for generations. Recently their business had been challenged by a young upstart who offered lower rates, a wider selection of caskets, and many other modern conveniences. My mother disdained this new undertaker's *falta de respeto* to traditions, and besides, he was not in the right political party. I hear all this as we drive to the funeral home. Already people are making the narrative of my mother's life fall into linearity; everyone knows or can guess what her choices would have been if she had planned her own funeral. She was an opinionated woman, so I do not doubt that she had made her thoughts on her own death be known. She would have joked about it. Do not let me be buried by that *fulano* who is only out to make a profit. I know she would have called the upstart a fulano. In the vernacular of gossip, fulanos and fulanas are the ones who do not deserve to have their names spoken with respect. And when someone is called a fulana, you know that she is fast becoming an outsider, to the person *hablando mal* about her or to the community—someone from so far outside the bounds of las costumbres or el respeto that she has lost her right to a proper name. My mother was a great manipulator of her own language, and she could use it like a scalpel.

The casket display room makes me think of the word *penumbra*. It is a room kept in twilight, with each box illuminated by indirect lighting from overhead strips of tiny bulbs, as if rays of light from the heavens are spotlighting the proper vehicle for the loved one's journey to the other side. I stand within a little circle of close relatives as we move in synchrony from one coffin to the next. Soon the director arrives, emanating busyness, along with his clipboard-toting assistant. He has, he told us, dropped everything, left a meeting in Mayaguez, to come meet us. Fanny—he calls her by her first name— was special to him. His family has known the Morot family for many years. He does not fail to mention that his family had also made the arrangements for my grandparents. Turning to me and taking my hand in his, he is the first to speak the phrase that I will hear dozens of times over the next three days: *Estoy con ustedes en su pena. Siento su duelo.* I am with you in your pain? No, in your loss, in your sadness. I will need to master the vocabulary of bereavement. *Pena* means grief, sadness, and also punishment or penalty. *Pena de muerte*, death penalty. Do not burst into tears in public, *bajo pena de*, under penalty of . . . *El duelo* means mourning or bereavement. *El dolor* means pain. *Duelo* as a verb means I hurt. I hurt. It means I hurt.

I become aware of a dull, burning pain in my abdominal area that begins as we tour the caskets, which, it turns out, are arranged from the most to the least expensive around the room. As we follow him, the director points out and categorizes the quality of wood and metal used in their construction. The most expensive casket is gunmetal gray, a huge thing that looks like it could survive a nuclear blast. Made in the U.S.A. It is massive; its main quality is its impermeability. Waterproof. Sealed like a time capsule. We pause in front of it for a long time; perhaps the director wants a response to this masterwork. I feel uneasy. It is the most expensive casket. Do we not want the best for my mother? I suspect that my common sense has evaporated. I know this for certain when I cannot not say what I am thinking. This is a monstrosity, an impermeable, indestructible abomination. Thankfully, my aunt speaks up, perhaps sensing that I might be reluctant to say no to the most expensive box, this ugly thing, and be thought of as stingy. Ángel has told us on the way to the funeral home that the choice of casket should be *la familia*'s decision, not just mine or his. He reminds me that my mother had an insurance policy to cover most of the funeral costs. I can see how painful this process is to him.

"No se parece a ella," my aunt whispers to me. It does not look like her.

I agree, although I know it's bizarre to say that a coffin looks or doesn't look like a person; yet in the half light, in the fake spiritual ambience of that salesroom, I understand exactly what she means. I will not bury my mother in a waterproof tank.

My uncle moves toward a white casket with renderings of the Last Supper etched on enamel at either end. In spite of its religious decorations, the casket looks feminine and somehow, with its fluffy pillow and white linen lining, more like a bed than any of the others. Although I would have recoiled at the idea of a pretty coffin in my previous life as a sensible person, at this moment I lean on my uncle's shoulder and say, "Sí." She would have liked this one, sí, éste es. And as soon as I say it, the director reaches inside the box and pulls out the product description and the price tag.

He asks Ángel and me to follow him to his office, where he prints a list of costs. He directs us to his assistant to talk about ordering flowers and to select the little memorial cards that will be handed out at the velorio and the funeral. How long for a velorio? he asks. My aunt said that sometimes a viewing can go on for days, especially if you have relatives coming de afuera, but I could choose to have it last one day. Everyone would understand.

Ángel and I agree to be at the funeral home at 7:30 a.m. the next day. The chapel will be open until midnight, and we are expected to be present the whole time. The priest will come at 11:00 a.m. to do a eulogy. The burial is scheduled for the following day at ten. I say *sí* to everything. *Todo está bien.*

The assistant tells me, "I understand that her hairdressers will come before eight in the morning to prepare her for the viewing."

I didn't know that, but it does not surprise me. I saw their tenderness with my mother at the hospital. They will make sure she is ready to be seen one last time in public.

The director is already putting our invoice in an envelope and digging in his pockets for his keys. A busy man. He stops to remind us, "You should go by the cemetery and make sure that her plot is ready. Don Ángel, you know that the cemetery workers will expect payment for this service? And one last thing. If you have photos of *la difunta*, and of la familia, bring them with you and we will display them." Gracias. Adiós.

I have a to-do list now. This is good. ¡Bien! I have always functioned best when I have an assignment or a list I can check off.

My stomach is cramping. I have not felt a pain like this since I had an ulcer many years ago, around the time of my father's death—a burning deep in the pit of my guts. *Dolor, el duelo* causes *dolor. Me duele, Mami.* How many times did I say this to her as a child? It hurts, I hurt.

Ángel asks me if I want to go home while he goes to see the cemetery workers. I tell him I want to go along. I went to see my mother's tomb several years ago. She and I drove there together on a hot July day, much like this one. She took me to see the newly completed plot that she had had constructed near her parents' graves. I remember being momentarily blinded by the harsh reflection of the sun on the white concrete slab and granite marker. Then I felt the shock of seeing that her name in black followed by one date, her birthdate, engraved on the stone, April 10, 1936, with a dash following it and a blank space. On that day she had been proud to show me her *tumba*, which had cost her a lot of money. She asked me if I was going to get one made near her. I could start paying for it now, she said. At first I thought she was joking, but she was serious. "Naciste aquí," she reminded me. I had been born there, and all my ancestors on both sides of the family were buried in the "old" part of the cemetery. Why would I want to be buried anywhere else?

"Mami, I live in Georgia now, and John, I imagine, will want us to be buried there." Half lying, I refrained from telling her that to be cremated was my only final "plan," if I had one, since I did not feel a need to be planted on any plot of earth, Island or mainland. To her, an old-school Catholic, cremation was a blasphemy. It is called *quemar al muerto* by the faithful, burning the dead one. We did not speak of it again, but her strange question stayed with me. It seems she truly believed that in the end I was going to choose to lie next to her. My afterlife would be lived as her daughter, on the Island; my epitaph would be in Spanish.

As we walk toward the family's gravesite, I am thinking about my dual self, how I live on this earth as two people: one life here on the Island and one life afuera. When I was on the Island my mother had felt connected to me as I had to her, but my other life wasn't as real to her. She knew I struggled to be true to each of my identities; yet to her, I was on loan when I was away from *casa*, and she may have felt it was her right to claim me for eternity. She would have me near her once I left my physical self, gave up my life afuera, and returned to my birthplace. She never really accepted the fact that I do not believe in eternity, or only in subatomic terms, and that what is left of me after my days are done is not my concern. Ashes, I prefer ashes.

It will be half of my divided self, not the eternal soul she so fiercely believed in, but a state of mind, a sense of locale for my self and part of my identity, that I will bury in this sturdy underground dwelling my mother had constructed. Standing at the foot of my mother's grave, I resurrect another cliché—part of me will go with her. I know I will never again feel the wholeness of being I felt when she was insistently alive and showing me again and again how to be at home in this place she had reinvented for us. I wait in the full sun, facing my mother's last *casita*, while Ángel conducts business with the undertaker. I feel my skin prickle, begin to itch from the white hot sun. I feel the sting of a mosquito on my arm. Soon I will redden and perhaps burn. "Te vas a quemar," she'd say to me if I went out without my layer of sunblock and mosquito repellent. "You will burn and you will be eaten alive, Hija. Porque you have American skin now. The kind mosquitos find sabrosa." And she'd laugh and bring me the lotions that would save my thin skin.

41 My brother, visiting our mother several months before her final illness, had found a photo that he scanned and sent to me. I study this photograph of my mother taken on her return to the Island as a widow in her forties. What do I see? A woman in a bright red top and black pants, neither smiling nor frowning, posed in front of a painted canvas. Her back is very straight and her hands, showing signs of arthritis in the slightly swollen crooked fingers, are spread flat on her lap.

Something draws the eyes to this woman's face. The camera has caught her in between emotions. We do not know whether she is about to smile or about to cry.

In *Camera Lucida*, Roland Barthes talks about the two planes in a photograph that interest him. The first he calls the "studium," and it represents the actual occasion, meaning, or intent of the photograph. But it is the detail that defies analysis, what Barthes calls the "punctum," that interests him the most.

The punctum is the point of intersection between viewer and image, that detail that draws us into the picture as a shared human event. It is the thing, whether intended by the photographer or not, that touches you or triggers a quickening of the pulse, an irresistible impulse to look closer.

When I was asked for photos to be displayed at the funeral home, I looked through her albums and found dozens of pictures, but I could not find one that had the right tone, the "air," as Barthes calls it.

The photo of my mother that my brother had sent me had been taken when she first returned to the Island after my father's death. She had told him that she did not like it but had not given a reason. She had kept it put away in a box. I looked at it occasionally, drawn to her haunting look of almost-revelation. This is an ordinary picture taken by a stranger, but the longer I looked at it, the more meaning it gained for me. Of the grainy picture of his mother that has come to embody her essence, Barthes writes, "It exists only for me. For you, it would be nothing but an indifferent picture."

She looked younger in this photo than I remembered her looking at that time in her life, maybe because she had taken to wearing conservative, matronly clothes and her hair pulled back while she spent her years as a navy-wife-in-waiting in the United States, her time in an immigrant's limbo.

But in this photo she has regained her true age. Her hair is shiny with only a hint of gray at the part, her tan arms are bare, and she looks slim and fit. But in spite of her rejuvenation there is a seriousness that belies the outfit, clearly donned for an evening out.

The punctum of this photo for me is the little spray of white flowers adorning her hair. Doesn't a woman have to be thinking of something celebratory or someone special to put flowers in her hair? I had never seen my mother indulge in anything quite so impractical and frivolous. In fact, she was as concerned about bugs on her body as any child who had experienced the parasite scares of a childhood on a tropical island. I looked at the photo for other signs of her transformation but kept coming back to the two disparate qualities: the hidden grief in her expression and the flirtatiousness of the little white flowers in her hair.

On the painted canvas behind her is an idealized seashore scene at dusk: a background of sinuous palm trees, placid ocean, and a black mountain range. Perhaps this is how our beaches looked once, before the litter, the hotels and condos, and the tourists. It may have been the image my mother carried in her mind all those years when she yearned to return.

An ordinary woman, she was a muse to me. It was her ineffable air of timidity and even fear, precariously balanced by passionate desires and dreams of living on her own terms, that I have been trying all of my years as a writer to capture.

But I cannot create the visual image I have in my mind's eye. I choose this photo to represent her in life at her funeral. I have to use an image taken by an anonymous photographer of a woman in the midst of a struggle, a new widow, alone in a place that had grown strange over the many years of her absence. It will have to suffice.

42 *The coquíes' song*

I gave up the practice of Catholicism as soon as I left my parents' house. Like many children of the sixties, I used the word "oppressed" often and liberally. I claimed to have been oppressed by the demands of the church, the rituals of sacrament and holy obligations. I went to confession on Saturdays every week from the age of seven, when all I had to confess was talking back to my mother, tantrums over toys I saw on our black and white TV and couldn't have until Christmas or my birthday (or until Papi came home and approved them), and other childish "sins." Of course as I got older, the sins became more private. We were warned about sinning in our hearts as well as sins we actually committed. I accumulated a lot of sins in my heart and hated telling the priest, who would likely recognize my voice and my accent. I was one of a few Puerto Rican students at St. Joe's, and the priests were constantly present at school and in our lives. Yet if I didn't confess and do my penance—dozens of Our Fathers and Hail Marys along with the Act of Contrition—I would not be able to take communion at Mass the next day, and my mother would know that I was walking around with a spotted heart, as I had been taught by the nuns to see my soul: a heart with something like the Bubonic Plague buboes on it or, if I had committed a mortal sin, a completely blackened valentine. Even as I questioned this absurd image, I could not fully dismiss it while I lived and breathed Catholic dogma. But the truth is that the rituals of the church, the sensory experience, mesmerized me. I have written often about the sort of trance I'd go into as the priest intoned the Latin prayers and the altar boys swung the censers over the kneeling congregation—all this was pre–Vatican II, before the rites were modernized and the services started being spoken in the vernacular. There were candles, chants, and smoke. A hypnotic ambience that was perfect for my daydreams, not always religious in nature. These experiences of sensory awakenings insinuated themselves into my imagination early in my life and later into my work.

In my mother's house there is plenty of evidence that she has become more attached to the symbols and rituals of Catholicism over the years. I knew she liked the social aspects of the church, the music, rites, and rituals; I did not realize how deep her faith had grown. Knowing she enjoyed collecting images of Mary, I sent her pendants with the Virgin's many apparitions that I found during my travels. I once found a sort of charm bracelet decorated with many renditions of Mary, from ivory-skinned Madonna to copper-skinned Guadalupe to the black Eastern European María. I justified encouraging her interest in the Queen of Heaven—better that she be attached to the goddess than to a patriarchal Heavenly Father. Hadn't we all had enough of the macho in our lives?

In the evening, after Ángel and I return from making arrangements for her plot, I sit on her rocking chair in the carport and listen to the *coquíes* begin their evening song. The thumb-sized frogs are indigenous and unique, a national symbol. It has always made me smile to think about how such tiny creatures can be so loud, loud enough to sound like a jungle full of either birds or monkeys—tourists have mistaken them for both. The coquí is an appropriate totem animal for us, a small and admittedly loud people. The coquíes' song seems muted this evening, and Ángel tells me that most of the coquíes have been frightened away by the population explosions in neighborhoods like this one. My mother had missed their song so much these last few years that he had gone out to the countryside and waited hours to catch a couple—a male and a female, he hoped—and brought them in a jar for her garden. We listen for them, and their song sounds sad to me this evening. I know that this is the pathetic fallacy we warn our literature students about—nature does not represent human emotion; we impose any meaning we wish it to have. Read "it was a dark and stormy night," and you know you are not in for a light and cheery story. But I wanted every tree, flower, bird, and frog in my mother's beloved garden to mourn her along with me, pathetic fallacy or not.

My stomach is hurting so much that all I can do is sit in the rocker and watch Ángel begin his own frenzied limpieza of my mother's house. Although I have already cleaned, he sweeps floors, mops, and hoses down the carport; he washes her car, and with infinite patience, he polishes it. Every morning of their lives together, he had gotten up to wipe down their cars. For the last two weeks, he has not been able to maintain this ritual. He wants everything to be clean and in order before the house is opened for the novenas, which will begin the night after the funeral. She would be pleased to know how hard we have worked to make her casa presentable.

43 Luto and las palomas

I remember how during my childhood, upon the death of any close relative, the whole family and anyone who entered was put into mourning in Mamá's house: no TV or radio for weeks, no singing or loud talking. If one of us violated the rule and dared to laugh out loud, we'd be reminded, "Mira. Respeto. Estamos en luto." Show some respect. We are in mourning. Papá wore a black armband when he went out. People treated us deferentially during el luto. That was what el respeto demanded.

On the day my mother dies, I wonder what I will wear until her funeral. Appearances and public demonstrations of respect for the dead matter a great deal here in this traditional pueblo. I didn't have much time to pack when I got the news of her illness. I have only my usual travel attire. Am I expected to wear only black? I did not come prepared for a funeral. Both my grandmothers kept el luto for life. I only ever saw my paternal grandmother in black, for she was widowed before I was born. Mamá wore black for three years after her parents' deaths, and thereafter she went to half-luto, dressing in only grays and dark colors. I never saw her in anything else.

Today, my whole being demands el respeto. I want silence. I want the blaring of radios and TVs turned off, I want people to stop talking loudly, singing, and laughing. I want candles, incense, and prayers. I retreat to my room with a cup of herbal tea, and I hang my brown skirt and black top in the closet. El respeto.

I lie in the dark, listening to the sounds of my mother's little backyard garden where birds always come to roost at the end of day. Hours later, it must be near dawn, I hear the dove, one of the pair of palomas that nest in a nearby tree, begin her call. I have always known this familiar three-note lament as mere background noise. But this morning, I listen closely to its incantatory coo, which is a mother's sympathy sound, a sound she may make to soothe the sick or restless child. *Sé-que-duele. Sé-que-duele*, says the paloma. I know it hurts.

44 I measure every Grief I meet
    With narrow, probing, eyes—
    I wonder if It weighs like Mine—
    —EMILY DICKINSON, #550

El Velorio is a famous 1895 painting by the Puerto Rican artist Francisco Oller. It depicts a child's wake as a fiesta. The child's body is on a table covered with a white cloth and is practically smothered in flowers. All around him are people of different ages singing, dancing, and eating. A child's wake is a traditionally called a *velorio de Angelito*, a wake for a little angel. Usually held for a child younger than seven—when innocence is said to end—it is a good-bye party, *la fiesta para un Angelito*. These festive velorios, the *baquinés*, were practiced in Puerto Rico well into the twentieth century. I heard my grandparents talk about them. My mother showed me a print of this painting once and said that no tears were allowed at an innocent's wake and burial because it was believed that tears would dampen his wings and prevent him from flying to heaven. "Las cosas de antes eran inocentes y bonitas," she would say of old customs. These old traditions were born of innocence and were lovely. In the old days, I had often countered, many things were also done in ignorance. I've done some research on *velorios*. In the homes of the poor, the body of the child was placed on the dining room table and the party went on until the smell of death drove people away. Then the novenas began. For the nine days and nights after a death, the spirit is believed to linger around the familiar, trying to attach itself to loved ones. It was necessary to pray, light candles, and lead the spirit gently toward its final destination. This belief is a vestige of the times when wakes were held at home, so the presence of the departed was heavily felt as families lived with the casket until the day of the burial.

I have a hard time entering the chapel at the funeral home where my mother's coffin sits in front of gray drapes and flanked by lamps on tall posts. The casket spray of red, white, and pink roses and white orchids I selected lies over it. *Coronas*, rings of various types of flowers, hang all around the room. On their ribbons are the names of the senders and messages to my mother: To my beloved sister, aunt . . . To our fellow member of the American Legion, the Progressive Women, the Voter Registration Association . . . We will miss you. Among the redolent flowers in the capilla, I feel the fullness of my mother's life. In front of the casket are fancy, flowered high-backed chairs and a settee. Behind them are rows of plainer chairs. It looks like a little theater. It is all tastefully done, but my anxiety is rising.

The solicitous director's assistant soon comes in carrying a stand for my mother's portrait. He places it on a little marble-top table at the head of the coffin. He puts a candle on its holder and a crystal vase in front of the picture. He takes a rose from one of the coronas and sticks it in the vase. He leaves and returns with an easel to hold a sort of bulletin board on which he uses magnetic frames to display the pictures I brought. Then he turns to us. "You may want to rearrange the pictures." And with no transition, he places a hand on the lid of her coffin: "¿Quiere que lo abra ahora?" "Would you like me to open it now?" He is asking us if we are ready to see her.

I think Ángel says yes or nods. I look in with trepidation. I don't know what she will look like after embalmment. But I am pleasantly surprised to see that my mother's face has relaxed into a semblance of life. Her skin is smoother, less lined, and her body seems to have filled out. Her green dress fits snugly, despite how thin she had become in the last few months. I do not want to think of the mortician's work or her night in the depths of this building. Her hair is flat and her gray roots are showing. She has no lipstick or any sort of makeup. "We were told someone was coming para arreglarla." The assistant has obviously noticed my distress. Someone will be coming to fix her, he assures me. I don't want my mother to appear as if she were dressed up for a party but had forgotten to comb her hair or apply makeup. I decide that I will do it myself if the beauty salon women do not show up. I will do it. Yo puedo arreglarla. The assistant's choice of words, arreglar, to fix, makes me recall what Eli had asked John when he was told that his abuela's mommy was very sick. He had asked if my mother could be fixed by a doctor. When John's father died, Eli had been told that sometimes even doctors could not fix a person. On hearing that my mother was gone, Eli had asked in disbelief, "Then abuela will not have a mommy?" Unthinkable to a three-year-old. To be motherless. This could not be. How old does one have to be not to feel orphaned?

The two sisters arrive dressed in dark colors and carrying their cosmetics bags, and after embracing us, "Estamos con ustedes en su pena," begin their work on my mother. They labor in perfect unison. Like surgeons, they lay out their bottles and tools on the table in front of my mother's picture. They work in silence, silently passing combs and brushes without looking up, and to my amazement, they even use a hair dryer. They are priestesses performing a ritual as ancient as any. As they begin to put their tools and bottles away, I remember the rosary in my purse. I hand it to one of the sisters, and she knows exactly what to do with it. She winds it around my mother's hands and says softly to her sister. "She always kept her nails so pretty."

Then they each kiss my mother. I stand between them so I can see my mother as they saw her. "Siempre estaba elegante y bonita," one of the sisters says. And the other adds, "I never saw her without lipstick and earrings." They have dyed her hair, put a glowing foundation on her face, and tinted her lips a rosy pink. It was a respectful "arreglo." They have ministered to her. They have touched her gently and given her the gift of their loving attention. It is a tribute to my mother's ability to connect to others that these women, her hairdressers, feel that they can treat her so familiarly in death.

On my way to the restroom, I see the assistant in the kitchenette making coffee. There is also a hot chocolate machine burbling, and a box of doughnuts on the counter. Food, yes. But there will be no musicians, there will be no singing, no dancing. Through the glass door, I watch several members of our family getting out of their cars. I rush to the bathroom, as my grief-induced symptoms now include nausea. Dry heaves. I have nothing in my stomach but still feel, as I will for the next two days, that if only I try hard enough I can get rid of that hard ball in my stomach. I feel as if I have swallowed broken glass. I can hardly straighten my spine. I can only get relief if I hunch over like an old lady. I walk down the hall with my hands on the sides of the walls to keep from listing. Psychosomatic symptoms, I tell myself. You are letting your emotions affect your body. But knowing the facts does not help me this time. My pain and nausea intensify by the hour. But I am determined to stay until the last minute of this *buen viaje*, this long, public good-bye for my mother.

Every day one of my aunts or my oldest uncle takes me aside and makes what they call "sugerencias," suggestions as to what has to be done next. I don't know if they met to decide to do this, and if each has an assignment, but I understand that it is done so that I will not have to look it up, the customs, my duties, the Spanish words, although I always do—and perhaps also to make sure I do not make any preventable errors. The protocols of death are complex and the expectations on a daughter, many. "Mira." My aunt finds me in the bathroom and places her hand on my forehead. "You are already getting sick. You must eat and stay strong so you can get through this." She takes me by the hand as if I am a child and guides me to a folding chair in the kitchenette. She gets me a cup of coffee. "Today will be long. You and Ángel will be expected to stay until the chapel closes. Several of us will always be here. Your mother was very involved in the community so there will be a lot of people. ¿Me entiendes?"

Yes, I understand. Many hours of talking about my mother, of accepting condolences.

"We think you should know that some palabras will be expected of you tomorrow. Es la costumbre aquí to have testimonios at the funeral. Do you think you can do this?"

Yes. I will find some words to say about my mother, and I will translate them and practice my enunciation.

"The priest, a family friend who grew up in our old neighborhood, will do a eulogy before the funeral."

Está bien. I have my assignment. I take my place on a wingback chair in front of my mother and begin my mental preparation for the burial by looking at her and trying to imagine what she must have remembered in her final hours. In the end, I hear, one's "moments of being" are projected on that proverbial black screen that will eventually resolve into the blinding source of light. Of course, it can all be explained scientifically as the effect of oxygen deficit and the flooding of the brain by natural endorphins. This is the agonal moment made bearable by our own brain and our own chemicals. Once again, my mother has secrets I will never know. I will have to choose for her.

45 *Before the storm*

Poetry has been an ongoing pursuit of self-knowledge for me. Whatever has confounded me, astonished me, brought me joy, or hurt me, I have usually examined it in a poem. The quest has been an obsession. Reading and writing have given me a way to locate myself in the world I live in, between languages and cultures. But my quest for knowledge has also occasionally distanced me from one of my most important sources, my mother. The more I read, the more I questioned and the farther I drifted from the things she cherished. It was not until I began to see my mother's self-definition as the pursuit of the proverbial truth and beauty that I had my most important revelation, and it changed our relationship. One of these insights came to me after I read Alice Walker's important essay "In Search of Our Mothers' Gardens." I began to think of my mother as one of those unrecognized artists of the self, creating, out of an unstudied need deep within herself, a meaningful way to live. In the title essay of a book I wrote on the process of becoming a writer, which was triggered by Walker's essay, I delve into that revelation. My mother had summoned me to Puerto Rico for a special occasion during hurricane season one year, and I got caught up helping her prepare for a massive storm. As the storm approached, we engaged in our usual heated discussion about God's will versus scientific facts. But observing her, in what seemed to me a futile act,

> She packed the bulging family albums with pictures that she could use to connect the dots of our family life, along with her talismans and totems; the religious objects that she had carried with her from apartment to apartment . . . as a Navy wife and later as a widow upon her final return to her homeland. I got caught up in the ritual. I handed her what she asked for like an acolyte in a ceremony, my mother a priestess going from station to station of our lives, making each ordinary event meaningful by telling its story.

It is all I do, all I can do. I watch, I record, I interpret, and I tell the story. I have to write my poems and stories, without hope for immortality. My work has to serve me, nurture me, and save me, if possible. I heard a Latina poet once make the greatest claim she could think for poetry. She said, "Poetry saved me from an ordinary life." She did not mean that it had saved her by granting her fame or fortune. It had let her see in a new way. It had given her a way of making meaning. My mother's life was ordinary, but in the way she infused it with meaning, it was not. She made art out of living. The poet's role is the same, to make the ordinary meaningful, to make it new. If it transcends beyond self-help and touches others, then it has a chance of becoming art.

I hope that in the end she remembered the times she and I had learned how to survive the storms.

46 *Proper attire*

As the people begin to arrive for the velorio, I stand next to Ángel, greeting each one. I look into their faces as they speak the now-familiar "Estoy con ustedes en su dolorosa pena."

It is suddenly crucial for me to know how each person came into my mother's life. Usually one of my relatives or Ángel introduces the person in terms of his or her association to her: "I'd like you to meet la Señora This or That, who worked with your mother en la política" or "Mira, this is one of our cousins on Mamá's side." Occasionally, I pull out a familiar name from far back in my memory. There are two sisters about my age, distantly related to me, whom I had known the few months of a school year when we had attended public school in the pueblo. By third grade, we were enrolled in a Catholic school in another town, one run by American nuns. In these women's faces, I see an alternate route my life could have taken had my father made a different decision. If we had stayed on the Island, I would now be in this circle of women in their late fifties. What would I be doing? Both of them are now divorced but proclaim without prompting that they are not unhappy about having another chance at a life as sister-roommates. They are catching up with life, finishing sentences for each other, free of the men who had limited them in their pursuits of a more enjoyable vida. "Te imaginas," one says to me, "that hombre I put up with while my children were still young even tried to keep me away from the church." This sister is part of my mother's prayer group and offers to say the Rosary one of the nine nights of the novena.

I am introduced to an older man who speaks to me in very careful textbook English, enunciating each word much as my father always had. Now a retired English teacher, he had been one of my father's high school classmates. I wonder if my father could have grown old here in this pueblo. I know he once had a dream of teaching. Would he now be joining this man and other friends at dominoes, reminiscing about the old days when they both played baseball on the school's team, or would he have been claimed by the plan, or by some predetermined fate embedded in his DNA, regardless of where he had found himself? *El destino*, or fate, seems to be a concept that works for both sides, believers and nonbelievers. *Es lo mismo*, my mother would have pointed out. It is the same thing, her destino and my science.

After a few hours, I go to the back of the dimly lit room to rest. I am feeling worn out from the coughing and my relentless stomach-ache. I believe my symptoms are all a result of stress and grief. I know will feel better as soon as my public duties are done. A man dressed like a *jíbaro*—an iconic country type found in paintings and sculptures to symbolize the innocent agricultural days—swaggers over and sits next to me. He appears to be in costume: straw hat, work pants, rough leather sandals, and white handkerchief in his hand. I nod and smile but keep my eyes lowered, pretending to read the little remembrance card that announces my mother's birth and death dates accompanied by a prayer for her eternal repose on the other side. For its cover, my uncle had suggested the image of el Divino Niño, a pink-robed baby Jesus standing on a fluffy white cloud inscribed with the words "Yo reinaré," I will reign. He is crowned with a large gold halo, his pudgy arms raised toward a baby-blue sky in triumph. My uncle seems unconsciously determined to keep muted all the things that surround his little sister's departure. He wants her swathed in soft, feminine colors, from the white casket and pink roses and carnations of the corona he had delivered to these cards that seem more appropriate for a child's funeral. He wants to remember her as the little girl he had once taken care of.

The man pulls his chair too close to mine and stares at me until I raise my eyes.

"¿No eres de aquí, verdad?" You are not from here, right? Without waiting for me to answer, he adds, "I can tell by how you distance yourself from la gente." His tone is disdainful, his campesino accent so exaggerated that I suspect it is mostly put on for my benefit. I do not answer. I am puzzled about how this man sees me and why he seems so angry. I can only guess that he must be, in his own eyes, a representative of the true Island Puerto Rican, a true patriot, one of the few who has not sold out to the imperialists in America. He is affronted by the impression I must have made—the daughter de afuera sitting apart, obviously trying to isolate herself at her own mother's velorio. He has come over to let me know that I am a stranger, an ugly American in his eyes.

Later, I see Ángel standing by the casket, being embraced by the same man. I wait until the jíbaro takes a seat next to another of my uncles, the one whose party affiliation is pro-independence and who was put in a federal prison once for protesting the U.S. Navy maneuvers, practice bombings on our *isla-nena* of Vieques. *Isla-nena* means baby island. The one-pueblo islands of the archipelago are considered the children of the isla-grande, the Big Island, the mother island, which itself is only thirty-five by one hundred miles. The family is the unit of measurement here, and to some people, such as my uncle, a serious, conscientious man, the American colonizing presence, and even its assumed paternalistic role, is untenable. *Palabras.* It is always a matter of the chosen word. My mother would call the Americans protectors, rather than oppressors. Yet she was on the front lines defending my uncle when he was arrested; the whole family, in spite of its major political differences, fought for his release. Passionate politics and political theater are a way of life here, and some choose to dress for their parts. I can't help but wonder whether the *jíbaro* is at my mother's wake to accompany us in our pena or to make a point. *I measure every grief.*

At around eleven that night, when I am as tired as I have ever been, a dark-skinned woman with rosary beads in her hand stands up in front of the chapel and announces, in a subtly accented voice (Jamaican, Virgin Islands?), that with the family's permission she would like to lead us in the Rosary for the soul of our sister en el nombre de Jesucristo. I have the center seat directly in front of the casket, so I respectfully place it facing the people, offering it to the woman. In what I interpret to be an annoyed tone, she immediately turns the chair to face my mother's casket. "Una falta de respeto," she says to me. "Disrespectful to turn your back to the difunta." Defeated by fatigue, embarrassed by my unintentional disrespect of the departed, I walk to the back of the room to sit by myself. Soon I start to go into a sort of trance, a dreamlike state induced by the repetitive prayers and the woman's incantatory intonation. I want more than anything to fall into a deep, dreamless sleep. Is this what I will face if I stay for the novena? Nine nights of hypnotic laments, praises to Mary and the Son and the Father, and admonitions to the faithful and the less-than-faithful. Ave María. At my grandmother's novena fifteen years ago, I had been both moved and alienated by the ritual, which I judged from the periphery of my vision. I wrote a poem, "Noche Nueve," to try to understand how I felt about the experience, but its tone now seems too flip, too dismissive. In the poem I speak of the rezadora who leads us in an endless loop of prayers to "God, the gatekeeper, Mary, the housemother, Saint Peter, / the hard-of-hearing custodian" as we try to stay awake, eager to rise from the "hard folding chairs branded with the name of the funeral home, to be returned." We do this because "we are negotiating for the key to the comfortable room / where our tired matriarch will spend eternity." At the end of the ninth night

> . . . We can toast
> her memory with the customary hot chocolate and crackers,
> kiss her photo on the little altar of wilting tropical flowers
> from her backyard and the FDS bouquets
> called in by mainland descendants,
> all the blossoms now equally redolent
> as flores para los muertos; and go home
> to face our private grief.

I have a choice. I could go home to my real life and do my grieving in private. I have a return flight scheduled in a couple of days. I could avoid going through a rite I believe is mostly superstition posing as religion. Or I could stay and pretend to believe that the soul wants to stay in this life, and that the prayers we say again and again will enlighten it as to its true destination. If I believed this, I'd also have to believe in heaven and hell and the resurrection of the body, wouldn't I?

The rezadora makes the sign of the cross and then goes to the casket and kisses my mother. She comes to me and takes me in her arms. "¿Por qué esas lágrimas, Hija?" She wipes my cheek with her hand, "Why the tears? Your mother was a believer. She is on her way to paradise. Let us rejoice."

I did not realize I have been crying. Too exhausted to notice tears. I am suffering from cramped muscles after the day-long vigil. The woman then asks Ángel, who has come over to help me up, "Shall we start the novenas the day after tomorrow?"

"What do you think?" Ángel passes the question to me.

"Está bien." Why had I waited? Perhaps I thought I'd be released from the long penance by the family, who must understand that my family is waiting, that I have done all I can do here. But I haven't, and I feel a sense of relief at knowing that I must, that I will, stay. I will stay for as long as I can.

At almost midnight, the lights at the funeral home are dimmed and people file out. I stay until one of the assistants comes in and quietly starts to close the lid on the coffin. I take one last look at her. I touch her face and her hands for the last time. Throughout the day many people have commented on how much I resemble her. I have said *gracias, gracias*. Someone said that she looked younger somehow, "La muerte la rejuveneció." A strange thing to say, "Death has made her young again." I had wanted my mother to live to be very old when she died; I wanted to see her age, and I wanted her to see me get old too. I did not want her to look young in a casket. It is time to close the lid. Time to turn off the lights.

47   Does anyone have palabras?
     I have palabras.

Back at the house I find the little stack of the books I had inscribed for my mother, most of them also dedicated to her, and I choose the Spanish translation of my book *Woman in Front of the Sun*. I begin practicing the lines I will read at the funeral. What I want to say with my poem is that there are a few things I knew about my mother with absolute certainty, the most important being that she believed in a yielding world, one that offered as many opportunities for joy as it did for pain. I have never attained this balanced vision, and now that she is gone, I am afraid that my measurements will be skewed, that I will be naturally drawn toward la tristeza. I will say only good things about my mother. I will thank Ángel for the care and the good years, la familia for their love and support. I will praise her, not because she was a perfect woman, but because she shaped the world she wanted to live in. I will eulogize but will not canonize.

As I wander around her house tired beyond any possibility of sleep, I experience a rush of memories. I recall vividly the day she called me to say that she had a lot on which to build a house. After years of struggling, she had secured a little piece of land and the loan for a house. It was the closest to euphoria I had ever heard in her voice. A house of her own. When John and I visited her that summer, she walked us around her property and described the little cement house she planned to build.

Over the years we helped her and Ángel furnish the house and even talked her into bedroom air conditioning units—every year I, *la gringa* that I had become, threatened to go stay at the nearby Hilton on account of the heat. She filled the house with knickknacks and covered the walls with family pictures. As I walk down the hall now, I see myself growing up and growing older. The latest pictures are of Eli, the great-grandson she was going to meet this year. How different this home is from the others we occupied during our transient years—our bare apartments in New Jersey filled with my father's silence. So much stuff and ruckus here. With the windows open, even at midnight there are radios to be heard, people calling out to each other, the frogs, the crazy rooster that crows at all hours. This is how she liked it: "La vida. Se oye la vida." You can hear life. Yet she had not returned to an island paradise. La Isla del Encanto of the commercials was a thing of the distant past, if it had ever existed. The vida she heard outside her home could also be dangerous; the crime rate, the drugs, the violence matched and surpassed that of even our urban jungle of Paterson, New Jersey, in the sixties. But the thought of living in a gated community, or especially in a retirement community, was repellent to her. She had had enough of the four walls of apartment life. She liked throwing open her doors and windows in the morning and letting the sounds of life fill her house. "Dar aliento," she'd say when she heard the voices of children on their way to school, meaning to give courage or energy. *Aliento* means breath. The sounds of daily life, the palabras spoken in her own language, were what she had missed in our locked and guarded lives. She was aware of the dangers, the lower standard of living, the political corruption, the power outages, and the hurricanes that beset her island, but none of this was going to keep her from declaring herself a winner in the immigrant's lottery—her prize was returning home.

She had little mantras that she invoked on different occasions. When we'd arrive at her house from our shopping expeditions or day trips, she'd always say, "Qué bueno llegar a casa."

How good it is to come home.

48 Whenever I visited my mother, I'd always go into her room before we went out, to see what she was wearing and to have her check my choices. I was very aware of her pickiness in clothing and of my cluelessness about appropriate attire for special occasions. I knew I was to dress modestly when she took me to visit our ancient church, which she liked to do often, since it sits on the highest spot in town, offering a great view of the town and a delicious breeze. This is the same hill where Nuestra Señora de la Monserrate appeared to a terrified woodcutter and a bull that was charging him and both fell to their knees. Steps had been cut from the hill and a shrine built to her on the very spot of the apparition. The mural scene was burned into my pupils as I sat in front of it numerous times in my childhood—woodcutter on his knees, bull on its knees, the dark-skinned Lady levitating over a tree. To my mother, it was sacred ground. I'd be reminded: no shorts, cover your shoulders, no excessive jewelry. Or if we were going out to a political event: don't wear red or green, those are the other party's colors. Blue was good; it was the Estadistas' official color. We made a game of this—I'd try to sneak in a little

red or green just to excite her into witty, scornful remarks about the showy parrot colorations of her political opponents.

On the day of her burial, I select one of the two skirts I had brought with me, a brown pleated skirt that looks very similar to the one I had worn as a school uniform during the short time I was enrolled the same grammar school that both she and my father had attended. I add one of my numerous black tops and head for her room to ask her what she thinks. A stomach cramp doubles me over, and I run to the bathroom only to find it already occupied by my brother.

"I'm in distress," I say to him through the door.

"We all are," he answers, perhaps automatically falling into the argumentative mode that often characterizes our exchanges. He may have thought that I was merely informing him that I was in emotional pain. Interesting that grief turns everything around it to grief.

I collapse into my mother's rocker and just let the waves of nausea pass over me. I let self-pity take over. "Me duele, Mami," I rock and repeat. "Me duele mucho." Time is folding on itself, like origami.

"What do you think of this outfit, Mami?"

"Hija, we are going to dinner at the Casa Blanca restaurant, not a service at the temple of Jehovah's Witnesses," she'd have laughed, "Why don't you ever wear colors? You always dress as if you are going to an entierro." Today is the day for which I have apparently always dressed appropriately. *Entierro*, literally to be put into the earth, *en la tierra*.

The chapel fills up fast. My youngest uncle, who is close to my age, points out the priest.

"Mira, we ran around, corríamos juntos, with el Padre when we were children. He ate at Mamá's table often because he was an orphan. His mother died when he was a baby, and his father, an American, went back to los Estados Unidos, leaving him to be raised by his abuela. They lived in the last little house at the bottom of the hill in our barrio. He was always outside when people came and went from the barrio. Even then he was giving blessings to travelers. '¡Vayan con Dios!' Do you remember?"

The priest looks vaguely familiar. Then I remember: he attended one of my readings long ago. Our age or a little older than us, he seems young in ways that I recognize as a byproduct of the religious life. Many nuns and priests I have known have a sort of youthful luster to their skin, unless they are missionaries in a harsh climate or working in combat zones. These chosen people seem hardly used by life. Perhaps it is a result of their faith and their devotionals and good thoughts. Meditation and prayer do have their rewards. I have noted the same aura lighting up the Dalai Lama and his monks. A healthy spiritual diet may result in a glow that nonbelievers lack. *El padre* takes my hands in his and speaks his blessing. His smile is truly beatific. He is here to celebrate my mother's life, I intuit, not to sermonize, and I am relieved. I can't bear to hear any ashes-to-ashes and dust-to-dust pronouncements today.

El Padre surprises me when he begins his eulogy by quoting from my first novel, a fictionalized account of my family's life in Hormigueros and in Paterson, New Jersey. He has chosen a passage that describes Ramona, the protagonist's mother, as a sensitive young woman who finds herself severed from family, culture, and language and thrust into an alien environment. In the cold city of her exile she learns not only to survive, but to re-create a microcosm of home for herself and her children, all while keeping alive the hope of returning to her casa on the Island. He then talks about how he had been a witness to the departures and homecomings of the heroic young women who had left *el pueblo* in anguish, thinking themselves weak and dependent, and had year after year returned as strong combatants. Made strong by life afuera, much like the men he had also seen leave as naive young soldiers and sailors and had sometimes seen return as confident men and heroes—when the American wars had not claimed their lives, that is.

From his grandmother's front yard, the priest had seen a generation come and go as they boarded the cars that would transport them across the island to the airport in San Juan and then across the Atlantic to *Nueva York*. These dramas were enacted in front of his house, as it was a rocky hill all the way up to my abuela's house at the top, with *casitas* on either side. Out of those casas emerged our parents as young people on their way into the unknown. He talked about how he had seen some of them collapsed in grief. They would have *ataques de nervios* during these departures, similar to those experienced by soldiers diagnosed with the Puerto Rican Syndrome. El Padre spoke of this particular cultural grief that outsiders could not understand. Even as a young child he had understood what made these young people weep and fall to the ground, as if leaving this island were more than they could bear. They were grieving for a time and place that could never be regained, and for a spiritual condition represented by family ties that would be stretched by distance and sometimes broken. They were not crazy. They were giving free rein to a sadness like no other. He spoke of *la tristeza por la familia y el país* that women like my mother wore with pride once they accepted it as their *destino.* And he praised my mother for having attained her dream of returning home and building her own casita. He said she had been rewarded for her sacrifice afuera. God had blessed her by letting her return to her beloved Island. He called my mother an unsung hero of the diaspora and thanked me for writing about her and our town and especially for honoring the name of Nuestra Señora, La Monserrate—adding, with a sly smile, even if I had fictionalized her a little—who was now welcoming my mother with open arms.

I am both honored and slightly embarrassed by el Padre's choice to deconstruct my novel in this setting, and grateful that he has called my mother a hero and blessed. He is a literary man, a man who has read widely and has also written books. Listening to him talk about what my novel has meant to him, I begin to see my work in a new light—that is, illuminated by the light of a single votive candle flickering in front of the statue of Mary in his church, one that I did not light, but neither will I extinguish.

49 The old section of the cemetery looks like a city of the dead with its mausoleums and statues of angels and the Holy Mother. She is everywhere. I recall when my mother and I visited this *cementerio* together for me to admire her recently constructed tomb. "Mira," she said, pointing to another tomb that was either particularly bizarre or

particularly poignant, depending on your point of view. "This was a young girl's bedroom, a gift her parents had given her before she died." She sighed. "If I could take it with me . . ."

"What would you take if you could, Mami?"

"Mi casita. Entera." She had laughed, and then crossed herself for laughing in a graveyard.

If she could have, she would have taken her entire little house with her. It had just been finished at that time. Modest, very small, a doll-house she had immediately filled with the tokens and talismans she had stored and preserved for so many years.

The ceremony at the gravesite is brief. The men of the family, including my brother, have lifted the casket out of the hearse and placed it near the open grave. Too deep, I think. She'll be so far underground. My claustrophobia kicks in, and a coughing fit. I feel many eyes on me, waiting for me. When the convulsions pass I wipe my eyes and glance up to see my father's ghost in the crowd. He appears to be my age or a little older.

"Prima," my father's nephew kisses me, and speaking in my father's voice minus the heavy accent, he says, "I am very sorry about your mother. Your brother sent me an e-mail and I drove here. Glad I made it in time." He steps back into the crowd.

I keep staring at him. He had been at the funeral home. I had seen him. But at that time he had not yet transformed into the ghost of my father.

I have not seen my cousin in years. He has grown into the Ortiz look in middle age. Fair skin, light hair, now peppered with gray, and a military bearing. This cousin, at least a decade older than I, is a Vietnam veteran. Most of the Ortiz clan was scattered by the military on the mainland and made their lives there. This cousin is one of the few Ortiz family members who has come back to Puerto Rico. He now owns land and animals in a town in the center of the Island, but because he travels frequently, I've rarely seen him on my visits.

I must look as weak as I feel because one of my Morot cousins comes over puts her arm around my waist. Testimonials are called for by the funeral director: "Palabras. Does anyone have palabras for Fanny Morot?"

Several people speak of my mother, her civic-mindedness, her generosity, her faith. A former mayor of the town talks about her *alegría*, how she made even the dullest political meeting seem like a fiesta with her enthusiasm. "And let us not forget that Ángel and Fanny were the salsa champions of the senior set." Laughter. I had been hoping there would be laughter.

I come closer to her casket and lay my book on it. I speak some palabras for my mother too. I thank la familia for their support, and my brother for staying to the end with me. *Estamos aquí, Mami.* I hold Ángel's hand as I express my gratitude for the good years he had shared with her and for being her *pareja*, her other half in life and on the dance floor. I mention the years of her exile and I speak my father's name. He is part of her story too. Then I read the poem I had written the year of the storm, when I had finally attained a bit of grace. I admit that perhaps this may not have been the kind of conversion she had wanted me to seek, but it is the only state of grace I may access through my work; it comes to me not as a tongue of fire, but as an understanding of how the ordinary may be transformed into art in anyone's life. I read from my essay about returning to her house, "Woman in Front of the Sun":

> She and I had both found a way to give meaning to our lives, and it was the same for both of us. We collected the materials for our collage, we looked for possible patterns emerging from the pieces, we organized them in a way that seemed right to us, and finally we hoped that the others, whose view of our work mattered to us, saw its beauty and value. . . .

"Before the Storm"
We are talking in whispers
about what is worth saving. A box of photographs
is pushed under the bed, and the rendering

of Jesus knocking at somebody's door, a hesitant young man,
that arrived with us in each new house, and another
of his dear mother holding his poor broken body
not many years later, are taken down
from their precarious places on the walls.
We surprise each other with our choices.
                    She fills boxes
while I watch the sky for signs, though I feel,
rather than see, nature is readying
for the scourge. Falling silent, the birds seek safety
in numbers, and the vagabond dogs cease their begging
for scraps. The avocados are dropping
from the laden trees in her backyard
as if by choice. Bad weather always brings in a good crop
of the water-fruit, she tells me; it is the land
offering us a last meal.

        On the outer islands, the fragile homes of the poor
are already in its jaws, the shelters we see on film,
all those bodies huddled in the unnatural dark, the wind howling
like a hungry dog in the background, make us stand solemn.
In the mainland my family and friends will watch
the satellite pictures of this storm with trepidation
as it unravels over the Caribbean. But I am already too close
to see the whole picture. Here, there is
a saturated mantle descending,
a liquid fullness in the air, like a woman feels
before the onset of labor. Finally,
the growing urgency of the sky, and I am strangely excited,
knowing that I am as ready as I will ever be,
should I have another fifty years to go,
to go with my mother
toward higher ground. And when we come home, if
we come home, if there's a home where we believe
we left one, it will all be different.

50 *The origins of grace*

All human nature vigorously resists grace because
grace changes us and the change is painful.

—FLANNERY O'CONNOR

I do not feel full of grace after burying my mother. If anything, I am empty and listless. I have met my duties, and now my sense of obligation shifts to the family waiting for me at home. I have the return ticket that I've chosen not to use. We have spent months planning a trip to Disney. Eli watched Disney documentaries in preparation and made a list of rides he wanted to go on—all this before he was taken to his first funeral and his wide-eyed wonder was focused not on Mickey Mouse or fantasy castles, but on the image of his great-granddaddy being put into the ground. He kept asking his parents if (not when) I was going to return. My family was grieving without me, yet I could not pry myself away from my mother's house, not yet.

After the funeral my aunts take me home and one of them asks Ángel and me for permission to contact the rezadoras, the women who pray the novenas, and tell them to begin the next evening. There was an unspoken assumption that I would attend only the first night.

"Es la costumbre aquí to pray the nine nights, and el Padre has offered to come here to say a Mass. This is unusual, a privilege not granted to many," my aunt addresses me rather formally in front of a group of relatives.

There ensues an effort to recall the last time a Mass had been performed at someone's house. No one could recall an ordinary person ever having been so honored.

"But el Padre can only do it on Friday night. We will all be here, so do not worry. The family will be represented every night of the novena. One of us can come and help Ángel prepare the house."

"I will stay. Me quedo para las novenas." I have spoken it, and it's become a reality. I have now committed to the nine days and nights when I had thought I'd stay for only one or two beyond my original plan. The family would have taken over this last duty. They had let me know that they understood my need to go home. I had not expected

the words to come out of my mouth. I didn't want the hours of repetitious prayers, the hugs and kisses from strangers, and the "estoy
con ustedes en su pena" on an endless loop like a snatch of song lyric
you want so desperately to forget. I wanted to go home. My home.
But my mouth opened and I said, "I will stay, and I will help Ángel
through the novenas."

51 The word *grace* is translated from the Greek in the New Testament,
charis, and it is the source of charisma, meaning a gracious gift. Grace,
according to Catholic belief, can be bestowed only by God through the
sacraments. Long ago I ceased taking the sacraments, and I no longer
feel an affinity to the practices and symbolism to which I dedicated
so much of my childhood. Yet at this moment, I'm overcome with a
longing for such rituals. It is a need imprinted on my psyche. This has
happened to me before. John and I had Tanya baptized even though
neither of us attended any church. I had felt a need to protect my
child from any repercussions of my nonbelief. My mother reminded
me that babies who die without the sacrament are assigned to Limbo
for eternity—Limbo, a nonplace where you don't suffer but can
never meet God, or, in other words, a concept obviously invented to
punish negligent parents with guilt. While Limbo is one of the many
Catholic fantasies, both kind and cruel, I no longer believe in, I could
not risk it being true. I am always surprised by my brain's devolutions
and by my propensity to rely on the eternal por si acaso I claim to
have outgrown. For reasons beyond the limits of my logical mind,
I want to pray for the release of my mother's soul, and I will sit still
and do so for nine nights. It is imperative. She had suffered nine days
before she expired; I will stay nine more days and complete my self-
imposed novena. I am invoking the winds of Dante's purgatory for
myself, and I know it. But I give myself over to it, research it, make
plans to tie myself to the mast.

Grace, to the believer, may come as a gift from God, whether you
want it or not. In some religions, grace has to be earned through
good deeds, spiritual practices, self-abnegation, and prayer. To the
nonbeliever, grace is a nonconcept, akin to the idea of luck. In any

case, I will stay and wait to see if I can see it, whatever it is, luck or grace, where my mother had apparently found it.

I call John and convince him to take the family to Disney World without me. I call the travel agent and change my return flight. Then I begin making to-do lists. There are specific things I can do to help Ángel get on with life. I need to make the house ready for the next nine days.

I schedule the hardest task first: the giving away of my mother's clothes and what are euphemistically called her personal effects.

52 Keepsakes and empty places

I begin with an inventory of her books, many of which I had sent to her via Amazon.com. It was one of our regular long-distance shopping rituals. I would call her while on the *Libros en español* website and read her titles. We compromised in her areas of interest and mine. She liked the mind candy of Nora Roberts and Danielle Steele, whose numerous books have Spanish versions. The books I wanted her to read ranged from Gabriel García Márquez (that is one talkative hombre) to Isabel Allende (she talks a lot too but at least has great women characters) to the contemporary writers whose stories I hoped she'd find familiar: Amy Tan, Julia Alvarez, Sandra Cisneros. She would often tease me by claiming that her favorite Latina writer was Isabel Allende. My part was to act offended so she could say, "I don't think of you as a Latina writer, Hija. You are my daughter, la escritora puertorriqueña." I loved her takes on the stories she read. She admired the strong female characters, but only if they showed respeto for their parents and did not reject their ethnic heritage. She enjoyed Amy Tan but did not like what she said about her mother, mainly about the broken English she spoke. Teaching English has made me a bit jaded about literary criticism, and so her deeply personal interpretations of books I often taught kept me going back to them for the human experience my mother extracted from her reading. I looked at every book that she signed with her name—she was a lending library to her relatives and friends, and she wanted her books returned. It was a bragging point with her that she received more boxes by UPS than any of her neighbors. There was still one unopened Amazon box on her little desk—one of my choices, a Steinbeck novel, *Las uvas de la ira*.

To give her all the books she ever wanted was a privilege I relished. I had been the one who had brought her the few books in Spanish I could find at the library in the seventies in the southern towns where we lived, and I'd seen how she'd plowed through Unamuno's dense philosophical works (Ave María. *Qué pesado*, heavy and pessimistic) and how she delighted in Lorca's poems. *Verde que te quiero verde*. Palabras, she needed to hear the Spanish in her head.

The books were her soul food. I packed the boxes in categories and put them in the hallway. I would tell my aunts, who would be coming to help me sort her things in the afternoon, what kinds of books each box contained, and they would divide them among the family. Romance, mystery, travel, philosophy. I felt good that I had helped feed my mother's hungry mind, for she had fed my imagination. Why was she so crucial to my work?

Sometimes we shopped together long-distance. I would describe an item to her over the phone, and she would approve it or not. Now I pull all her clothes out of the closet and lay them on the bed in categories: formal, party, casual. I set her nightgowns aside to dispose of along with her underwear and stockings. I do not want anyone else touching these items. Ángel has given me leave to do as I see fit with clothes and books. He wants Tanya and me to have the few good pieces of jewelry. I notice that he is wearing her favorite ring on his little finger.

I also put two of her hand fans, her *abanicos*, which she had with her constantly, in my suitcase. The fancy hand-painted fan, the one she took to church, I will give to Tanya, and the old one that she kept next to her chair, the one that has a coffee stain and still smells of cigarette smoke, I will keep.

It hurts me that the essence of my mother is tainted with the poisonous stain and smell of nicotine. It lingers in her clothes despite the lavender sachets in her closet and dresser drawers.

She had kept the inexpensive jewelry I had sent her as souvenirs from my travels in their original boxes. Earrings, bracelets, pendants of coral, onyx, Native American silver, and turquoise from San Antonio, Las Cruces, San Francisco, New York, Atlanta. I place each box on her dresser, mementos of my mother for my aunts and cousins. I feel as if I am dismantling her life one object at a time. This is her collection, her personal collage, made up of everything she thought worth keeping. I am uncomfortable putting objects that had connected us over the years into boxes and bags to give away. I tell myself I have to do this for Ángel's sake. He will continue to live in her house, and I cannot selfishly choose to leave it as a museum to her memory for me to visit sometime in the future. It has to remain a home for him.

Her presence is strong in this room full of her possessions; here I see and smell the paradox of my mother, who loved life but could not or would not face the habit that would kill her. I did not idealize my mother in life; I will not do so in death. There is, in the very fabric of things she held closest to her, more evidence of her poison of choice. I discover a half-empty pack of cigarettes in one of her purses and I crush each one before flushing them. Although I wash my hands repeatedly, I smell the tobacco on my fingers all day.

As a car bringing several female relatives pulls up, Ángel calls me to the dining room. He points to what he calls her altar, a credenza covered with *miniaturas* and religious objects, pictures of all of us, and souvenirs, and he whispers, "Por favor, no quiero huecos. I do not want holes in the house." At first, I don't quite understand what he is saying, until he points to the objects and to the picture-covered walls. He doesn't want empty spaces in the house. He wants the things she had so lovingly collected for their home to remain as she had left them. I understood that the empty spots would hurt him more than seeing it all where it had always been for the two of them.

"Está bien." I promise him that I will not give away anything other than what had been in her closet and in her dresser drawers. I show him the boxes and the clothes on the bed. I ask him if I can have the photo albums of my brother's family and mine.

"Sí, está bien. I will not miss what I do not see every day. I just do not want to look at empty spaces."

While my relatives and I carry boxes and bags to cars, Ángel sits at the table, occupying himself by trying to fix a wall clock that had stopped sometime during the week before she died. I read that it was the custom in times past to stop the clocks at the time of a person's death, to draw the curtains, to drape mirrors with a dark cloth so as to keep the spirit of the deceased from getting trapped in the looking glass. A black wreath would be placed at the door to announce that the house was en luto.

But all we need to do is give away what we can no longer bear to keep, and look again and again at the things we need to hold on to. After everyone leaves, I sit down with the bulging photo albums, which tell her story and our family's in no particular sequence. I look for the points of intersection and departure in these images. I see her as younger and sadder, and then older and happier. I grieve for the lonely girl in exile and feel pity for the orphan, me, before I was an orphan. How old can you be and still call yourself an orphan? I am parentless. And the strongest tie I will ever have to the country of my birth is gone. I am no longer at home in my native land without my mother, no longer at home in my mother tongue.

In these old albums and scrapbooks she valued so much, I look for myself before the fork in the road, before duality became my main mode of being, before I had a divided self. I experience what is sometimes called marginality as time travel, a vortex where I am living in the past and present at once. My past is intrinsically connected to her, and now there is a hueco, an empty space like the ones Ángel does not want to face. In trying to find a sequence and a timeline for her life, I start to see why my mother became whole as I became divided. She knew who she was and where she belonged from the beginning. No matter where she found herself, she was always heading back to that place. She kept an idea of home alive in her imagination—an instinct, a memorized map. And she would reinvent the place if she could not find it where she had left it so long ago. I have no dream of place. Home to me is where the people I love are, at any given moment in time.

53 The excursion is the same when you go looking for your
sorrow as when you go looking for your joy.

—EUDORA WELTY

The photos do not reveal the huecos in our lives. Their original
purpose was to record the days we thought worth remembering.
Sometimes they reveal more, but by accident. Here are my brother
and I posing with our mother in one of our living rooms in Paterson.
The room is uncluttered, and the view from the window—that white
shade was almost always down, so the photographer (my father?)
must have needed more light—is of a gray building and rooftops
beyond. It became a family joke that the dismal city view almost
always triggered one of my mother's dramatic sighs, usually followed
by "Si tuviera alas." Yes, we knew, if only she had wings, she would fly.
She would certainly fly home.

She stands very straight, chin up, attentive to my father's directions, but she is not smiling. Photo after photo taken in those days
show a lack of focus on her face. To me, she looks like a woman waiting for life to happen, but I don't think she would have agreed with
my assumptions. She did not intellectualize; she endured, and her
philosophy was basic. Así es la vida, that's the way life is—or was—
was an almost automatic response to complaints about things that
had to be accepted. She usually brushed aside my questions about
her loneliness during those years, but recently I had asked her again
how it was to live so far away and without her family. She had said,
"Me sentía defraudada." She had felt defrauded? Robbed? Of her
right to pursue her happiness in her own way? The word casa echoed
through our many temporary homes. Going home to her mother's
casa was my mother's singular goal during her self-designated exilio.
But when she did finally return permanently to her mother's house,
she felt stifled by the maternal vigilance. The loving matriarch was
also an old-fashioned woman who believed in luto forever and disap-
proved of my mother's new set of wings. Soon after her return to the
Island, my mother began to prepare herself for an independent life.
I was surprised to hear that she wanted to leave the place she had

dreamed of returning, Mamá's casa. I heard only snatches of stories about Mamá's attempts to re-establish control over her middle-aged daughter's life. "She waits for me on the porch when I go out," my mother told me, "and later complains that she is not getting enough sleep because of my gallivanting."

My mother's *gallivanting* mostly involved church-sponsored events, political rallies, and dancing with friends—but once she excitedly told me that she and a woman friend had stopped at a nightclub to use the restroom one night, a place called El Otro Mundo, and the other world turned out to be a gay club! She had had a glimpse of women dancing with women, and men with men, and kissing! She had enjoyed this excursion into a different world, perhaps even more so because her mother would have been out-raged. Even though I feared for my mother as she tried out those nascent wings, I saw that she was going through a belated adolescent rebellion. She had married so young that she had missed the opportunity to face off with her possessive mother, and vice versa. Although I loved and admired my strong-willed grandmother, the woman who taught me the power of storytelling and whose strength of character I have often written about, I understood that for my mother to survive in a country she had left as a very young wife and mother, she was going to have to learn to fly. Our weekly phone calls in those days, when I was trying to get through graduate school with a toddler at home and only John's income to support us, were two-way therapy sessions. She encouraging me not to give up on my dreams of teaching and writing, and I coaching her on becoming a liberated woman. It must have felt like both a victory and a betrayal when she finally rented a little house in the middle of town, under the shadow of the church on its hill. "I can hear el Padre say Mass from my porch! I can also hear the jukebox from el café down the street." *Ay vida.* There is life to be lived and savored. Mamá would still send her hot plates of food daily via one of the grandchildren, and my mother visited her every day, which was a tribute my abuela exacted from her children until she died. She was the center of our family and remained on her throne until the end.

She had not needed wings: her kingdom was her casa, and we all arrived there, and returned there, like homing pigeons.

I will never return to my mother's casa. Even if I come back, it will be to her widower's home, and even if Ángel keeps everything just as she left it, I will see only objects, not her hand upon them.

54 *Novenas and las costumbres*

On the day of the first novena, I look for my mother's spirit in her home. According to old beliefs, the soul will have to be given light and directions if it is to find the way to its next destination. I remember her lighting a white candle for her parents' spirits.

One of my aunts has left a list of what we'll need for the first novena: a candle, a Bible, a picture or statue of Mary, holy water, and flowers, all to be placed on a table covered with a white cloth. I search the house for these items. Ángel has produced a little glass bottle with a cross on it—the holy water he had at the hospital, with which he'd make the sign of the cross on my mother's forehead every morning. He goes to town to buy fresh flowers (I ask him to try to find azucenas) while I find her Bible (on her dresser), a plaster statue of Madonna and Child (on her dining room "altar"), and a candle (a drawer full in her kitchen in case of power outages or spiritual needs). I can't locate an all-white tablecloth, so I call an aunt, who says one of them should have one and would bring it that night. I hear a commotion outside and see that the funeral home workers have arrived with the folding chairs, which they stack against the wall. They hand me the traditional *panderetas*, the hand fans stamped with religious prints in front and an ad for the funeral home in back. Ángel comes home with the flowers and asks if I want to go to the grocery store with him, as he is not familiar with the items my aunts had specified. We are to get a particular kind of hot cocoa mix, which is traditionally prepared on the last night, and a large tin of soda crackers, plus *queso de bola—es la costumbre aquí*, my uncle had told me, to serve this type of cheese at novenas. We should also buy water and soft drinks, as people would be very thirsty after praying for hours.

The grocery store seems to make Ángel sad. He has never been the one to shop for groceries, and even now, he chooses items we need at the house from her specific list of brands: only Colgate toothpaste, only jabón de Castilla (castile soap), only Old Colony grape soft drinks, *uvitas*. He tells me her reasons, and I see my mother's hand shaping her reinvented world down to the last detail. These were brands we had used when I was a child, during the times when she had enjoyed a reprieve from our father-directed lives on the mainland. She was preserving the illusion of a return to casa by re-creating the past in detail, down to the familiar smells. In my writer's mind, I identify this effort to keep faith as the driving force in her life: she had to believe that she had achieved her dream, and an illusion can be as good as reality. I know this with certainty. It is my work. I too create an illusion of life, and I believe in it as if my life depended on it. If not, what is the point? *Mi prueba.*

At the supermarket I experience a growing impatience with the constant socializing that goes on around the news of a death. In every aisle, around every corner, are people who know Ángel and knew my mother, who have heard of her illness and unexpected "passing." They all have to embrace us, offer their condolences, and then launch into a "last time I saw her" story, punctuated by "¡Ay benditos!" which, like "¡Ave María!" can be inflected to express anything from petty annoyance to horror. I find myself analyzing these words for honesty, measuring the level of real grief they might or might not contain. I count the clichés, willing myself to endure the lengthy discourses, while Ángel explains calmly what happened in the last two weeks and invites everyone we meet to the novena. I practice smiling and nodding and holding my tongue. This is my prueba, a trial I will endure for her, I tell myself, after the cashier holds up the line to talk at length about the last time she had seen my mother, and to exclaim, "¡Ay bendito! Tienes la misma cara." You look just like her! A declaration that makes the people around us stop and stare at me. Actually, I have my father's facial structure and skin color. I only look like my mother to others because of our thick black hair and petite body type.

But I understand what it's like to see her everywhere. I nod, agreeing that I look exactly like my mother. I thank the cashier for her words. *Gracias, muchas gracias.* I am emotionally drained by the exchanges that are required of the grieving family. *Gracias, muchas gracias,* I want to scream out. *Basta.* Enough. It is the mental fatigue of the unfamiliar that is making me impatient with people who are only doing what they think is proper and right.

In my growing irritation with the slow-motion life in this pueblo, in the costumbres de aquí, and even with my own constant struggle to find the right words in Spanish, I see that my mother's death has created a widening divide between me and my so-called cultural heritage. The role of pretending to be a native is wearing me out. I understand that I am what they suspected, I am de afuera. De afuera, that's right. I am the daughter from the outside. Even the son from the outside is not expected to do what a daughter must. Everyone understood that my brother had to return to his job and his life, and he did.

The fact that I had a professional life and a family waiting was not in question, but I had the role of *la hija buena* to play, a role assigned to me and me alone as the daughter and as the eldest child. *Es la costumbre aquí.*

I am torn between my need to stay until everyone who has known and loved my mother is convinced that I have done my duty and an urgent need to fly home to my own family. But there is no real debate in my mind. *Estoy aquí.* Here I am, and I am bound to stay. My last duties to my mother entail acting as if I believe that her spirit is waiting, like a lone traveler at an airport, to be prayed toward the right gate. I can do this. But I know that her presence, and her essence, which are near and strong, were and will be conjured by my imagination.

55   While I do not believe in an afterlife, I do believe in preserving the stories that shaped us, and this involves remembering and recording the parts played by those who preceded us. Our individual life stories are made up of our collective memory; we keep others alive

in us by weaving the narrative threads together, theirs and ours. The only immortality I know is remembrance. I do believe in the power of grace, or something like it, to alter us, to makes us better. It is what happens on those rare occasions when I have gotten the words right, especially in writing a poem. There is nothing equal to it. It is a sort of lifting above the ordinary, an illumination or transcendence that is as close to a Pentecostal moment as I will ever know. Getting the words right is mostly a matter of total absorption in the task, plus a little luck. It's the little luck that makes all the difference. I have read that the skeptic will put grace in the same category as luck, a nonconcept. But I have come to think of grace as a condition achieved through determination and self-abnegation. By humbling yourself to the task of getting it right. Lately, I've been feeling that my store of grace may have run almost dry. Approaching my sixtieth birthday, I've been struggling to tap into that wellspring from which my poems and stories have flowed. While I can still imagine lives and craft stories, I have been feeling out of touch with that rush of excitement, that moment of heady discovery that addicts writers to language in the first place. That little eureka moment, the tiny flame burning above your head that lets you know that your words have somersaulted into something bigger than yourself, is what the writer lives for. That feeling is what I got out of bed for every day of my adult life. But like the vigor of youth, the elasticity of my skin, and the acuity of eyesight, my ability to suspend my disbelief long enough to admit grace has been waning. While I've still been writing to the best of my ability, I have started to feel a lessening of my powers of concentration and, frankly, of my creative energy. While I have written hundreds of poems and dozens of essays and stories based on my childhood in between worlds, I have recently struggled to regain my faltering voice. The only poems I wrote in the last year were about old women losing their ability to connect with life. "The Muse of Nada" is a decrepit old woman who sits in a bookstore looking for the poems she inspired in a book she will not buy:

Old Mary, all in black, a crow
perched over poems no one will ever buy, the book
having lost its place in the shelves.
"Basta," she says to the lines. Enough
to what? Beauty, truth, wisdom, delight?

Another poem, "Twilight of the Queen of Corona," is an equally
dark look at the end of truth and beauty:

She sits alone by the hotel pool,
her head inclined toward another time—a time
of unruly nights and deliciously slow
awakenings; an elastic time
that always snapped back to its former shape,
without vacuums or holes or losses.
Her body, once a bridge,
separates her more and more,
from the lives moving deliberately
out of her reach.

I sent these poems out as a matter of routine, a long-standing practice: you work on a poem until you abandon it, and abandoning it,
unless you are Emily Dickinson, means casting it out into the world
of literary journals, hoping someone will think it worth sharing with
the invisible, unknown public. They were returned by editors, and
whereas once I would have immediately cast them out again, instead
I put them away indefinitely. And I have not looked at them again
until now. I have decided that these tired characters I created did not
have the necessary energy to engage the imaginations of others. That
tired old muse and exhausted queen of nada.

Nada. Nothing can be made of language if there is no passion driving the words—there has to be a transformation. I realize as I write
this that I have been given another chance, a gift, but at what cost?

56 *The acolyte*

In my Catholic life, I learned the steps needed to erase the spots on a sinful heart. I am hoping they can also be used to relieve my burdened heart. There would be the self-abnegation, the giving in and giving up. "Giving up for Lent" was a good model. Give up things you enjoy, and you will earn the grace needed for redemption. What I yearn for now is a nonreligious awakening so that I can grieve for my mother fully and properly, so that I can begin to reimagine her. How can I connect with her again? There is penance to do first. I will now give up my desire to be home with my family, give up my need to be understood without having to translate, give up my need for privacy. I will also have to commit as well as omit: I will practice patience; I will practice stillness and silence; I will offer my assistance to Ángel; I will serve as an acolyte in the rites and rituals for her soul's release; I will rededicate my work to a task greater than merely that of filling and refilling my nearly empty cup. I have a growing need to tell her story anew—to enter her secret heart—but this time I will not have her as a living source to feed my imagination. I will have to re-create her from memory, fill in the empty place with my imagination.

But I feel incapable—worse, I feel vulnerable, nearly sick from many sleepless nights and the nausea that wakes me whenever I manage to doze off. I do not want to see a doctor here. Since I arrived, I have spoken to doctors only about cancer, about imminent death, about their inability to identify my mother's killer in time to do anything about it. I had been relegated to supplicant in the throne rooms of the rulers of the kingdom of the sick. In any case, I know that my insomnia and even my cough and nausea most likely have one source: a weakened immune system directly attributable to the stress and emotional drain of the past weeks. I know how to find my symptoms and diagnose myself. I have spent many dark hours searching through the magic looking glass of my iPad for guidance in matters others might call spiritual; the irony of looking up the meaning of novena, prayers for the dead, and how to say the Rosary on my electronic device does not escape me. Online, I read testaments of the faithful;

I watched videos of fervent prayer sessions, the faithful counting the rosary beads, chanting the Mysteries, eyes closed. I put myself in their place and studied the rituals like I did my notes for school exams, until I felt confident that I could pass this test. Reading and research have been for me the route to power ever since my early days as translator for my mother, reinforced when I turned myself into a scholarship kid who would, with an education and a mastery of English, break through the boundaries between languages and cultures that imprisoned my parents.

I have a hunger to connect with the power source that fed my mother's passion for life, which seemed to grow with age until cancer struck her down, felled her like a tree that crushes a house. She has been my channel, my medium, connecting me to my culture and language, the triggers to my creative work. As it turns out, what pulled me away from this place is only half my power; the other half has come to me through threads that quietly connected me to this place, these people, threads that I can only see and feel now that they have been torn. In the past, I wrote about my mother in an attempt to learn her secret to leading a fully engaged life — the opposite to my life of the mind, to my impulse, almost always thwarted by my job and other demands, for near reclusiveness. I admired her way of being, but that admiration was contingent on the fact that I assumed her being was separate from my own. Now I realize how much her life, her energy, made my own life possible. I have no more conduits to the culture and language and costumbres of the place of my birth, this ancient pueblo that holds on to tradition with a fierceness that is both admirable and irritating. It wants both a miracle and the Internet. It wants absolute loyalty from hijas who must observe las costumbres and also *mujeres profesionales* who follow the rules in a man's world. It is a place of beauty *and* contradictions, and it's now almost foreign territory to me. Without her to guide me, I feel like a denaturalized citizen of my native land.

57   Ángel sets out the chairs in rows on one end of the pink-tiled porch in front of the little altar my aunt, cousin, and I have set up. The same mosaic tile table where she had sat for her cup of coffee and cigarette is now covered with a white cloth and reconsecrated by the placement of her Bible, a candle, holy water, and a vase of roses. At the far end of the carport is *la marquesina*, which is mostly outdoors and is the beginning of her minuscule botanical garden, with its orchids, hibiscus, roses, miniature palm trees, and shade trees strung with hummingbird feeders and chimes. La marquesina is where most gatherings and parties are held, in the fresh air; where children learn to dance, where young lovers court, where you greet visitors, and where you say good-bye to the ones leaving on their journeys.

The novena is scheduled for 7:00, when we hope it will be cooler. We set up for refreshments on the kitchen counter. I hang my mother's portrait from the funeral on her dining room wall in a prominent place, and I feel her sad eyes on me as I come and go. When I look at the portrait, I try to focus on the flowers in her hair, her festive clothing, her manicured nails. She is dressed for a party. She will always be dressed for a party.

At 6:30 two women walk up, and I rush outside to greet them. They are my mother's age or older and identify themselves as members of her Rosary group. One of them fixes her gaze on me and gently pulls me down onto the folding chair next to hers. She says in a strangely intense way, "Eres una buena hija." You are a good daughter. All I can think to say is "Gracias," but I have an uncomfortable feeling that I am about to be caught in a spell of need. She has the "glittering eye" of the Ancient Mariner. She has arrived early for a reason; she has a story to tell. I've seen this glitter in the eyes of audience members who approach me before and after readings to tell me their own ideas for poems and novels. But this woman is not approaching me as a writer. She calls me "Hija" when she tells me that she saw a picture of Tanya at the funeral home. "Bella," she calls her. Her hand holds my arm; her friend's hand holds her arm. I feel the heat and pressure of her fingers. I feel as if the three of us are joined by a live wire.

"I had a daughter too," she begins.

It is a story that will bear no interruptions. A mother recounting the horrors of her own private tragedy, she becomes an oracle. She speaks as if in a trance. The grieving mother speaks and speaks of months of agony beyond language: "Ay, Hija. She would not come back to the Island so I could care for her. Her husband had to make a living, and she had small children. I went to that cold place and stayed by her bedside to wait for God to take her. I witnessed how my daughter, beautiful like yours, como tú, Hija, was consumed from within by the cancer. In the end, she was no bigger than she had been as an eight-year-old. I could hold her in my lap. I had to come home because my husband became ill with grief and could not travel. But Nuestra Señora gave me strength to do this, and my compañeras raised the money for my trips. My belief in the Sacred Mother and my friends was my support and my comfort. These women embroidered baby clothes, also pillowcases and tablecloths, and sold them. Without their help I could not have been with my niña at the end."

I see Tanya's face. I try to imagine my daughter ill beyond hope, but it is too devastating to comprehend. I can imagine this mother's pain, but I can't share it, not fully. I can't become this woman, and she can't know my pena. But we can try to inhabit each other's minds through our stories, for the moment. Grief is a country with one citizen and one ruler, and they are the same.

Why has she chosen to tell me about her tragedy? Not to add to my pain, but to connect with a fellow sufferer. The bereaved fear disconnection, being left alone in their pain. They also feel shame for the sadness they bear visibly like a rash that others may think is contagious. So who is left to share their pain? Other sufferers. The lepers, the ones touched by death, seek the ones who will not run away and form a community of *tristes*. What is the symptom most recognizable in the carrier of grief?

The need to make herself excruciatingly vulnerable by telling her story.

After I offer my condolences, avoiding the prepackaged phrase of "I share in your pena," I tell her that as the mother of a beloved daughter, I understand her tragic loss. The woman then offers me her blessing. "Prayer is the only thing that helps, Hija." Then I go in the house and sit across from my mother's picture, watching through the window as cars pull up and people gather in front of the house. Soon I hear greetings and the happy Ave Marías of unexpected reunions. "I have not seen you in so long. ¡Hija, tanto tiempo sin verte! How long has it been? Look how tall your daughter has gotten." I try to calm my mind, but the images the grieving mother has transmitted to me have aroused a growing fear for my family's well-being. "One minute you are celebrating the birth of a grandchild," the woman had said, "and the next watching your child die. Así es la vida, Hija."

It is almost time to greet the guests. I help my cousin and aunt set out the paper plates, the plastic cups, the "party supplies," on my mother's dining room table. My aunt comments that there have not been this many people here since my mother paid off her *promesa*.

"When this house was finished, she organized an open reception, to thank la Virgen de la Monserrate for letting her make her dream of a casa come true. All of us contributed. I brought a cake, your other aunts made pasteles and huge pots of rice and beans. She hired musicians—she said you had sent her money for la música. She opened the doors to todo el mundo. The priest came and blessed the house. I wish you could have been there. It was a great fiesta."

I had known about her plan to have this party, but I had not stopped to think about the significance of the celebration. It was the culmination of her main wish in life: a house of her own, no less an important event to her than having my first book published had been to me. But I had been busy with my life.

Now it sounds like the beginning of a party in the front yard. People gathering in her name, who cannot help but smile at one another, comment on their lives since they last saw one another, mention the happy events, the births and weddings, issue invitations to festivities, even laugh. Life in death, death in life—time folds on itself like a fan. I take one of her fans and go stand at the kitchen door leading to the carport. This fan was a souvenir from Tanya's wedding. Tanya and her groom signed the fans and gave them as favors for the guests to use on that hot July day—a gesture my mother had liked, for it showed that Tanya's Puerto Rican heritage influenced some of her choices.

My aunt whispers to me that the sister of my childhood friend is going to lead the prayers on this night. "You probably know that her oldest sister, the one you played with, died of breast cancer a few years ago."

I brace myself for the violence of grace and walk out into my mother's life.

58 The custom of counting prayers on a string of knots is an ancient one practiced by many religions. In Catholic school we learned from a visiting friar. I remember the day clearly because he arrived on a frigid winter morning in Paterson wearing only his brown habit and thin leather sandals. I stared at his red toes the whole time he spoke. He told us that the monks in olden times had kept track of their prayers on a knotted cord or belt. The word *rosary* comes from the Latin term for a garland of roses, with which Mary is associated. It interests me to learn from my Internet research that *rosarius* was also used to designate an anthology or collection of stories or prayers.

From my mother's book *El Sagrado Rosario* I learn this: there are five decades in the Rosary sequence, beginning with the recitation of the Apostles' Creed on the Crucifix. The Our Father is said on each of the large beads that separate the decades of Hail Marys on the small beads. You say the Glory Be after the three Hail Marys at the end of the Rosary and after each decade of the small beads. Each decade represents a mystery or event in the life of Jesus and Mary. The Mysteries of the Rosary are the Joyful, the Luminous, the Sorrowful, and the Glorious. The rezadora announces each of the Mysteries before starting a decade. The Mysteries are said on specific days of the week. Ave María. The rezadora opens the session with "Ave María Purísima." We reply, "Sin pecado concebida." We are in agreement that Mary is the most pure among the pure, and conceived without sin. She is worthy of being our liaison to her Son in heaven.

My mother's novena starts on Thursday. This will be the beginning of the Luminous Mysteries: the Baptism of Jesus in the River Jordan.

"This is my Beloved Son, with whom I am well pleased."

The soft voice of my childhood friend's sister intoning the Ave Marías, the Padre Nuestros, the calls to profess the faith, and the proclamation of the Mysteries blends with the heat of the night and the motions of dozens of hand fans. I sit to the side, near the garden, so I can feel the breeze on my neck. Letting the ritual play in the background, I allow myself to succumb to an irresistible lethargy, a kind of trance. It is an out-of-body experience I know from the long church services of my childhood. I had evaded tedium then by immersing myself in the sensory bath that was a Latin Mass—the Latin chants, the overwhelming scent of incense, the flickering candlelight. Once again, I let the experience overtake me. I am there and not there. I have heard that the point of repetitive movement and chanting in religious rites is to induce a state of self-forgetfulness and a sublimation of the senses, an alternate state that aids the soul's communion with the deity. I experience a brief reprieve. I have no visions, no awakenings.

I rouse from my word-induced torpor when the rezadora stands up to claim this night of prayer for my mother's soul. Everyone crosses themselves, chanting in unison. They recite a prayer to release all the restless or lost spirits, to free those souls who may not have yet found their way to the Holy Mother's arms.

Then the many titles of Mary are proclaimed in a hypnotic litany— Mother of God, Virgin of Virgins, Queen of Heaven, Our Refuge, Our House of Gold—and an amen is given to each:

Santa Madre de Dios,
Santa Virgen de las Vírgenes,
Madre de Jesucristo,
Madre de la divina gracia,
Madre purísima,
Madre castísima,
Madre Virgen,
Madre Incorrupta,
Madre Inmaculada,

Madre Amable,

Madre Admirable,

Madre del Buen Consejo,

Madre del Creador,

Madre del Salvador,

Virgen prudentísima,

Virgen digna de veneración,

Virgen digna de alabanza,

Virgen Poderosa,

Virgen Clemente,

Virgen Fiel,

Espejo de Justicia,

Trono de la eterna sabiduría,

Causa de nuestra alegría,

Vaso espiritual,

Vaso de honor,

Vaso de insigne devoción,

Rosa Mística,

Torre de David,

Torre de marfil,

Casa de oro,

Arca de la Alianza,

Puerta del cielo,

Estrella de la mañana,

Salud de los enfermos,

Refugio de los pecadores,

Consoladora de los Afligidos,

Auxilio de los cristianos,

Reina de los Ángeles,

Reina de los Patriarcas,

Reina de los Profetas,

Reina de los Apóstoles,

Reina de los Mártires,

Reina de los Confesores,

Reina de las Vírgenes,

Reina de todos los Santos,
Reina concebida sin pecado original,
Reina llevada al cielo,
Reina del Santo Rosario,
Reina de la Paz.

Amén, says the rezadora, and as if released from a trance by the snap of fingers, the somber congregation resumes its animated chatter.

Water, soft drinks, and cheese and crackers are passed all around. With tray in hand I offer the cheese cubes like communion wafers. I collect kisses, hugs, and blessings like church offerings. After the last guest leaves, I help Ángel fold the chairs and clean the kitchen. Only then do I allow myself the reward of looking for the daily photo John sends me, usually of Eli. I see that either Tanya or her husband has taken one of John holding his happy grandson in front of Cinderella Castle, an almost exact replica of the one my mother has of John holding Tanya in the same spot. I pull myself out of the depths of this yearning place and go to my room to read and look through photo albums. I come across an old picture John took of a site of Mary's apparition in another town on the Island. There is a little well at the shrine where a schoolboy supposedly saw a divine apparition of a beautiful young girl wearing a white gown and blue veil, rosary beads wrapped around her hands. A search on "Puerto Rico, Mary Apparitions, Pozo" found many YouTube videos of the crowds at the site, plus one fascinating clip made from an old newscast of the boy, now a grown man in the film, describing the vision in such an articulate way that it sounded like he had memorized a script. He said that the young girl he saw was *muy bella*, with dark eyes and brown skin. Mary looked like a pretty Puerto Rican woman. Of course she would. It is a documented fact that in most of her apparitions, Mary looks like one of the natives. Blonde in northern Europe, copper-skinned in Mexico, and in Puerto Rico she would have café con leche skin like my mother and her sisters. John took a photo of the site of the well. A sign in front read, "El pocito está seco." The well is dry.

59 *Certification of la nada*

Grace, I was taught in catechism class, is to direct kindness toward someone without expecting it in return. In the days following my mother's funeral, I am made aware of the official business assigned to the "surviving members," that of deleting the dead from the official rolls and records of the living. There is the death certificate to be requested in person in the town where she had been *pronounced*; there are copies to be made of *el certificado de defunción*; there are *sellos*, seals, and more stamped documents—proofs of your right to inherit, even if there is little or nothing to inherit. We will need to present these documents at the Social Security office and at the bank where she and Ángel have joint accounts. There is her funeral expense insurance to be filed, requiring copies of both their birth and marriage certificates and driver's licenses. *La papelería*, as I had heard her refer to the business of life's paperwork, the bills, the forms, the endless filing for insurance benefits. She had become good at these clerical and accounting tasks in her second life on the Island. During our years on the mainland, my father had been the record keeper and I his reluctant assistant. I had translated bills to be paid and forms to be filled out.

Ángel sets out file boxes for me to look through. Although he knows where she kept it all, he has not ever done la papelería. I ask him to sit across from me at the table so I can explain her system to him. I see how meticulous she was, and I also learn some things about her she had never discussed with me. Although she lived on her Social Security check and my small assistance every month, she had managed to contribute modest amounts to the church, an orphanage, and several other charities. I find certificates for civic duty and one certifying her for work with disadvantaged children. I label and alphabetize folders so that Ángel can find things easily in the future. Then we begin our pilgrimage from office to office to remove my mother's name from the official books of lists. At the cemetery, I saw a statue of an ángel holding the heavenly Book of Lists, where all humanity's good and bad deeds are recorded for God's reference at the Last Judgment. Eternal bureaucracy.

We drive to the demographics office, the first anteroom to hell. There should be a sign in front quoting Dante's words on entering the Inferno, "I had not thought death had undone so many." Everyone in this waiting room has been in one way or another undone by death. The space is kept frigid by a noisy, rattling window AC unit, which freezes the sweat on my skin and has my ears buzzing, and the atmosphere is made further unbearable by a ceiling-mounted TV blaring a talk show about elder abuse. Although it is early in the day, rows of chairs in the waiting room are already filled with glum people, and there is a long queue just to sign in. Ángel finds me a chair and takes his place at the back of the queue.

I try to read but have to listen to the dramas unfolding around me. The young woman sitting next to me is being held tight within the arms of a young man. She looks pregnant, but from the bits of conversation I overhear, it is her recently born child that has died. He says more than once, "You should have stayed home," and she keeps shaking her head, no. There is a man behind me telling another that he has given his wife a Xanax and left her passed out at home while he got *el certificado de defunción* for her mother. It is high time the old lady died, he proclaims, apparently to the whole room. The dementia had made her combative, and for the past year she had been telling him, in vulgar terms, what a loser he was. "Hombre, I almost left home. Mi mujer would not let that vieja go to a nursing home, and it was driving me crazy. She even took to agreeing with the crazy old lady about my character. I feel like the one who was abused." He chuckles about what's being said on the TV. "Some of these people need to be locked up when they get to be that old and crazy." A woman behind him calls out loudly in an angry voice, "Cállate, estúpido. What if it was your mother?" There is some clapping from the crowd and forthwith ensues a general discussion on the care of sick parents. The brash man goes outside to smoke a cigarette after giving the whole room a disdainful look. The same woman who spoke up earlier shouts to the room in general, "Don't tell him when they call him up. Let him miss his turn." More clapping and laughter.

I am stunned by yet another demonstration of the communal mind at work and the cultural approbation that allows you to glide smoothly between grief and joy. As frustrating as I've found it, it is also a gift, this ability to let humor and laughter enter even a room full of those recently touched by losses and death. The young woman is called up before anyone else, although she had arrived just ahead of us, and no one complains, no one claims a spot in front of this level of tristeza.

My mother's death certificate makes it official. There is the span of her years, both dates filled in. The document is permanently filed, and thus she is removed from the lists of the living. We take the form from office to office. We have all her documents stamped with "Difunta." The customer has passed on to the kingdom of Nada: no more financial transactions, no more medical bills, nothing else will be added to her records. No need to send her bills or advertisements; no need to call her about special deals or lower interest rates. Put her in the file labeled inactive, move her, after a decent interval of time, to the "to be destroyed" file. This is how we move out of this world—our paper trace is deleted. Nada. We become nada.

60 *On cooking*

What now? Ángel and I have been living like people stuck in an unwanted vacation where bad weather was forecast—stuck in a place where the time is spent preparing for departure and sitting in offices answering the same questions, like tourists whose identity is being questioned. Ángel and I have been subsisting on fast food and contributions from neighbors and relatives. It is time to help Ángel reestablish a sense of normalcy, a routine. Food is important to him. I am what my son-in-law, an ecologist, calls an opportunistic eater, like an animal in the natural world: I eat when I am hungry. I do not plan around meals, and I am no cook. Growing up, I preferred Chef Boyardee from cans and bologna sandwiches on Wonder Bread to my mother's limited repertoire of rice and beans with this and rice and beans with that. My mother, who was no great cooking enthusiast herself, attempted to teach me how to cook when I was a teenager.

This is one of the few memories I have of my father giving in to one of my unjustifiable demands: I asked to be allowed to concentrate on my studies instead of becoming a "slave to the stove." No to being *una esclava de la cocina*. I told him that cooking interfered with my homework time and that my grades would suffer if my mother added that task to my many duties. I knew how important education was to him, and it was the only leverage I'd ever have with him. Sure enough, it worked. Later, I eavesdropped on my parents:

"I hope this señorita will marry an understanding man who will hire a cook," my mother said.

And then my father said something astonishing, especially given his conservative views of women: "Maybe she will make enough money to hire a cook."

Instead of hiring a chef, I had the good fortune to marry an understanding man who is an accomplished cook, having learned the skills to help his working parents in the care and feeding of his younger brother and sisters at an early age. When I met him, I was skinny and homesick. He said I looked like one of those paintings of a big-eyed melancholy alley cat that were so popular in the sixties and seventies. (I had one on my wall.) John's inspired cooking also won over my parents when they first met him. From him, I learned that cooking is not always a task, that offering food you make with your hands is a way to connect and nurture. I could not learn to think of it as art, however. I have learned only survival cooking. Even as I accept my good fortune, cooking is not my gift.

I know that my mother had taught Ángel to cook some basic dishes, and I decide that it is the right time to get him to practice feeding himself (and me). I ask him if he'll cook us a meal. Hesitantly at first, talking himself through the steps, he gains enough confidence to make a delicious beef stew, with rice and beans, of course. When we sit down to eat in front of my mother's picture, he says, "Dios quiera that this tastes as good as her food." It is good.

I make a list of what he'll have to do when I leave, although house-keeping is no problem for him. He is always in motion, sweeping, mopping, washing dishes, and working in the garden. But the care of houseplants and the laundry had been her province by choice, so we do the laundry together. He worries about the things he had heard her worry about: the right cycle to add laundry softener, the right hour to hang the clothes before the daily downpour. We hang the clothes together, noting the time of day. He does not fail to remind me to use sunblock because, as my mother had always said, I am the *blanca* in the family. Hearing her speak through him, I'm reminded of how we embed ourselves in the minds of others, our spirits lingering beyond the end of our physical selves, in echoes.

No matter how many times I remind him to water the indoor plants, it is just not something he is accustomed to doing. So I suggest that we make a potted plant garden in her front yard; that way, even if he forgets to water them, nature will take over. I am no gardener either, but putting my hands in soil and feeling the cool water gives me a small thrill of recognition—this is what she had wanted to come home to do, this simple pleasure of the sun and soil of her country, the little garden that had been denied to her during that lifetime of apartment living. An American garden, even a large one like the farm I live on, would not have sufficed. I begin to understand that even a dream long deferred, if it's modest enough, can eventually become a dream fulfilled. *Una casita, un jardín.*

61 *Rituals of la vida*

One of the advantages the child has over the adult is limited perspective. Growing up in Paterson, I did not have the capacity to yearn for anything else until, as a teenager, I learned to contrast my circumstances with those of my classmates at St. Joseph's school who lived in the suburbs. Only then did I feel ashamed of our inner-city address. The years of months in Paterson punctuated by months on the Island were a normal way of life for my brother and me—we readjusted after each move with relative ease. My mother, on the other hand, was deeply changed by place. At her mother's house, she was a vivacious, talkative woman who allowed us to run free with our cousins and neighborhood friends. Back in the city, she became a bookworm, almost furtive in her demeanor, letting us answer the phone and do

the talking for her de afuera, outside the family circle. Of those apartments, I retain a sensory memory of linoleum floors, hard furniture,
and dark staircases and landings. Winding staircases and hallways
lined with doors still inhabit my anxiety dreams. I vividly remember
one of my mother's nightmarish warnings: "Always look at the number on the door before you try to enter. You never know if it's a good
person or bad living there. You can be grabbed and dragged inside in
an instant." And yet we lived in a better part of the city's core, among
Jewish businesses, not in the barrio with its raucous El Building. But
the lack of light in the old buildings, the dearth of natural beauty,
and the unnatural silence my father imposed on our lives must have
made her feel like she was living in constant luto. May as well drape
the windows and mirrors in black crepe. Her house was in mourning.
"Si tuviera alas," she'd say, looking down upon the slush-covered gray
streets from our window.

What did she do all day in those apartments while we were at school?
She read and reread her few books. She crocheted and embroidered—
we had doilies under every object and slept on pillowcases embroidered with brightly colored garden scenes. She watched the black and
white TV, all those shows with women doing a bit of housework in
pearls and high heels—no telenovelas then. She said she tried to follow the complicated lives of the characters in *The Guiding Light* and
As the World Turns, but nothing really dramatic happened to those
people in their nice houses. Mainly, they talked. Talky soap operas
seem like bland newscasts in comparison to high-drama telenovelas.
What else did she do in those days?

One place where she got to see things growing, but not to touch
them, was in an apartment in a building managed by Pete, the color-
ful Italian landlord I have written about in both my autobiographical
book *Silent Dancing* and my novel *The Line of the Sun*. He was a real
presence in our daily lives, as opposed to the ghostly rent collectors
in the other buildings we had lived in. Pete was talkative, vivacious,
and an ardent gardener. He grew his vegetables in what would have
been our backyard if he had not had the earth turned, roped off, and
filled with black topsoil. From the back stoop we'd watch him in his

straw hat and sandals looking like an Italian peasant—at least that's what she called him, *un campesino italiano*. She'd say it with a nostalgic smile as if that was what she wanted to be, an Italian gardener. We could smell the fresh earth as he turned it. He'd fill a big basket with his bounteous harvest of cherry tomatoes, green and red peppers, and cucumbers to share with all his tenants. How she must have longed to join him in that little garden. But it was strictly off-limits to all, especially the children. Pete became a monster if he caught anyone trespassing, which some of the children made a game of doing. We'd hear Italian invectives and threats of calls to the police. Italian is close enough to Spanish that she would call us in and turn on the radio or TV to shield our ears from the words—survival language we had already picked up in the streets of the neighborhood.

62 Paterson poets William Carlos Williams (whose mother was Puerto Rican) and Allen Ginsberg, of whose existence I was oblivious during my years in that city, both mention the Passaic River and Falls and Garret Mountain in their works. To Williams, Garret Mountain seems to have been a green place of beauty and a respite to the soul; the falls, as described in his eponymous poem, were a place to experience synergy between nature and poetry. In Ginsberg's "Paterson," Garret Mountain becomes the setting of his imagined resurrection after dragging his world-weary soul through the dregs of other devastated American locations:

> . . crowned with thorns in Galveston, nailed hand and foot in Los Angeles, raised up to die in Denver,
> pierced in the side in Chicago, perished and tombed in New Orleans and resurrected in 1958 somewhere on Garret Mountain.

Neither of these visions of the local landscape would have made sense to us in Paterson of the 1960s, as Paterson was by then a troubled place, racially torn and being considered as a candidate for urban renewal, if not urban resurrection. My father considered Garret Mountain a good place to "air" his family. When he was home on leave, we'd get in his Oldsmobile, usually on Sundays, and head out for a scenic ride and hours in the sun. Coincidentally, we would go to lovely, suburban East Rutherford, William Carlos Williams's hometown, to get our treat at the Dairy Queen—always a banana split for me, a pleasure I remember distinctly. Then we'd ride around the streets of neat houses on their manicured lawns. I longed to live in one of those houses, which I imagined were full of light, and to invite my friends for sleepovers and other American pleasures. I don't recall my mother expressing any enthusiasm for a life among strangers, no matter how appealing it all looked from the outside. Her small dream of home was guarded inside her, and her husband's big American ambitions would not sway her.

Garret Mountain had green fields, playground equipment, and panoramic views of the city, as well as Lambert Castle, a nineteenth-century mansion turned into a museum. My parents would sit at a picnic table and wait for us to do something. I remember sitting on a swing and looking out at the cityscape and, on clear days, the skyline of New York City. I swung and waited out our prescribed playtime. I do not know what my parents talked about as they lit up cigarettes and watched over us. I do not remember what else I did on Garret Mountain. I breathed in air perfumed with the odd combination of green grass and cigarette smoke.

On my return to Georgia a few weeks after the novenas, it seems like the dark cloud has followed me to the mainland and settled over my family again. I hear in the news that great floods have been devastating Paterson. I still have relatives living there, so I follow the reports closely. As the situation grows progressively worse, I call my cousin to ask how they are all doing. She tells me that her family had had to be evacuated by police boat. Familiar streets and landmarks on the television and sweep me up in a rush of memories. Paterson has always inhabited my imagination. It shaped my character and my worldview; I like to think that it made me tougher. Whatever it did to me or for me, it is the setting for much of my work, although I was there only through age fifteen. But as Flannery O'Connor said, "Anybody who has survived his childhood has enough information about life to last him the rest of his days."

I thought I had written Paterson out of my system long ago, but memory has a way of looping back like a boomerang, of returning you to the starting points in your life. As I watch the waters trying to wash away Paterson, I reconstruct the city in my mind and place us safely inside one of our tall apartment buildings, in one of our small, dark, temporary shelters. It would not have been washed away by the mighty Passaic River, as have been the lovely, fragile houses of East Rutherford that I once envied. My mother would have stood at the window looking down on the waters, wishing she were a seagull. Yet, would I have traded places with the residents of East Rutherford then? In a flash. It was my mother who did not want to trade up or down. And her dream was nonnegotiable.

63 A sueño is a message

Before one of the novenas, my cousin whispers to me, "I dreamed of her last night. She was with Mamá and Papá, our grandparents. She is fine." During the evening one or another of the older relatives repeats the good news, "He dreamed of her, and she is fine." It's as if she sent a text message from the beyond: *I am with Mamá and Papá. I am fine. Spread the word.*

I want to resist this offer of closure, although I see relief on the faces of the ones who believe that dreams are the soul's Internet connection, the wireless access to the spirit world. I understand that this dream gives my mother's family a way to start thinking of her as having finally arrived safely at her destination after a perilous journey. My *primo*'s offering of this vision to ease my grief moves me. I read somewhere that dreams are a kind of empathy, a way to connect to the raw human experience through symbols shared within a culture. My mother believed in dreams as harbingers and message boards. I believe that my cousin had a dream of my mother within the loving embrace of her dead parents because he knows that some of us need the dream; his sharing of the dream is a consolation he offers to the family, particularly me.

Portentous dreams and visitations by the dead are not just a Puerto Rican tendency. Even learned friends in academia and fellow writers have talked about feeling the presence of a departed loved one. The dead do haunt us by opening up a longing in us that can be satisfied only by their return. As for me, I know that my mother's spirit will be summoned by my urgent need to encounter her again, fully alive, called forth from memory through my fingers, onto the page.

64   On this night, the rezadora is the dignified black matron with a patois accent. It is obvious that she is the chief church lady; she walks in a regal manner and holds her chin up, almost in defiance. She has the unlined face of a young woman. I had over the years heard about these ultrapious women who are the keepers of the houses of God. They are at church for the sunrise and sunset services and also in between, to clean, to cook for the priest, to launder and iron his many vestments. There was a time when I would have thought of women like these as weak and servile, allowing themselves to be used. But this week, when they've come to pray for my mother, I've tried to understand what drives them toward this life of church service and prayer, for it is a direction my mother seemed to have been headed in.

I have read about the difference between religiosity and spirituality, and the categories are beginning to make sense to me. Organized religion, with its strict definitions of right and wrong, is what I rejected long ago. The rituals of appropriate dress, of performing spiritual rituals publicly, under the watchful and judging eyes of others—these social exercises have come to mean little to me. But there is another way to belong to a church, and that may have been what my mother had discovered among these women. The church can be a community that provides you with a frame of reference for what you need to believe at a certain time in your life. It is evident to me that my mother had come to a crossroads and had sought and found appropriate companions. Were they seeking a spiritual renewal even as their bodies failed them?

Not all the rezadoras glow with the light of the Holy Spirit. One night one of the ladies in my mother's prayer group sings the Ave Marías in a high, tremulous voice. She is obviously performing. When I mention it to one of the other rezadoras—that I enjoyed the singing, a break in the routine—she answers in a snippy tone, "This one likes to show off her singing, always has." Competition among God's handmaidens?

The rezadora with the accent stands in front of us with my mother's Bible in her hands and in a forceful voice asks us to meditate on the Glorious Mysteries of the Rosary, which guide us in the ways of a strong faith, the virtue of hope, and most of all in the daily renewal of our zeal for the glory of God. She is like a preacher in a revival tent. Her eyes shine and her arms gesture histrionically. She points to my mother's Bible. "Our sister's eternal peace depends on the sincerity of our prayers tonight." People sway in assent, nod their heads, and say amén. I almost applaud. She is a powerful speaker. What a loss to the Catholic Church not to allow women like this into the priesthood. She has achieved something I have rarely seen in priests or nuns, a healthy spirituality that erupts from her like spontaneous laughter. In fact, she laughs when she says that she has instructed her family to throw a party when she dies, for she will be headed to a place where there is no pain, no sorrow. No *lágrimas*, she has ordered. No tears for her. This is no pious church cucaracha but the embodiment of the archetypal prophet; she truly believes, and her faith makes her powerful.

After the Rosary I offer her a glass of water, as she is hoarse from the passionate praying session she conducted with such brio. I ask her where she was born, and she says, "If you are asking me de dónde soy, I will tell you that my life began in las Islas Vírgenes. But I'm no longer *from* there."

"I hear an accent." I say this respectfully, as her guardedness about her birthplace may be a warning that she does not want to discuss it.

"In my other life, Hija, I spoke patois. But when I married a Puerto Rican man and came to this town over sixty years ago, I was forbidden to speak it. My mother-in-law warned me that only Spanish was tolerated here."

"Did you miss your native country?"

"At first I missed my family and the food, yes. And you know I was treated like an outsider because of the way I dressed and spoke. But now, I feel like a stranger when I go back to my island, even though," she chuckles and looks around, "there are many more people there who look like me than here."

A little circle of listeners gathers around us, and several ask the rezadora questions about her early life. She seems surprised by their belated interest, almost abashed. But eventually she tells the story of her immigration and her years of loneliness. *Sí*, she had felt *sola* until she met the women who became her spiritual sisters—the same ones who had never heard her story until now. There are expressions of surprise that this well-respected matron, whom they have known for decades, has turned out to be an exotic foreign woman who can speak in a strange, lilting dialect at will. They had assumed that she was de afuera but had never presumed to ask from where, and she had never offered them her story. She had become one of them, and over time, her differences had become invisible to them.

65 *The meaning of* de afuera

When does one stop being de afuera and become one with a culture? Within the inner circle of a family and close friends, things like appearance and accents matter less and less over time and are rendered psychologically invisible by affection. My Latina appearance and the accent I can no longer hear in my voice inspire questions in both my cultures: "Where did you come from?" Puerto Rico, New Jersey, points in between, and Georgia. In most cases, people ask questions because they are simply trying to connect with me. On rare but memorable occasions (I can recall each incident clearly, as prejudice marks the psyche), my otherness has caused me annoyance, irritation, and even anger. At an airport: "Do you speak English? Didn't you hear them call First Class passengers only?" Apparently I had blocked the way for a woman dressed like a rich tourist on her way to the Caribbean—a different Caribbean than mine, obviously. "These people . . ." People like me, on our way home, were in the way. But this is nothing, only the most recent episode, small and almost insignificant. I have been followed around by clerks in stores where no one who looks like me "should be" able to afford the merchandise. I have been ignored by the same clerks when I had a question about an item. Knowing that there are ignorant people in the world, I let it go, but the humiliations that my parents endured, which were mostly kept from us, were not just in the category of impolite behavior by stupid people. My father was denied the rental of an apartment because the landlord didn't want "the Spanish" (as we were called before the terms *Hispanic* and *Latino* were popularly used) "infesting" the building. The incident involved a scene I heard my father recount enough times that I came to understand that it was, and would always be, an open wound. The landlord had said to my father, "I don't rent to Cubans." My father had corrected him: "We are Puerto Ricans." "Same shit," the man spat out, slamming the door on his face. Occasionally, my father would make a bitter joke when anyone mentioned Cubans or any other Latino groups in the United States. "Same shit, we are all the same in this country. Same shit." On a trip from New Jersey to Texas, where he was going to be stationed for a year, my mother, my brother, and I were sent to a "Colored" bathroom at an Alabama gas station because she was darker than us, and so we must be mixed. My father was furious, but there was a rifle prominently displayed on a rack behind the mute man sitting in his office. Growing up, I heard many stories about the sexual harassment of female "Spanish" factory workers by their boss men who thought that the way they dressed and walked meant that they wanted male attention—the "hot tamale" stereotype. Perhaps these Puerto Rican women dressed in louder colors and more provocatively than these men were used to, but it was thanks to cultural differences, not as a signal of sexual availability. There had not yet been the great multicultural awakening, nor were there any sexual harassment laws protecting women in the workplace. It was an American man's world.

From the complexities of language acquisition to the little personal and social survival skills that make all the difference, becoming American takes a lifetime. Island girls, take note: In the States, you should wear little or no makeup at the workplace unless you are seeking attention; no low-cut tops showing your very fine cleavage; no tight pants that accentuate that fine bottom. Otherwise, you'll be verbally and physically mauled by the predator who is also the man who can fire you, and who doesn't understand that back home, showing your assets is not an open invitation. Of course, this is not to deny that there weren't cases when the costume was designed to attract precisely the consequences that ensued.

66 *Poetry and prayer*

And when the day of Pentecost was fully come, they were all with one accord in one place. And suddenly there came a sound from heaven as of a rushing mighty wind, and it filled all the house where they were sitting. And there appeared unto them cloven tongues like as of fire, and it sat upon each of them. And they were all filled with the Holy Ghost, and began to speak with other tongues, as the Spirit gave them utterance.

—ACTS 2:1–4

These nine days after my mother's funeral are an intensely lived retreat for me, but not a retreat from experience. I am living in a state of high alert, like a refugee returning home after a prolonged absence. Along with grief, I am experiencing a sort of reverse culture shock. What I manage to retreat from, almost to the point of disengagement, is my real life back in Georgia. I miss my home and family. Like a soldier sent to a faraway place to complete a mission, I have to let go of nostalgia and either focus or fail. I practice my Spanish, research what I no longer remember or never knew about my native culture, and dig in for the duration. I begin to feel a sense of satisfaction at accomplishing the minor things I can do to restore normalcy to my mother's house. I also practice yielding control, and I see Ángel grow stronger each day as we trade roles and he becomes teacher and guide to me. I show him how some of the huecos left by my mother's death can be filled again, and he shows me which can't be. Some of the things she had done for him he can do for himself now. This is the easy part. The other empty places, the ones we can't see, will be what time may or may not take care of.

Ángel begins to cultivate the garden again. He once worked in a plant nursery, and he shows me how he keeps the plants healthy and pruned. By the end of the week, I hear him get up at dawn, wipe the moisture off the cars as he has always done, and then start working among the plants. He also goes back to the wellness center, as had been his habit before her illness, to walk and work out. Not a full return to his previous life, at least it is an indication that he is fighting the stupor we both fell into during our long hospital vigils and in the aftermath of her death.

I believe that the Rosarios have helped awaken us both. *Hay vida*, my mother used to say about the hubbub of daily life around her. There is life. The novenas have brought family and friends to the house and filled it with vida. Even though the gatherings are in the name of the dead, there is conversation and even laughter. Each night during the incantatory prayers I've closed my eyes and allowed my memories to come to me. Anytime I prepare to do creative work, I have to separate myself from all distractions. I often listen to sacred music, usually Gregorian chants, before turning to the page or screen: the background sounds of human voices rising in expectation of grace aid me in my meditations. Listening to the prayers for my mother's soul, I begin to feel the notes for this work coalescing into a narrative. And I know that my reawakening is a gift.

67 The many names of grief

Es pentecostal. She is a Pentecostal, evangelical Christian. This is why one of my aunts is not reciting the Rosary. Sitting in my mother's rocker, which I cede to her, with her head bowed, respectful but silent, she is steadfast and dignified in her isolation. The word *Pentecost* reminds me of a body of religious paintings that has always attracted me: I like to study the many versions of the Feast of the Pentecost, usually depicting the circle of Apostles with a little tongue of fire over their heads, and above them, the white dove representing the Holy Spirit. It is the perfect symbolic representation of inspiration, an artist's much-hoped-for eureka moment. After they had prayed and fasted together for nine days, Christ's followers were given language. They were given a way to tell their story.

The Mass at my mother's house will be performed by her priest, the same friend from the old barrio who spoke at her funeral. After this final rite, I'll get ready to go home. I will meet my family back in Georgia, as they will be driving back from Disney World at the same time I am flying home from the Island. I try to think in English again. I answer some of the many e-mailed condolences I am receiving from my university colleagues and students. I have been corresponding only minimally with people other than my immediate family during the novena. I find it hard to think about my life in Georgia without a sense of dislocation—a conflict of emotions that is hard to describe. I want to go home but feel disloyal yearning for a life that has nothing to do with my mother. I want my final good-bye to be free of cultural dualities and doubts. I want to live in Spanish until the last moment in her house on this island. But I also desperately want to reunite with my family, to be in my quiet house in the Georgia countryside with them, and to re-enter the language and culture I will now have to accept as where I am from. Together we will make sense of so many losses in such a short period of time.

Tanya's text says that her father seems to be getting sick and she is concerned. When I speak to John on the phone he plays it down—a bad cold, nothing more, and heat exhaustion from walking around Disney World in the relentless Florida sun. But the worm of fear is now burrowing its way into my brain; the poison it carries is manifested in an increasing sense of foreboding and extreme homesickness. I have two more days until the end of the novenas. My airline ticket is confirmed. I will meet my family back in Georgia after completing my final duties to my mother.

68   Homesickness is called a sickness for a reason. It can be either brief or chronic, and when it becomes a permanent part of one's life, as it must have for my mother and perhaps my father, it turns into what has been labeled by sociologists as cultural grief or bereavement, and by my native culture as la tristeza—that is, a sense of loss that does not abate. In trying to understand what my parents must have felt when

they left their culture as young people, I researched cultural grief, "el duelo cultural," and found a list of symptoms and behaviors familiar from our early lives on the mainland. In Spanish, the symptoms sound like a religious litany: *El duelo por la familia y los amigos, El duelo por la lengua, El duelo por la cultura, El duelo por la tierra, El duelo por el contacto con el grupo étnico, El duelo por los riesgos físicos, El duelo por la pérdida del proyecto migratorio, El duelo por no poder regresar.* Grief over the loss of family and friends, over the loss of the mother tongue, over the loss of culture; grief over the loss of the homeland, over the loss of contact with your ethnic group, over the fear of physical danger; grief over the loss of the original dream, and the grief of no possible return.

69 *The Ulysses Syndrome*

The difference between my mother's and father's cultural bereavements may have been a result of the total loss of hope I believe my father experienced. His depression deepened the more he struggled to give us the ideal American life he had envisioned, and loss and grief became the cycle of his life. He could not return to the Island, as my mother wished, because his dream was too big for him to achieve, though it may have been a modest ambition for others. He wanted to cross over from the brink of not quite poor into solid middle class— to own a house, to send his children to college. Mainly, he wanted to have accomplished something other than mere survival. But la lucha never ended for him. His pride would not allow him to admit that he had failed. My mother kept her dream small, and by doing so she may have avoided the collapse of hope that finally defeated him. He suffered from *el duelo por no poder regresar*, the grief of no possible return. Her sadness was not complicated; hers was simple grief over a temporary dislocation. She was irritated by her inability to express herself. She yearned for family and friends. *El duelo por los riesgos físicos* was her constant companion; she feared being sick and being unable to get help for one of us if we fell ill. I can still hear her litany of precautions. The por si acaso mentality ruled our lives: just in case, here is a list of phone numbers; just in case, here are canned food, flashlights, candles, first aid kits. But my mother also knew that la esperanza was always flapping its wings somewhere in the vicinity. Hope was just around the corner. She had her plan.

She believed she could and would return. And this, in my view, is the difference between simple homesickness and the complicated *duelo migratorio* at the core of my parents' lives.

70 *History of dominoes*

There is another psychological condition experienced mainly by immigrants that some sociologists have called the Ulysses Syndrome, which in retrospect seems to encapsulate my father's tristeza.

I have been grieving backward for my father ever since his mysterious early death at the age of forty-two released my mother to pursue her *Sí, se puede. Se puede regresar.* You *can* go home again. But sometimes the cost of the passage is almost more than you can bear. She got to go back home, alone.

In my poems about my absent father, which are mainly about my mother waiting for him, I have portrayed him as Ulysses/Odysseus. In a sequence I titled "A Sailor's Wife's Journal," I imagine her as the long-suffering Penelope stuck at home, sequestered in "My ship, Odysseus, / a ship that goes nowhere," while he sails around the world, encountering adventure, meeting new people. It took experiencing loneliness myself—empathy *is* the core of compassion—to begin to envision my father as trapped in his ship, yearning for home, for us. I think I finally got it right, decades later. I struggled even all those years later to find a vehicle for my grief, as I could not express it directly any more than in the simple words I had spoken so often to my mother, until she could hear me no more. *Te quiero.*

In '62, my father, called to duty at sea, left his game in Puerto Rico forever, and learned that *embargo* is an American word. *Sin embargo,* he had also drawn a double six in his last hand. Aboard his ship, there were no domino games. No one played. He later said the ivory pieces in a cigar box under his bunk clicked like the bones of the dead all that long October month, when the water between the islands got rough. I can still see him studying the black-and-white faces, twenty-eight in all, representing all possible number combinations, ranging from double blank to double six. I never saw him play again. My father's bones lie under a headstone listing all the wars since his last game. He did not lose his life in a war, but he lost his love of the game. My father's ivory tiles, twenty-eight in all, feel like dry bones in my hands. I cannot play. It is lately I learn that six-six is the luckiest domino of them all, predicting happiness, success, and prosperity, while the direst of omens is a double blank with danger, despair, and death all to be written in black ink on an ivory page. This is an old game. The first record of dominoes comes from twelfth-century China, where they were used for divination. In their Western incarnation, dominoes have tended to be far more popular as a game. Certain tiles are thought to be lucky for the player, regardless of the outcome of the game.

—from "Dominoes: A Meditation on the Game"

71 *Numinosity*

I do not ever intend my work to be a sociological report on the immigrant experience. How can I know what my parents really felt about their dislocation and losses? I know only that there were real setbacks that diminished them and must have caused them to question their decision to leave all they had known behind for an uncertain future in a foreign land. Now I am using memory, imagination, and the accelerant of my grief to try to find meaning in the life I shared with them. I must find a sequence, try to create a shape out of these events, even if eventually all of it was the result of a game of chance. *Así es la vida.*

Both my parents are now gone. I try using the word *orphan* to describe myself, but it does not seem to be adequate. Motherless, fatherless, denaturalized, truly de afuera now. If I return to this island again, it will be as a visitor, not as the daughter coming back to her mother's casa. Yet I long to go back to my home in Georgia; adopted or native, the place where our loved ones are waiting becomes the real thing eventually. My grief is complicated by this other, ambivalent duelo. I am prone to sudden anxieties, waves of loneliness, and a recurrent dream of being lost or imprisoned. In one, I find myself alone on a ship, where I wander up and down passageways and knock on cabin doors. In another, I am locked up in what seems to be a cathedral, lit only by candles. I want to dream of my mother, but she resists me. I miss her most in the morning, when I long to hear her footsteps and the familiar sounds of her making coffee, the door opening so that when I get up, the house will be full of light and the noises of her busy neighborhood. One morning, desolate after a night of dreams and waking up to a tightness in my throat that led to a coughing fit and tears, I call John and ask him if he believes I am ever really coming home. It is a strange question, but he understands that what I need is a firm answer, not questions in return. He says yes. I will be home soon. They are all waiting for me. I realize that my sense of reality is becoming shaky from lack of sleep and the demands of constant socializing. I have kept myself barely in control by doing the familiar things I know how to do: read, research, study, and write.

I have learned ways to cope with the pain of missing her at the sight of everything she once touched. I let her voice enter my mind and tell me the story behind the picture or object. In spite of the laws of physics, it is possible to go back in time and to retrieve what you need from the rooms you once inhabited. This retrieval is to a writer a sort of mining for grace. The mother lode is yours if you can bear re-entering the landscape of what was and what may have been and bring it back as language.

Although the messages from Tanya and John contain a certain ambiguity, mainly about John's health, I am focused on completing my offices. Two more days and I will meet my little family in Georgia. From the "big" city of Augusta, we will drive into the Georgia countryside and then down one mile of dirt road lined with so many trees and vegetation that we joke that centaurs and ogres live in our woods, like in a Harry Potter book. We will finally enter our house surrounded by a pond and a forest of pines. I will then let the quiet and the green begin to heal me.

I am almost at peace by the time the priest is scheduled to say Mass at the end of the novenas.

My relatives bring a rectangular table that will serve as an altar. El Padre wishes to perform Mass in front of my mother's garden, although it is a hot, humid day and not likely to get much cooler by evening. The Rosary ladies arrive early, all abuzz. This is a special occasion, a private Mass. We set up extra chairs and prepare to serve refreshments to a bigger crowd than the usual thirty to forty people that had been attending the Rosaries. There is a muted excitement among the people. It seems that this is a sort of minimal Pentecost. Their efforts—praying hard and praising God and Mary and all the Heavenly Host—are being rewarded and blessed by the priest himself. My mother's spirit is about to be set free, like a kite that has been tangled in the limbs of a tree. Disentangled. Her wish to have wings and fly away will finally be granted. I do not know how many of those present really believe that this is all factually true, but I have learned to focus my eyes and attention on the believers. They are the channels for the strength I need. I have stayed in order to find comfort in the repeated rituals, in the words said with such conviction that I now know how to find meaning in them. *Pray for us sinners now and at the hour of our death* means, Do not let me be alone at the end. These sessions have not led me back to religion but have allowed me to suspend my cynicism and taught me to open myself to a new acceptance of the mystery of faith. The word *numinosity* comes to mind, a word that sounds like it should mean "infused with light." Is that what I am seeing on the radiant face of the woman leading the prayers?

Numinosity, as I understand it, is an overwhelming emotional reaction of wonder in attempting to grasp and articulate the inexpressible, drawing the believer toward the religious experience of grace. Supposedly the Apostles achieved the goal of grace by opening their minds to wonder, suspending their disbelief. And thus able to speak in tongues, they began telling their stories. And infused with the Spirit, Peter announced, "I will pour out my spirit." I read my mother's Spanish-language Bible and looked up the translation. I have not picked up a Bible since my first year of teaching, when I was assigned "World Literature from the Old Testament to the Renaissance: A Survey." I lectured on the Book of Job as the beginning of narrative as we know it. I had identified with the pesky Satan, the Questioner. Why not test Job's patience, God? Why not kill his family and inflict on him every imaginable pain? The Bible seemed to contain every promise and every threat, grace and grief offered in equal measures.

The idea of the holy is the result of being able to suspend our rational minds in order to experience wonder. This, the experience of the numinous (a word I doubt my mother would have known), means an attempt to explain the mystery of human existence, to express the unutterable, to work toward the fascinating and terrifying state of grace. The saints are said to have mortified their flesh and martyred themselves to attain it. But I believe that grace can also be as simple as the feeling of oneness achieved through prayer and ritual, or even through poetry.

72 *Ashes*

My heart is crushed as ashes. The priest arrives carrying a bag with the instruments of his service and enters my mother's garden. He is both courtly and jovial as he touches the heads of children and blesses them, kisses the cheeks of old women, shakes the hands of men, and makes his way toward the family and finally me. He tells me that he loves my mother's garden because it represents the beauty of the Island. He speaks of her house and her garden in the affectionate diminutive, *su casita, su jardincito*. My mother had been a tiny woman, barely 4 feet 11 inches tall and petite, and so was her house, her garden, her small dream that she had made come true. The priest smiles when my uncle the photographer asks if he could take our photo—"Para los nietos," el padre says, winking. For the grandchildren—a typical Puerto Rican joke: laugh with me at who I am; it is an offering. No children or grandchildren for him, but he appears a man at ease with his childless, wifeless condition when he says this. Or perhaps he agrees with Francis Bacon's dictum, "He that hath wife and children hath given hostages to fortune." I have known both kinds of priests; two of my former pastors left the church to be able to give hostages to fortune. And there are others, like my mother's pastor, who walk into rooms full of happy and unhappy families like affectionate bachelor uncles, happy to receive everyone's attention and just as happy to go home alone. This is a sort of grace.

He performs the Mass joyfully and sings the requiem hymns in a strong, clear voice. Dressed in his white and purple robes, he is a dancer in God's Court. He raises his arms over a silver chalice and proclaims that the Savior is among us, is a guest in my mother's house. El Padre asks the Holy Spirit to descend on us. Surely the Heavenly Host will bring us consolation.

I am satisfied with the magic. I wanted her to have this—a Mass said in her name. In her garden. How she would have reveled in it.

Oro supplex et acclinis,
Cor contritum quasi cinis:
Gere curam mei finis.

My heart is in ashes. I have done all I can. I have sung the hymns, partaken of the rituals, said the prayers. I have performed a daughter's offices according to my mother's faith. I watched over her body. I buried her in her chosen plot of native earth. I gathered her family and friends to pray and pray for the release of her soul. I gave away what could be given away and kept what had to be kept. The priest came down from the church on the hill to say a Mass for her eternal rest, and I will hold the final night of the novena tomorrow, *tu despedida, Mami*, and serve the special cheese, *queso de bola*, with saltine crackers, and the thick chocolate, which will be mixed in a huge pot by the loving hands of your sister. Then I will go home and rest. Not in peace, but I will have to rest.

After almost everyone has left, my cousin and her friend ask me if I want to ride around the pueblo, as it is a clear moonless night and she has something special to show me. She promises me the beautiful sight of the church on the hill appearing to levitate above the town as the black hill on which it sits blends into night. I agree to go; this might be my last view of the town for a very long time. I'll have no compelling reason to return anytime soon. To get to where we can see the supernatural sight, we circle around the perimeter. The highway takes us through a business district that can be found anywhere in the United States. I have seen the same stretch of road from Georgia to

California: the KFC, McDonald's, and Burger King; a strip mall with a Kinko's, Pep Boys, and Radio Shack; and farther down the road El Mall, the shopping mall that has now replaced the traditional plaza as the social gathering place for throngs of people, mainly teenagers. My mother and I had shopped there occasionally, and I had felt claustrophobic in the elbow-to-elbow crowdedness of the place. I have felt that way about most of the public places on the Island. There are too many houses, too many cars, too many people everywhere. The population of the pueblo, a midsize town by Island standards, is almost three thousand souls per square mile. This number bothers someone now used to living in a sparsely populated part of Georgia, but to my mother and others, crowds on a tiny island are a given, like grains of sand on the beach. Still, an exploding population and an eroding economy have made the place I had gotten a fleeting glimpse of in my childhood, an almost tropical paradise of pristine beaches and miles of cultivated lands, a thing of the past. One of Puerto Rico's leading writers and social critics, Ana Lydia Vega, said in one of her newspaper commentaries, "El Paisaje, precisamente el paisaje, es lo que está ausente." It is the view, precisely the view, that is missing. She points out that it is almost impossible to see a field that is not designated "under construction," an unpolluted river, or uncontaminated seashore. The Island of Enchantment from the Chamber of Commerce TV commercials is mostly a fiction now. Although I agree with Vega's pessimism, and she is the expert witness, I have tried hard to find the view. I have looked around the condos and found turquoise waters; I have made John drive along precipitous mountain roads so we could glimpse fields of plantains and coffee beans growing on hillsides; I have followed my mother to the source of an underwater well where her grandparents obtained their drinking water. We had to go through private property to get there, but we found it. Her optimism made her see as a poet sees.

My cousin takes me to the spot beneath where the church rises, on a narrow street where the town becomes ancient and the old houses sit at the feet of the Basílica de la Virgen de la Monserrate like a kneeling congregation. I can imagine my mother here as a teenager on her way to Mass, trying not to glance over at the boy in the café as he puts a nickel in the jukebox to play their love song, "Dos gardenias." I would hear this song again and again on my mother's portable turntable on many of those gray Paterson days when I'd come home and beg to play my own records—Paul Anka, the Beatles. "Dos gardenias," sung in the voice of la tristeza itself, embodied by Daniel Santos, the tormented icon of the love ballad, would haunt our homes for the duration of her exilio.

The church does seem to float above us like an apparition as we sit in the darkened car. I feel like I did as a student when I looked at the stars through a telescope and was told that what I was seeing was in the past: the configuration of the stars, the nimbus of colors surrounding them—none of it existed in real time; it had already happened thousands or maybe millions of years ago. It had taken the light that long to reach us. I am seeing what my mother may have imagined, looking out the windows of the many places that she would not call home: a view from the past, suspended in time—one she could come back to.

The church looks exactly the same as it did in my childhood. And this moment clarifies what Flannery O'Connor called one of the "peculiar crossroads where time and place and eternity somehow meet," out of which the writer's imagination operates. I see what my cousin, who chooses to stay on this island, sees: beauty out of time.

73 *No puede ser*

It is a pitch-black night, darker than any night has been since I arrived, and as I approach the house I realize that there are no lights on anywhere. My cousin explains that it is an outage, a common occurrence, and that power will be restored soon.

How soon? My main concern is the temperature of the bedroom. Sleepless as I've been all these nights, I relish lying down in the only cool place in the house and doing my customary reading in bed. There are always things to look up online, and only this distraction keeps me from consciously worrying about my family. It is also the time when I can contact them with text messages and e-mails, a silent conversation we have at the end of the day. Often there will be pictures of them enjoying Disney World, although the heat index there seems dangerously high, and in some pictures John looks flushed.

I sit on my mother's porch rocker until I notice lights beginning to come on in the distance, like blinking stars. The house starts to hum as I begin my preparations for bed, and my phone rings. It is Tanya. I know something is wrong from the way she says "Mother?" My own tone as I answer her—I hear my voice rising, "Tanya, Tanya, what's wrong?"—alerts Ángel, who comes running into the room, alarm on his face.

She tells me that John had left the restaurant where they had been having dinner for a breath of air, and when he didn't return, she had gone to the car to find him collapsed on the seat and incoherent. They got him to the ER—by following an ambulance through the unfamiliar city—and found he had a fever of nearly 104 degrees.

I feel my knees buckle under me, and Ángel rushes forward to hold me up. "Take care of him, Tanya." She assures me that she will not let anything happen to him, and that she will call me with updates as they hear news.

I sit in my mother's rocker to try to absorb the shock. Ángel sinks into a chair from the funeral home and pulls up close. We wait in silence for what seems hours. At some point Ángel says almost to himself, "No puede ser." It cannot be.

Tanya's next call is to tell me that John has been admitted to the cardiac unit of the Orlando hospital where he had been taken to the ER. Even as they diagnosed him with viral pneumonia, he had gone into severe atrial fibrillation. He will have to undergo a battery of tests before he can be released.

Should I get on a plane now? I doubt that the tiny propeller planes have a round-the-clock schedule, so I will need a ride to San Juan. But my daughter has assumed command of the situation for now. The same strength of will and sense of purpose that allowed her to become a scientist is now focused on getting us all through this crisis. I am both sad and relieved at having her assume this painful duty. I know exactly how she must feel—still grieving over the loss of two grandparents and now having to deal with her father's sudden crisis. One begins to feel forsaken. "No, don't change your plans yet. I'm hoping he'll be stabilized and we can drive home by Sunday. We'll meet you there. We have to make sure he is seen by a cardiologist immediately." She is doing everything to get her father safely home. Home. If only we can get home, things will be all right.

74   I try to avoid thinking about death by recalling one of the last excursions we took with my mother and Ángel on the Island. It was our custom to rent a car at the airport in San Juan and then maneuver through the terrible traffic jams that paralyze the highways for hours, called "los tapones de tráfico." A tapón is a plug, and sitting in an unmoving sea of cars indefinitely, you do feel as if someone had put a giant plug on the flow. As soon as there is a reprieve, a mad dash will ensue, with drivers flashing by, even using the exit and emergency lanes, as if winning an inch were worth risking their lives. *Así es la vida* in modern Puerto Rico. In the Puerto Rico of my childhood, the dangers were different, but the macho drivers' attitudes were the same. Now, the macho drivers are of both sexes. As a child bouncing without a seat belt in the backseat of my father's car, I was a witness to many hair-raising standoffs on narrow mountain roads, with a precipice to the ocean on one side and falling rocks on the other. After his first stunning encounter with the Island's wild drivers, John learned how to drive in this automotive war zone and took pride in getting us out of the maze of San Juan and onto the Autopista. The Autopista cuts through the central mountains and, after numerous tolls, emerges on the southwest shore of the island. It was always an adventure. My mother insisted that we call her at intervals to make sure we had survived the dangers, which she enumerated each year, adding gruesome details to make sure we got the message. "Mira, someone was yanked out of her car at a stoplight and kidnapped just last week. If they know you are de afuera, they will think of you as prey. Mira, the drogadictos are everywhere and they are desperate." Every year she was more reluctant to drive to the capital for the huge political rallies and musical extravaganzas she enjoyed. The Isla del

Encanto, which had been coveted by both Spain and the United States as a crucial port of entry and military base, is now a paradise for drug smugglers. The *New York Times* reported:

> High murder rates are not unusual in Puerto Rico. Between 1980 to 2005 the average annual homicide rate was 19 per 100,000 in Puerto Rico and 8 per 100,000 on the mainland. Murders on the island declined early last decade, only to spike again recently for the same reasons they did 20 years ago, when drug trafficking, gangs and carjackings rocked Puerto Rico.

In spite of her fears, in the last year before her health began to decline, we had convinced my mother to spend two nights with us in a beautiful hotel facing the cruise ship docks in San Juan. At first she had resisted, but the hotel had a casino, and she loved playing the one-armed bandits. I recall the night we dined on a terrace over-looking the docks with their huge cruise ships unloading hundreds of tourists to spend their money in the shops and restaurants and to walk the cobblestone streets of Old San Juan, where Ponce de León's house is still standing—the mansion he never lived in, busy as he was looking for gold and the fountain of youth and then getting himself killed while on one of his *aventuras*. She would walk into every shop and insist that we take *piragua* breaks; she's have us sit on a cement bench to enjoy one of the ice cones topped off with thick tamarind syrup. When I was with her I felt like an insider, although John and I still acted like the tourists we were, marveling at the Spanish architecture, the ancient fort El Morro, and the cobblestone streets—an ancient core within a twenty-first century city. Even the slum ironically called La Perla looks alluring from a distance, framed as it is by miles of sparkling seashore. Her owner's pride of the beauty of the Island reinstated mine, at least temporarily, in spite of the frightening crime statistics.

I know John must share my complicated sense of loss of our relationship to this place. Without my mother, we will be merely tourists.

As I steel myself for another bout of anxiety and fear over John's illness, I think about the toll this stress has taken on him. I know very well that the body is totally immersed in the grieving process. I feel it in my persistent cough, my sleeplessness, and the lingering pain in the pit of my stomach. I suspect that John's collapse is related to the body blows of his father's death quickly followed by my mother's. Trying to carry on without me, he has extended himself by spending long days in the Florida sun, making sure our little grandson has a few good memories of this summer. The heart does break under intense pressure. I am afraid that another cliché is going to rise and attack us. A rule in thermodynamics states that an exact price is paid for each action; if you transfer energy to one place, it is depleted from another. The eighteen days I have spent trying to bring order to my mother's house and peace to my mind have depleted me physically and emotionally.

Notes from my frantic phone calls with Tanya become an outline of our plan of action. I will travel back to Georgia on Sunday while they drive back at the same time. I have the hospital phone numbers, the password for inquiring about his status, and his nurse's name for the night. I call several times, but the answer is always the same. He is stable at present. Yes, his heart rate is still erratic. A cardiologist will see him first thing in the morning. Tanya will call if anything changes. I am beginning to feel almost as dissociated from my body as one does after a vivid dream. *No puede ser*, I tell myself, this cannot be.

75 Teach us to care and not to care
Teach us to sit still.
—T. S. ELIOT, "Ash-Wednesday"

On the day of the last novena, I receive a text message from Tanya that John's arrhythmia has not yet been stabilized. The doctors are considering surgery. She does not know if she can get him back to Georgia. The next twenty-four hours will determine all. I need to be ready to change my travel plans on short notice. A heaviness descends on me.

Into my head, I can only pour death poems and the words of the requiem. I can't move and I can't sit still. My heart and mind are racing toward the next hurdle—or is it a precipice?—but I am externally paralyzed. I am also strangely vacant. Dry eyes, dry mouth. This is a familiar feeling from past occasions of extreme stress—that I have left my body. It happened when I was a young mother and baby Tanya was running a fever of over 103 degrees on Christmas. We could not get a doctor to answer and had to rush her to a hospital. As I held my burning child in my arms, I felt as if I had passed out but was still awake. I heard John calling my name but could not respond. A psychologist called it depersonalization, an unusual but not uncommon response to psychological duress beyond what the body is prepared to handle, a state of shock similar to what happens when one loses a lot of blood. I was so afraid of losing Tanya that I had gone into shock. Now, the idea that John might die has put me in a similar place. I force myself to go outside and sit in my mother's garden and bear the full force of the sun. I need to feel again, even if it means letting my skin burn. I think of her voice—"You will burn, Hija"—the voice I will never hear again, and I allow myself to cry. I need to cry. I also need to be strong for the new prueba. What would she say? "La vida es una prueba." Life is a test. Face it. Deal with it. Clean the house, cultivate your garden. Give light to your restless spirit.

When I am able to rise, it is time to prepare for the last novena. I help Ángel wash the tiles, set up the chairs, and put a vase of fresh azucenas on the little table, and then my aunt and cousin arrive to make the huge pot of hot chocolate. I slice the cheese and arrange the crackers around it. We make platters of cookies and the sliced jelly roll called *brazo gitano*. We are preparing for a bon-voyage party. The final night must be a celebration. The whole time, I carry my phone in my hip pocket and occasionally feel a "phantom" vibration. It is like a second heart, a defective one with a murmur. I am in anticipatory anxiety. On many occasions as a child I had followed my mother or grandmother around a church, pausing to pray at each Station of the Cross, distressed by the depictions of the tormented Christ, his agony growing with each panel. This is how I walk through the last novena: bent over from carrying a burden heavy with past and future grief. Tomorrow I will be flying home, and then there will be another hospital vigil. But in the meantime, I going to say adiós to mother and country.

As the family spokesperson in my childhood I learned how to select words carefully. As the bearer of messages from my mother to the world and back, I went in and out of the family cocoon in each of our temporary homes with a sense of caution: the outside world was a minefield. Most important of all, I had to project confidence. Small for my age, I used language to defend myself. In my classrooms, I still use this trick. Students have often told me that they don't realize how short I am till they have the occasion to stand next to me. I use words to project power. Language is my armor. The English language, that is. It has become obvious during the past eighteen days, encompassing my nine-day vigil over her body and the novenas for her soul, that I have lost ground in Spanish; I am again a child in Spanish, and people respond accordingly. Before I can think of the right word, they jump in offering their best choices for what they assume I am trying to say. My mother and I had gotten used to our role reversal, and it had seemed natural. Her powerful personality and cutting wit had emerged in her native tongue, and it had been a revelation I'd witnessed with pride. She had given me the necessary clues to the culture, just as I had helped her negotiate the mysteries of English. But now the struggle to communicate is draining me. I finally understand at the level of bone and blood how she must have felt all those years away from her language, unable to fully express herself, *sin palabras*. I miss my vocabulary. I miss my writing, which is how I have defined myself for most of my adult life.

I do and don't want to leave my mother's house. I want to fly home to my sick husband and distraught daughter, but I do not want to say a final adiós. She never liked saying adiós after my visits; it was always *nos vemos pronto*. We will see each other again soon. Even when it'd be a year before my next visit. I do not want to leave my mother's house because when I do, it will cease to be her casa. No matter how welcome Ángel makes us, it will be his house that she had inhabited so fully that there were no huecos, no spaces that were not imbued with her touch. No empty spots, Ángel had said. And I understood. He wanted to keep her with him through the objects and plants she had magically transformed by assigning them meaning. This is Judith's hibiscus. Do not cut it; let it grow. My hibiscus is now taller than the roof of her little house. This is what she wanted to see.

> . . . spirit of the garden,
> Suffer us not to mock ourselves with falsehood

Let me let her go. I think of her hands—her nervous, strong hands that held ours so tightly when she walked us to school, transmitting both her fears and her determination. This is what I can take with me, the memory of her physical self. She is dead. Gone. I will never see her again. I have been taking the narcotic drug of ritual and repetition and have almost achieved an altered state. From this place, I can believe that my mother has "passed" into another dimension, one vibration of the universe away from me. But I can't live with this false notion. She is dead. Gone. I will have to go on with my life as a wife, mother, and grandmother, but not a daughter. Eventually my own daughter will have to redefine herself as motherless, and so it goes.

I wait in my mother's garden for the people to arrive. Her spirit will remain there, if spirit is in the work. She had worked hard on her garden.

My aunt calls me in to taste the chocolate. Thick and ultrasweet, it tastes like the chocolate of my childhood. The swirling pot reminds me of the videos of Marian apparitions I recently saw. Mary's profile had been spotted in a pot of chocolate somewhere. It had been captured on film and posted on the Internet. A woman lovingly described what she saw: the mouth, the nose, the eyes, and the veiled head. I almost saw what she described, the familiar veiled oval of her face, but it soon dissolved. Now, looking into the chocolate burbling on my mother's stove, I see nothing more than goodness to be poured into little cups and shared.

I greet the people as they arrive. Many are new ones offering fresh condolences: I feel your sadness; I grieve with you. You have no idea, I want to tell them. It's complicated. You cannot know my grief multiplied a hundredfold by my anticipatory grief. I am afraid. I am so afraid. Luckily, I do not possess enough vocabulary in Spanish to indulge in self-pitying discourse. I accept hugs, kisses, and blessings. Then I sit down in my usual corner to try to remember, to pack my brain like an expanding suitcase with as much as I can fit in. I pack while they pray loud and passionately, firing at heaven their one last round of protestations for the release of my mother's soul from whatever was trying to keep her bound to the world of the living. Me?

Teach us to sit still
Even among these rocks

I try to sit still and concentrate on letting her go without letting go of the images that will allow me to begin telling her story again.

77 *Counting down*

The last novena is a particularly passionate performance. The rezadora sings between prayer decades, and the group joins in. The crowd is making a concerted effort to be heard, as if their voices are the jet propulsion to my mother's spirit, the Hail Marys and Our Fathers the countdown to her liftoff. I feel it but don't believe it. I have experienced aspects of a conversion during these two weeks immersed in the alternate reality of the faithful, but I have not become one with them. I understand that religion is culture here, and inseparable. It makes me yearn for unity in my life, for the ability to make the disparate aspects of my life come together seamlessly. This is no longer possible.

I have not practiced Catholicism since college. Now, dazed by grief, I have rocked myself calm to the rhythms of prayers and songs I have not heard since childhood. And I have opened my mind to a possible transformation, not in religious terms, but a qualitative change in how I see my own identity. I was shaped by all this. While I am the observer outside the circle, I have worked hard to win even this place of mindful observer. I have made myself vulnerable. I have stripped myself of the arrogant mantle of titles, education, and the privileges of being an independent woman. I have learned to sit still and practice humility, to be my mother's bereaved daughter de afuera, who needs help with language, who has to be led toward the appropriate action in her now-foreign native culture. To honor my mother, I have sublimated a lifetime of training in the opposite direction. I am a convert to the spiritual practices of sitting still and of acceptance. This change I will carry forward, and it will be of use to me in the difficult weeks to follow.

I have learned that my body is also capable of a less beneficent conversion. Apparently, I have transmuted my grief into physical symptoms, a painful cough that brings tears to my eyes and an ache in my stomach that accompanies me everywhere. I know that this pain is half grief and half fear of more grief. I do not want relief; the pain is part of the prueba. And this acceptance is part of the conversion also. To sit still even among the rocks. My discomfort is yet but a pebble.

78 I serve little cups of thick chocolate to my mother's friends and relatives. I hand one to Ángel, just as he served me a cup of hot chocolate that first night at my mother's bedside when I was so cold and so afraid. He was her good companion, and I wish him peace. I stand next to him and say adiós to all the people who have come to give light to her spirit. When they are all gone, my aunts and uncles stay awhile longer to talk about my mother. They arrange their chairs in a circle around my mother's rocker where I sit.

"Lo has hecho todo bien, Hija." One of my aunts speaks the words I need to hear.

My uncle takes my hands in his. "You can go to John now. Your mother is at peace."

How strange the protocols of death and how we adhere to them as if they are natural laws. I feel as though I have been released from a sealed room. There is a time to let go of the dead, but we don't know when that will be. It is not the same as letting go of the grief, which is a process that will take its required amount of time; but to physically separate myself from my mother's house, I need to hear the right words spoken, the spell broken. *You have done everything right.* No, in the past, I have not done everything right, nor am I likely to in the future. But for eighteen days, I have done everything I could for my mother—more than I knew I could—and it has been pronounced good. *Bien hecho, Hija.*

I can't believe that she has been transmuted into a being of light and is now in the company of angels, but I can feel her presence here, in her house. I take one last look at the photo of her with flowers in her hair. I am moved again by the vulnerability of her expression and the openness of her posture, at a transitional moment when she made her debut as a free woman, when she bade farewell to fear of loneliness. I step outside into the dark night and walk blind in my mother's garden. I feel her there, too, in the cool of the evening. I call forth her voice exclaiming how good the cool grass felt under her feet, and how good it was to watch things she had planted with her own hands grow. How good it was to have her own casita to come home to.

Ave María. Let me learn to relinquish her physical presence. Let her be the dew in the grass, the seed in the rich black earth, the shade of the tree; let her be in the ephemeral bloom of the hibiscus plant she named after me, with flowers that fold unto themselves each night and are renewed each day.

Notebook Two

Time is the longest distance between two places.
—TENNESSEE WILLIAMS

On the last day I spent in my mother's house, I got frequent texts from Tanya: John had undergone a battery of tests, the cardiologist would see him in the morning, and then a decision would be made about getting him home. Every time I tried to reach John, he was undergoing yet another test or sleeping off another procedure. Tanya was by his side, while her husband kept their three-year-old occupied. It would soon be my turn to take up residence once more in the kingdom of the sick.

This is where I should be writing the epilogue. Were this not a true story, it would have a neat arc. We should be well into the resolution by now. Before the call about John's collapse, I envisioned returning to our home in the country to begin to heal from our summer of funerals and help my family do the same. There would be the rites of closure. I would give Tanya some mementos of my mother's life I had put in the red drawstring bag where Mami had kept her little treasures, and I would show Tanya the photos of herself as a baby, a child, a teenager, and a bride, always holding my mother's hand, even when she towered over her abuela by nearly ten inches. My tall daughter and my tiny mother were always very close in spite of their cultural differences and the fact that my mother had the bare bones of a formal education while Tanya had a doctorate in mathematics. Their mutual love and respect for each other transcended all of it, and Tanya is devastated by the loss. Eli will not get to know his Puerto

Rican great-grandmother, who had intended to introduce him to her part of his ethnic heritage. And Tanya has also felt deeply the loss of her paternal grandfather, on whose gift of land we built our home in Georgia. Two major figures in our lives gone within weeks of each other. This is a bereaved family.

But it is not to be, not yet. John's heart has sounded an alarm. How did it happen? They had been at Disney World. John had carried a cold to Orlando but was taking antibiotics. The heat had been extreme, but they were taking frequent breaks. The photos they sent me show a happy family in familiar settings: the Dumbo ride, the Mickey Mouse Magic Show, in front of Cinderella Castle, at the Pixar car races. These pictures have provided me with little moments of reprieve from the solemnity of the novenas and the constant stream of mourners at my mother's house. What has happened at the Magic Kingdom, where no one grows old or sick and time is suspended?

They had gone to dinner after a day at the park. John went outside for some fresh air but did not return to the restaurant. Tanya found him curled in a fetal position in the car, with the heater on full blast. He was trembling and on fire with fever. She tried to get him to sit up, but he was incoherent and too weak to follow her instructions. He insisted he wanted to go back to the hotel, but by the time they got him up the stairs it became evident that he was very ill. They got him back in the car and to the nearest ER. There was no time to call for directions, so they followed an ambulance they had spotted on the road. It led them to a hospital specializing in cardiovascular disease. In the center of a vast population of retired elderly people, it made sense to have a center specializing in heart problems.

2   *The vast azul*

I board the tiny propeller plane in Mayaguez. Looking down at that vast *azul* sea of variegated blues, I see the green eye of my island looking at me, fixing me with a vision of place I will take to my grave. In half an hour we are on the other side of the island. We pass over the old city of San Juan, on whose blue cobblestone streets fortune seekers from all over the world have walked. There are narrow alleys lined with old warehouses that once stored rum and spices and are now stores that sell trinkets to the tourists. There are imposing condominiums and hotels, and there are cruise ships disgorging the masses whose dollars keep the Island's economy afloat. And just below us, as the avioneta dips and descends toward the airport in Isla Verde, is El Morro, the Spanish fort built by the Spaniards to defend their rich port. I watch it recede in the distance until it disappears. When it does, I look forward toward the horizon, letting my heart lift at the thought of home. I don't know now that it will be two more weeks before I will sleep in my own bed again.

The last message I get before boarding the flight from San Juan to Charlotte, where I will change planes one last time, is that the diagnosis has been definitely confirmed as pneumonia. Tanya reassures me again that this is something doctors can treat efficiently. He'll recover and then they'll be on their way to meet me. John will then be under the care of our family doctor.

I accept my daughter's words with gratitude. She is in command of the situation. She is a pragmatic woman. I do not have to be completely in control this time. She will make sure John gets the best treatment. Still, I feel fear rising and doubt that all will be well. All has not been well for two months now. I have not heard John's voice for two days. Now he is in an emergency room far away from home, and I am feeling, to use my mother's word, defrauded. Cheated of the peace we so desperately need. Why are we being slapped down again? I want and believe I deserve closure. When I write fiction, I know the moment when a turn in the narrative will allow the reader to intuit that the end is coming. When the writer fails to give us a hint of possible resolution, the reader feels cheated. But life refuses to follow the classic arc. This narrative's arc had shot straight up like a geyser. Death, death, illness, but, please, not death again.

In my state of premonitory fear I am not surprised when upon landing in Charlotte I turn my cell phone on and it immediately begins ringing. Tanya's voice is no longer as calm as it had been. "Daddy has been readmitted to the hospital with extreme arrhythmia. His heart rate will not stabilize. Mother, you have to get on a flight to Orlando. Now!" I must make some sort of anguished sound because the cabin attendant rushes to my seat and demands to know what is the matter. I tell her that my husband might be having a heart attack and I need to change my flight for Orlando. Her expression changes from annoyance to understanding immediately. She makes a call to the terminal and gets some sort of process started. When I run to the service desk there is an agent holding a boarding pass for me. He says, "You have fifteen minutes to make this flight, and the gate is on the other side of the terminal." I run, barely making it to the end of the boarding line. My heart can only be described in a series of clichés: it pounds, it seems about to burst, it is in my throat and at my temples. It is breaking like a windshield in a high-speed crash. I can barely see and I do not know if there is a road ahead or a dark chasm. But I am heading to my next prueba at 360 miles per hour.

3   *Broken heart syndrome*

I keep running over the events in time, trying to find some logic in the sequence. John's bad cold escalates to pneumonia, the pneumonia compromises his already stressed system, and his heart begins beating erratically. Atrial fibrillation is the initial diagnosis, a condition that could have killed him as it increases the risk of stroke five-fold, had it not been for the "lucky" coincidence of his pneumonia, and the other "lucky" coincidence of landing in a hospital fully equipped to deal with heart problems.

The sidewalk to the hospital feels like quicksand. The modern hospital building is painted in cheery tropical Disney World colors, pink, green, and turquoise. No statue of the Holy Mother, no renderings of the Holy Family anywhere in sight. I'm in the neutral zone of an American public space, where all are equally welcomed, especially the well insured. I follow Tanya through the glistening hallways to John's room, and the too-familiar smells and sounds begin to suck me back into a state of anxiety. *No puede ser.* How could this be happening again?

There lies my husband of forty years, a healthy, athletic man for most of that time, attached to tubes and IV drips, an electronic monitor on his finger. Upon entering the room, Tanya immediately shoots her eyes to his heart rate monitor, a nervous tic that will become my habit during the next week also, along with the absurd, fatigue-induced magical thinking that if I concentrate hard enough, I can bring the numbers down to normal range. John greets me with an apology: he is sorry to be causing me more pain.

I understand his feelings of guilt. It had been his mission to keep our little family from falling too deep into grief, to escort the rest of them through the Magic Kingdom until we could reunite back home and enjoy the last days of summer in the peaceful setting of the farm. But his heart has betrayed him. It has burst into an electrical storm—what Virginia Woolf called in her famous essay "On Being Ill" *the great confessional*. The sick body reveals us. It uncovers our secrets. Woolf says that the sick feel like and are perceived as deserters. I think John must have felt this. In spite of his struggle to keep his grief to himself, it exploded in his chest. And I feel that I deserted him in staying away for so long. It is a circle of guilt.

All I can do is settle in my hard, plastic foldout chair for the duration. I am here.

It may sound like I'm romanticizing grief and illness, but studies have shown that arrhythmia, breakdown of the heart's electrical synchrony, may be linked directly to emotional distress. Excesses in adrenaline-like chemicals produced by a body under stress may result in cardiac arrest. In fact, there is a syndrome first noted in Japan called takotsubo cardiomyopathy, or "broken heart syndrome." In each case, the symptoms, occurring in otherwise healthy people, could be traced back to high levels of stress, usually related to a death in the family. The more I read, the more frightened, almost paranoid, I become about the infectious nature of death. Bereavement is an illness. Death breaks our hearts. Death may kill us.

Virginia Woolf said we must invent a language for pain.

The cardiologist, a self-possessed small man with a Russian accent and a tendency to rock on his heels, makes a little speech by John's bed. Tanya listens closely while keeping her eyes on the heart monitor. It is morbidly fascinating to see the numbers shoot up, revealing John's responses to the doctor's words.

Fibrillation is caused by a complete breakdown in electrical synchrony. An electrical storm. Electrical impulses misfiring. Palpitations.

Tachycardia is chaos. The natural rhythms break down, and this is what causes the wildly fluctuating numbers on the monitor.

Unless we discover the reason for the tachyarrhythmias, a sudden stroke or sudden cardiac arrest may ensue.

Tests. A procedure known as cardiac catheterization will determine whether there is a blockage. A stent may be introduced. Or bypass surgery may be needed.

"He is lucky we discovered this potential problem before it kills him," the surgeon says. John's numbers jump high. My own heart begins to beat wildly. The broken heart syndrome is spreading through the room. I watch Tanya's brows furrow. She takes John's hand in her own and pats it.

We are finally allowed to ask our questions, but there are no conclusive answers. Tests, exploratory procedures. Wait for results.

All I can I do now is what I have learned to do when nothing else can be done. I sit on the hard hospital chair and practice being still. I read and I wait.

4   Patience has never been my forte. I have always chosen action. Confronting a situation is the best course for pessimists; I have always expected the worst and tried to prepare for it. I was infected early by my parents' por si acaso mentality. Just in case, I have always prepared for storms, real and metaphorical, and my "go" bag is always ready by the door. But this summer the dominoes collapsed before I could react. And now I witness John signing the form that states in print that he may suffer a stroke, respiratory or cardiac failure, embolism, life-threatening infection, or postoperative complications—that he might die while they attempt to find the roots of what could kill him.

For days John's cardiac rhythm has been flitting in and out of atrial fibrillation. They try every medication they can think of, all injected into his veins through the IVs, and still the monitor looks like aerial views of the Himalayas: peaks and valleys. It is obviously more than mere heartbreak syndrome. The avuncular internist, an Indian man whose copper skin and kind eyes remind me of my maternal grandfather, speaks softly to us about the possibility of a congenital condition that had gone undiagnosed. So many dark secrets our bodies keep. My mother's black spots revealed too late. What is John's heart hiding?

Tanya's eyes turn to her three-year-old son when she hears about the possibility that her genes, and therefore his, may be carrying a time bomb. I understand her fear. My own thoughts alternate between concern for John and fear that Tanya may also be affected. And so it goes, this cycle of hope and fear. John answers questions about his health history and his habits. He is shown diagrams and graphs. Yes, he understands the risks of the procedure, and he will sign away his rights to sue or protest should any of the potential catastrophes occur during the more-or-less routine procedure of cardiac catheterization (with the option to implant a stent or perform a bypass should they find a significant obstruction). The ultrasonic transducer–tipped catheter will be snaked up his torso into the heart and, "if all goes according to plan," will reveal every twist and turn of the inner walls of blood vessels, letting the cardiologist know if there is any plaque or blockage. A stent, a stainless steel tube to widen the passage, might be inserted. Do we understand everything?

5   No matter how routine, any invasion of the body is a frightening prospect, although I am more afraid of the results than of the process itself. So we focus on the positive. John's pneumonia has abated after aggressive antibiotic therapy. He should be able to tolerate the anesthesia well. If all goes according to plan, and if no major obstruction is found, we may be able to travel home within two days. We have already extended the hotel stay a week beyond the original vacation. We are taking turns at the hospital, but my cough has gotten so severe that I've had my doctor call in a prescription for codeine-based syrup that makes me feel lightheaded and unsteady on my feet. But it is a relief having my family by my side, especially my strong

daughter, whose clearheadedness and determination keep the nurses' attention focused on her father and give me a reprieve. But the fear of another loss haunts and depletes me.

No puede ser. My need to know exactly what is happening to John prompts me to continue reading and researching, although the facts about heart disease are even more frightening than what I learned about cancer. Approximately one quarter of Americans die suddenly from undiagnosed or ignored heart conditions. Many are victims of a rhythm suddenly gone chaotic. Is this what I am looking at on the monitor? Misfiring, one of the doctors called it. Firing, misfiring, invasive. Military terms are lobbed at us over John's bed like grenades into a trench, and all we can do is surrender.

The phrase we hear repeatedly is "atrial fibrillation," which is defined as "a complete breakdown in electrical regularity." Chaos. Potential sudden death. *¿Cómo puede ser?*

Lying in bed late, you will sometimes read to me
about a past war that obsesses you;
about young men, like our brothers once,
who each year become more like our sons
because they died the year we met,
or the year we got married
or the year our child was born . . .

> Death was a slogan
to shout about with raised fists or hang on banners.

But here we are,
listening more closely than ever to the old songs,
sung for new reasons by new voices. We are survivors
of an undeclared war someone might decide to remake
like a popular tune. Sometimes, in the dark, alarmed
by too deep a silence, I will lay my hand on your chest,
for the familiar, steady beat to which I have attuned
my breathing for so many years.
    —from "Anniversary"

6 This fall will mark our fortieth anniversary. Four decades. I have come to appreciate how much of our lives has been exceptionally good. We raised an intelligent, self-motivated, and accomplished daughter, and we built a home on the family's land deep in the countryside of Georgia. The dream of this home was what kept us going during our difficult first years as a young couple, when we were struggling to get our educations while raising a child.

John and I married at nineteen in a small church ceremony organized by his mother. She even gave me the money to buy a simple dress at the best store in town, White's Department Store, where my mother and I had never shopped. I selected a storm-cloud-gray ankle-length dress, and the few relatives still in town contributed flowers for my bouquet and hair. The ceremony was quick and simple. My parents were not there; they were in New Jersey. The depression that would result in my father's mysterious fall from a building was the crisis forthcoming, and for once, I would have a companion as I tried to help my parents across another rickety bridge.

Sitting next to John's hospital bed waiting to know his heart's secret, I realize that everything had changed for us that terrible night when we drove my wounded father from New Jersey to Georgia listening again and again to Don McLean's "American Pie." The change was like the subtle redirection of a train, how the passengers barely notice that they are suddenly headed in the right direction, the one printed on their tickets.

For forty years we have been building a life. We both had to learn our roles, especially since, like most young people, we did not want to imitate our parents. We had hippie sensibilities with preppy ambitions that came with Tanya's birth, when a laid-back attitude about money, adequate shelter, and health care would no longer do. We quickly discovered that we would have to make major adjustments to our plans so that we could both get our educations. One of us had to work full-time once we had a child. John took on the task of providing while I finished my degrees. My parents helped with childcare, financially, and in every way they could for the first two years, before my father's mysterious auto accident and my mother's return to the Island. How intense the days were then, what a vortex of memories. Somehow, we worked and we played and we got ourselves and our child safely over the rough waves and onto dry land. It was hard, hard, to fit in my dream of being a writer when all that was left of my days were the couple of hours at dawn when no one needed me. But I worked at it without hope and without despair. Well, maybe with a little hope, word by word, line by line, as I made my poems and stories. We felt that every goal we met, no matter how small, moved us a little closer to the life we wanted: John's dream of a degree in math and a house on his family's land, and mine of teaching and writing. Tanya gave meaning and purpose to our days, and our dreams kept us moving forward in inches. It took a long time for me to become the adequate provider that would allow us to switch roles. John and Tanya attended college at the same time, and finally, John, in his forties, got to do what he had wanted to do since our college days—teach math in Georgia. It took three of the four decades for our plan to be fulfilled. Our path was the long and winding road of the Beatles song I quoted when we experienced setbacks, dead ends, and derailments on our way to the future.

My mother's and his father's death, and now his illness, have shaken me awake from the daze of high-speed travel. We have been moving at warp speed all these years, and now what?

7   Illness means waiting. But waiting doesn't necessarily result in answers. We wait by John's bedside while they fill and refill his IV bags with a pharmacopeia of medications. We wait, and we watch the monitor, which jumps like a startled animal even while he sleeps. The lowest reading we see is a pulse rate of 140, twice the normal. I try not to think of the term *sudden death*, but it haunts me, making the electronic readings seem like coded threats. We wait for tests. We wait for the nurses to come in and look at the machines. They volunteer only what we already know.

Finally the day of the procedure arrives. John says little. He looks exhausted. Tanya and I stand on either side of him. We have both chosen pieces of my mother's jewelry to wear. I wind my mother's gold chain around my wrist, and Tanya wears one of Mami's favorite necklaces. Tanya says uncharacteristically that she knows Mamá would want to be with us today. She has chosen to suspend her disbelief, to sublimate reason and just open herself to whatever she can believe in, if momentarily. We are weary. We are in the fog induced by bedside vigils without end. Grief and anxiety have drained us relentlessly for nearly two months.

As I watch John slip into unconsciousness under the anesthesia and be wheeled into the operating room, I silently begin the Rosary repetitions, prayers still fresh on my mind. Santa María, Padre Nuestro, Espíritu Santo, anybody, let's make a deal: if I say these magical words will you spare this family another loss?

We wait to hear what secrets they have found in John's heart. At some point we are told to meet him back in his room. While we wait for him to wake up, a nurse hands us a printout of the procedure.

A 6-French pigtail catheter was utilized for performing left heart catheterization and left ventriculography. A 6-French JL 5 coronary catheter was utilized for performing left coronary angiography and the larger French JR-4 was utilized because the patient has a big aorta. At the end of the procedure a 6-French self-tightening suture auto-seal was placed in the right femoral artery.

In four pages of medical jargon, the only place where I detect that John has been seen as anything more than a "59 year old white male who was referred for catheterization for symptoms of cardiac distress" is in the brief statement about his enlarged aorta.

Eventually the cardiologist comes to give us the diagnosis in person. John's arrhythmia is caused by a congenital defect, a branch of the coronary artery that is deviated and constricted.

He has had it since birth, but only now, under the stress of pneumonia and other factors, had it caused severe enough fibrillation to "present" abnormally. The immediate course of action is to stabilize John with medications until a cardiologist in Georgia can see him. No surgery advised for now, but immediate referral to a cardiologist, and a lifetime of supervised drug therapy.

After giving rise of the diagonal branch coronary artery and after giving rise of septal perforator branch coronary artery the left anterior descending coronary artery continues as a small-caliber vessel and has some muscular bridging in the mid and distal portion with some systolic narrowing of the left anterior descending coronary artery but not complete systolic obliteration.

I am weary to the bone and word-drunk. Oh, I say to myself, *gracias a Dios*, no complete systolic obliteration. Can we go home now?

8   John has had enough of the poking and probing, tests and procedures. The day after he is pronounced not in danger of immediate death, we find him out of bed, still attached to his IV rack but insisting to his nurse that he needs to walk.

Eli takes his grandfather by the hand and we parade around the room and down the hall. I notice his pallor and the unsteadiness of his gait. He seems to be fighting motion sickness. His pulse rate is still erratic, though the numbers are not as high as they had been.

"We are going home tomorrow," he says, and the nurse on duty, a compassionate Indian woman who tries to answer our many questions and appears to really see John as a person, offers to call the cardiologist. In the meantime, John asks me to pack his belongings. I do, although I have lost confidence in things going right. I know that we are not the decision makers in the autonomous nation of the hospital. "I want to go home" means nothing if the all-powerful doctor, almost always a ruler in absentia, does not approve a release.

My usually calm, gentle, practical husband is by afternoon the proverbial caged animal. The young nurse of the second shift keeps up the work of faxes, e-mails, and phone calls to the cardiologist, as she can see that he is becoming more and more agitated. Finally, by that evening, we get the news that he will be released under advisement— the family is responsible for taking him to a cardiologist in Georgia immediately. In other words, the powers-that-be have washed their hands thoroughly, like the fastidious health care providers they are, of our case. Take him home, but if something happens . . .

Tanya and I debate whether I should stay with him in Orlando for a few more days, as she and Dory have to get back to Chicago within the week to start teaching.

"We are going home tomorrow," John insists, the monitors behind him drawing his desperation in peaks and valleys.

While we wait to discharge him, I visit the hospital gift shop and buy Eli a stuffed bear dressed in blue scrubs. When you squeeze one of his paws he sings a few lines of the Robert Palmer song: "Doctor, doctor give me the news / I've got a bad case of loving you." I want him to have at least one good memory of this week, something other than the memory of his strong granddaddy felled by illness and diminished by thirty-seven pounds—the total he has lost in the two weeks since his "cold" began. That's practically what Eli weighs. More than once Eli has expressed his fear of another person being put in a box. He holds on to John's hand the whole time we wait to be released.

Tanya takes her place in the driver's seat of the minivan John recently bought so that we could travel as a family. John climbs into the passenger seat, still too quiet and very pale. Dory is in the second row with Eli, who is safely strapped to his child's seat. I climb over to the last row—what we call the grandmother seat. I recall how my mother had crossed herself and said a prayer when we had piled into my father's Studebaker to make the perilous trips over mountains to her mother's house, across the island in Puerto Rico. *Vamos con Dios, Santa María, Jesús, y José*, she'd always say. Here we go with God, Mary, Jesus, and Joseph. Then Papi would always say, "This car doesn't hold that many passengers, Querida. It's either your santos or the children." She never smiled at this.

I allow myself a bit of hope. We are going home at last. Like Odysseus, we have met the Cyclops, the Lotus-eaters, and myriad other monsters on our journey, but we are on our way home. Satellite radio provides us with a vast choice of music on the long ride. John has a prodigious memory and can recall the titles of songs and what he was doing when he first heard them. But even as we listen to the hits of the 1970s and '80s, his head stays down. In the grandmother seat, I try to fill the hours by thinking of the decades of my American life with John and Tanya.

I look at Tanya in the driver's seat, determined to get her father home, and I remember the terrifying night when John drove my broken father from New Jersey to Georgia and proved his love and devotion not only to me, but to my not-normal, definitely not all-American family. In the four decades since that night when I knew I was not alone, I slowly began to believe that I had a chance at a "normal" American life. It is strange to say this about the hectic years when we were juggling school, jobs, and a young child while at the same time I was trying to write my first poems and stories. Looking back, I call up an image from old movies: calendar pages flipping away as time speeds by, the years passing in seconds. The flashback may be described in a word that makes my students smirk when I let it slip out, as it now seems so dated and particular mainly to my generation—psychedelic. Somehow, even while we rushed through our days, John and I managed to become a part of the culture, to immerse ourselves in the times—a phenomenon most people would consider "natural," but as the daughter of displaced people, I had lived under the bell jar of difference. I have written about the dissonance of my life in the 1960s from that of my classmates. To them, the Beatles, Woodstock, *Hair*, and Vietnam War protests were the defining moments of their generation. While I was aware of these events, my family's concerns were much more immediate. In the barrio, Woodstock was talked about (if it was mentioned at all) as a ridiculous show of ingratitude by spoiled children. We were concerned solely with our survival. Although my father was in the navy, he did not discuss military or political matters with us. We were always either planning a trip to Puerto Rico while he was away or returning from one, and we were always the new kids trying to catch up. It was not until I married John and had Tanya that I began to see that I had the option to enter the greater world. Unlike my mother, I had not attached myself to place—in fact, inadvertently perhaps, by making me the child interpreter, my parents had prepared me to more than survive in the world of English.

9   After we married and Tanya was born, America was no longer what was experienced by the others outside my parents' Spanish-speaking, microcosmic Island home. I was still umbilically connected to mother and to the Island through her. Even after my father died and my mother returned to her mother's house to reinvent herself, I was aware of the ties that bound me to my family there and to my native language. None of these things were abandoned or forgotten. In fact, when I discovered that my dual identity was a dynamic source of creativity, I began to mine this rich vein for poems, stories, and novels. But I have begun to see now, in my grief, how much of a cultural limbo I have lived in. I was not like my mother, living the life of my mind in expectation of a return to a specific "home," and I was not like John, living fully in his time, for better or for worse, since he had experienced his childhood and young manhood as part of his country's history. Meeting him gave me a taste of what it means to be fully engaged in the culture and history of your times. The first concern we faced as a couple was his imminent draft. Having barely avoided this threat, we began to count the missing among our college classmates. For a time, I wore a bracelet with a soldier's name. It provoked discussions, both pro and con, and it connected me with the anti-war movement in a visible way; it made me feel like I was a playing a part in our American history.

In the first two decades, John worked and I studied and wrote my little poems while we watched Tanya change from pretty baby to pre-cocious toddler to athletic teenager. I recall all this as fragments that I can arrange and view in any number of combinations. Fractals. I remember John calling dozens of stores all over the country to try to locate a Cabbage Patch doll to be shipped overnight for Christmas morning. I remember all the Barbies and Kens and the Dreamhouse with a thousand pieces—some (all night) assembly required. I remember the beads Tanya strung into necklaces, the outfits for recit-als, the Brownie troop, the dozens of cookies baked and pumpkins carved—every holiday observed so that our daughter could expe-rience all either one of us remembered or had missed. There were Michael Jackson's "Thriller" video and *Grease*, to be watched every day after school. There were late nights that made me write spells against death while I waited. There were the heartbreaks and exultations of first loves, college admission, graduation, and so much more as she became her own person.

In the third decade, I got to see John finish his math studies and fulfill his goal of teaching high school mathematics. Tanya got her doctorate and met the man she would marry. On her wedding day she looked radiant, even after a downpour that forced her to walk around barefoot in her wedding gown—a barefoot princess with her handsome groom by her side. They headed north for their first teaching jobs in Chicago. Eli was born, and I saw Tanya's life become truly and uniquely her story. Her decades to count, her fragments to collect.

We worked and studied and raised our child, and I wrote when I could find an hour or two. It felt like we were running toward the future in those days. We would sometimes pause to discuss what that future would bring. John's version always included a house on the land he would inherit in Georgia. I just wanted to be in one place and have time to write. It took thirty years to make that happen. By the fourth decade we thought we had achieved balance in our lives. This summer, the plan had been to gather our little family at our house, take our grandson to Disney World, and then visit my mother on the Island.

IO   In the front seat, John moans. Tanya parks at a gas station so Dory can help him get to a restroom, where he vomits in spasms that leave him too weak to hold his head up. He does not want to go to a hospital. *Home*, he keeps saying. Tanya drives without a break for the next eight hours. From the set of her shoulders I can tell that she is fighting panic and fatigue. I feel the guilt of a parent at her child's distress. Aren't we supposed to protect them? How has it all come unraveled? Have we made the wrong decision to subject John to the long trip from Florida to Georgia?

"I want to get home," is all he says when we suggest stopping at an ER or at least at a hotel so he can rest.

II   Our house was built with almost no money. Once I accepted a position at the University of Georgia and Tanya was in college, we made a couple of crucial decisions. All of our resources would go toward achieving the two main goals of our lives: John would return to college for a math degree, and we would build a house in "the piney woods." The house took shape with much help from his family. His father, who had bought a Victorian house for materials, donated the beautiful aged wood for our floors and two fireplaces; his brother, uncles, and cousins donated their labor; and his sisters helped paint and decorate it. In 1991, we were able to have a country Christmas in our own living room with windows overlooking a pond John's grandfather had made from a natural artesian well.

    It is like no place I could have imagined in my Paterson days, when we had to leave town and go to Garret Mountain to see "woods." It is a simple house, but like my mother's casita, it represents the fulfillment of a goal. I see its symbolic value, although I know that I don't feel my mother's or John's passion for house and place. I believe that I will forever feel that I exist in between places. For me, home is a state of mind more than a location. It is how my history shaped me. I am at home where the people I love want and need to be, and where I can function at my best potential. My recent losses and the renewed fear that comes in waves like John's nausea on this long trip home have made me feel even more rootless. It is as if I am on a ship lost at sea, and the sighting of land is no more than a mirage.

12   We make it home, but John is so dehydrated and so weak that he cannot stand on his own. The one doctor on duty at the ER in our small hometown hospital is unable to stabilize John with the usual treatment available there and tells us that he needs to be sent by ambulance to a university hospital in Augusta.

    Once again, I become a witness to a scene that seems to happen outside of me. I sit next to the gurney and feel myself floating above the room.

    I see John pale as death below me.

I see myself on a chair, eternally on a hospital bedside chair, waiting. I see Tanya pacing the halls, talking to nurses, trying to get answers. Then I hear her voice calling me back. "The ambulance is here. You have to ride with him. What's wrong? Are you OK?"

It is a psychedelic ride to Augusta, sitting next to a driver who knew Mr. C., as John's students call him, and who had read my work in his English class in high school, and who wants to talk. I don't really know what I'm saying to him. At the Augusta hospital, I follow another gurney to another room.

I wait for doctors. I wait for a diagnosis. One is offered: an infection picked up at the Orlando hospital, most likely. Gastroenteritis.

He will not hold food down for three days. He will lose more weight. We wait out the purging of his body while the cardiologists observe and examine him, and while the gastroenterologists run tests. John sleeps most of the time.

I sit and try to sleep on yet another hospital fold-out bed. One night I dream of my mother. She speaks familiar words to me: "Así es la vida." In my dream, she looks like she does in the funeral photo. She smiles her hesitant smile from the photo and says, "That's the way life is," her standard answer to my questions about the inevitable or inexplicable. "Así es la vida, Hija." For whatever reason, the dream snaps me out of my self-pitying daze. As I wait for John to recover, I remember how to sit still in my hard hospital chair. On the steno pad I always carry, I start taking notes. I review the notes I kept during my time in my mother's house, and I make lists of the images and sounds I want to remember. I listen to the Spanish words I recorded so that I can make sequences (and meaning) from them: El Santo Rosario. La gracia de Dios. El Pentecostés.

13 *Where time and place and eternity meet*

At almost sixty, it seems absurd to consider myself an orphan, or even motherless. The standard response I get from even close friends is some version of "parents die, get used to it." In the American culture, where extended mourning is considered a pathological condition—it even has a name, "complicated grief"—you are supposed to bury the dead and get on with life. But perhaps those of us who acted as intermediaries for parents lost in the new country, who felt they were on the fringes, whose lives were lost in translation, feel as if we have lost a dependent, more like a child or a ward than a parent. As a child I always felt responsible for my mother, especially since my father was absent so much of the time. Over the years I have experienced a sense of pride as I witnessed her self-empowerment—her belated liberation and, in her later years, her choice to embrace her Catholic faith again, on her own terms this time. She and her women friends invented a tribe of faith and good works. They formed a circle of companionship and support, and they were there, surrounding her with the prayers, rites, and rituals that would comfort her until she took her last breath and, they believed, beyond. I have a difficult time accepting her death because I feel that I had so much more to learn from her. Our roles alternated over the decades, and I was just getting ready to try to understand how she had achieved balance in her heart and mind. Religion had something to do with it, but not all. She was devoted, but she did not wear her religion on her sleeve. She kept God in his place, and the Pope too. Awareness but not piety. What I was beginning to understand about her was that she had prepared all her life to accept grace in small measures. She never had to learn to sit still. Thus had she gotten through the waiting that made up most of her life. My American life has been driven by big goals and great expectations; it always has to be a race to the end. The days I raced through now seem like a collage, with snippets of songs and images to mark the decades. The only place I've ever managed to slow time is in my writing, and my mother's reserve of memories was my treasure chest.

I have no fear of nonbeing. I fear the huecos, the chasms, left behind by death. They are sinkholes that the living fear falling into only to emerge lessened, like Alice. Diminished by longing. I am writing about the losses, the empty spaces, in attempt to fill them.

I am too old to be an orphan. It is too late to bemoan my motherlessness. But I miss the energy she brought into my life by just being who she was. I can bring that back in my work. Although I do not believe in a heavenly afterlife, I know that energy cannot be totally eliminated, and that it can be harnessed. I believe in the power of storytelling to preserve and conserve the energies of personality. Writing is continuing a conversation with the dead through the conduit of language. The work of returning my mother's energy to the world will be my small goal.

14   When John and I finally drive the one-mile unpaved road to our home, I have to slow down to wipe my eyes; after so many days of sterile hospital rooms, the deep green of the trees and the blood red of the earth make my eyes water. I see John stare hungrily ahead to the pond and the house beyond. We both feel like survivors of a devastating natural disaster. He looks paler in the sunlight than he was among the blanched surroundings of the hospital, and very thin. And I am bone weary, still coughing that dry, interruptive cough that clears nothing in my head or chest. A Spanish word comes to mind, náufragos, which sounds like a drowning person's gulp for air, and means shipwreck survivors. We are náufragos, and we are finally home.

15   As a writer, the hardest thing for me is to begin—and even harder, to begin again.

The academic year, its natural rhythms, the ebbs and flows and even tidal waves of our lives as teachers, has forced us to think of the end of summer as the beginning of the next race. I have adjusted my writing routines to this schedule. When Tanya was a toddler, when I first discovered that I needed to write the way some people need to run every day, for both my physical and mental well-being, I established a ritual that has remained unchanged for most of my life. I get up a little before 5:00 a.m., which used to give me two hours before Tanya awakened and the demands of "real life" sucked me into the daily vortex. Two precious hours to write. Until recent years, getting a few lines down for a poem or two pages of prose (my daily assignment) made up my matins, my daily offices, my meditation, my mental run. In the past couple of years, I have begun to feel more and more reluctant to go where my imagination and my memory have always led me. It is not a writer's block—I have always flippantly announced at Q&As and in my writing classrooms that I believe writer's block to be a leisure activity. I have never had the time for it. But now, at the time in my life when I have the time to write without alarms or a to-do list involving ten to twelve hours of nonstop duties, I have been having trouble finding something new to say. I have somehow written a new young adult novel and some poems on aging, but I am not experiencing the exhilaration of discovery. I have forgotten how to sit still before the blank page.

While keeping vigil by hospital bedsides, I've been reading and making notes to try to see patterns. In the end, I have discovered that although the losses have made me fragile and vulnerable, the grief has been like a forest fire, the kind that clears space for new growth. I thought nothing would be left of me after the losses, but what has burned away was the illusion of plenty. I do not have plenty of time. John and I are not invulnerable. Like his father and my mother, we have a timeline, and we do not know when it will end. Electroshock therapy is supposed to jolt the depressed or catatonic person out of their torpor. I have read that the patient wakes up weak as a newborn from this violent procedure. The violence of grace is not unlike a convulsion-inducing electrical shock. You may awaken in pain, the hurt itself letting you know you are alive.

Weak as newborns, John and I decide to take leaves of absence from our jobs and stay in our home in the middle of the woods to do something we have never done before in the four decades of our marriage: nothing, whatever we want. As soon as we settle down to do nothing, the waves of grief that were put on hold during John's emergency sweep over us, our own private little tsunamis. It is not only grief over the deaths of parents, which, as we have been told dozens of times, are expected and normal; I think we are both saddened by the loss of our own sense of time without end. We saw our life clock ticking down on the monitors attached to John's heart.

The waves of sadness hit us at different times. A phone call from a concerned friend sometimes triggers one, as we relay the list of our summer's woes. Sometimes objects bring the sadness, especially photos. Sometimes we talk, but we also learn to respect each other's need for solitude and silence. When Tanya tells us that she had undergone the agony of passing a kidney stone soon after arriving home, she says she chose not to share this with many people because she herself was suffering from sympathy fatigue and felt that the litany of our losses and sorrows was exhausting to others.

16   We hang on through the little tsunamis by turning to our routines. John settles into his new schedules of medications and oxygen and heart-rate monitoring. And he tends to his roses, which have wilted during one of the hottest, driest summers on record in Georgia. I sit down with my notebooks and with the boxes of mementos and photos I had mailed back from my mother's house, trying to overcome the torpor. Post-traumatic stress, said one of my friends when I described the symptoms; he recommended directed, purposeful activity and perhaps antidepressants. The unremitting stress of a string of crises will sometimes result in apathy. Why do anything if there is nothing but bad news coming? Spiritual aridity, said another friend, a woman of faith. You miss the solace of ritual and prayer. But I reject both diagnoses. I will not convert to either the cult of pharmacopeia or to a faith-based cure for my existential malady. I do not need my serotonin to be redirected, nor a novena to water my arid soul. I do not want to treat my tristeza with medications or therapy. I know that my apathy is a fear of commitment to the work I know I have to do. My traumatic stress is not post; it is present. I am facing my own mortality and trying to decide whether I still have the power to make something worthy from language. On an online discussion forum about bereavement, someone said that the grieving person undergoes a crisis of faith, even if she is not religious. My crisis, as I slowly begin to understand it, is a growing suspicion that I am now homeless. That with the loss of my mother, I have also lost my last legitimate connection to the language, place, and cultural heritage that has fed my work. My imaginative life has been orphaned; my "complicated grief" involves an identity crisis. I am at a crossroads and have to find my way to that intersection *where time and place and eternity somehow meet.*

Accepting doubt, allowing the flow of words to begin again, painful periods of aridity, demoralization, and the exultation of finding my way back to language—these have always been part of my discipline as a writer. In the study of literature I have found a path to meaning, a way to establish a sequence to the chaotic events of my life, and language has also led me to the wild excitement of discovery. In the reading and writing of poems I have found timelessness. The discipline of writing has given me a sense of stability. I lost my footing this summer, but I have gained my sea legs. I learned some things by following my mother's quotidian routines: When your spirit is troubled, clean your house, cultivate your garden, and feel the cool water on your hands, the hot sun on your skin. *Esto es vida.* Offer your soul the candlelight and good scents it craves. Give your restless spirit a quiet place to rest, and also open the windows and doors so it can hear the sounds of *vida* outside. Remind it frequently, *hay vida.* Give it silence and music and light. Learn to sit still and let prayer and song sway you gently, back and forth like an abanico in a woman's hand. Let ritual and prayer dance you to a rhythm your whole body will recognize as primal.

17 *Así es*

La vida can be measured in decades, I can hear my mother saying, punctuated by the Joyful and Sorrowful Mysteries, and sometimes even the Glorious and Luminous! The days can be counted like rosary beads as they slip through your hands. *Así es la vida, Hija.* This pronouncement was usually followed by laughter. Her laughter was a mystery to me, accustomed as I was to the high seriousness of academic life, with its insistence on specialized knowledge and the narrow focus on logical thought and straight-faced pronouncements—or, as it's otherwise called, literary criticism. My mother believed in heaven, hell, angels, and demons and laughed at her own blind faith. She did not question her outrageous cosmology and superstitious beliefs but thoroughly enjoyed questioning my certainties. It was her way of keeping us on the same level. She loved puns, jokes, and prayers. "Tú sabes como era," I heard again and again from the people who knew her and told me stories about both her love of fun and her unshakeable faith. "You know how she was."

How she was. What shall I call it? Inadvertently profound? Her observations and casual remarks about *la vida y el mundo* peppered my writing. I once wrote an entire poem around her claim that the blue of the sky above her island and the various blues of the ocean belonged to her when her eyes were upon them. *Mi cielo, mi mar*, she had said to me, pointing at the sky and the sea. I took her sky, her sea, and made them mine in my poem.

> If I say *el azul*, you may not see the color
> of *mi cielo*, *mi mar*. Look once upon my sky,
> my sea, and you will know precisely
> what *el azul* means to me.

I am writing this as I near the end of my appropriately named leave of absence; I have taken leave from the normal world of job, writing, ordinary duties and routines, activities that have come to seem incongruous after these months of death, illness, and mourning. The huecos that Ángel feared he would have to face in the house that had been so completely filled by my mother are metaphorical holes I have brought back with me. The empty spaces left by grief are what cause the disequilibrium in the bereaved. Some people can refill themselves through faith. They can find comfort in the belief that there is something beyond this life; the fear of death is assuaged by the promise of an afterworld without end.

I came home to face the heretofore unacknowledged fact that death is not a surprise; death is the given. It hovers over everything and everyone. Someone quoted Saint Benedict's injunction during the Mass or the novenas and I wrote it down: "Keep death before us." Before us. Do not mask it. Do not rush through the grieving and put it past us. Keep it before us. In order to work again, and to engage again in the quotidian, I have to believe that the lyrics to the song that played one terrible night in my youth when I believed they were meant for my father, "This will be the day that I die," could apply to me, on any day. It is only the date that is uncertain. Death is the one certainty I have now.

Because I am dying, because we all are, I will claim my bit of grace, which I extract from my mother's gift of abundant grace, and which has propelled me through this story during the pruebas I was given by el destino, or perhaps just my luck—one of the lay definitions of grace is luck. In my mother's Bible, there was a highlighted passage from the Gospel according to Mark. One short sentence, the blind man's response to Jesus' question, "What do you want from me?"

"Déjame ver." Let me see.

It is what I want too. I want to see again.

18 *A dream or la verdad?*

For me memory turns on the cloying smell of boiling beans
in a house of women waiting, waiting for wars, affairs, periods
of grieving, the rains, *el mal tiempo*, to end, the phrase
used both for inclement weather and to abbreviate the aftermath
of personal tragedies. And they waited for beans to boil.
My grandmother would put a pot on the slow fire
at dawn, and all day long, the stones she had dropped in, hard
and dry as a betrayed woman's eyes, slowly softened, scenting
the house with the essence of waiting. Beans.
I grew to hate them.
—from "Beans: An Apologia for Not Loving to Cook" (For Tanya)

There is a story I sometimes tell at my poetry readings before reading a poem called "Beans," which I dedicated to Tanya. I wrote the poem by way of explaining to her why I don't cook. I was pleased with my little feminist manifesto, but, as always, I felt the impulse to share my revelation with my mother. I wanted to hear her say, "You are right! I was one of the victims of the hot stove, shackled to the oven! Hija, you got it right!" But it was not to be. My mother's impish spirit swam across the Atlantic and entered my ear through the phone receiver. Through gales of laughter she said, "Hija, what an imagination you have. Dios te bendiga! Oppressed? The days I spent in the kitchen with your grandmother were a blessing, a retreat, a vacation from children and men. But you cannot know this secret about women, how they can find peace in their kitchens, because you chose another sanctuary for yourself among your books and papers— a lonelier one, ¿verdad?" *Ay, Dios mío.* I laughed with her but published the poem anyway.

We come to the truth in our own ways. Food, poetry, *es lo mismo.* It is all the same, and all true. ¿Verdad, Mami?

19   Language is a skin: I rub my language against the other. It is as if I had words instead of fingers, or fingers at the tip of my words.

—ROLAND BARTHES, *A Lover's Discourse*

Prayer has a hypnotizing effect on me, the same as poetry. I love the language. Listening to prayers and the seductive dream state induced by the repetition of words may have originally awakened my desire for making poems. The passionate recounting of mysteries and miracles may have planted the seed in my budding writer's mind. I may have fallen in love with the word at the feet of the passionate women counting prayers on their rosary beads, the beauty of the language: annunciation, transfiguration, Epiphany, Pentecost. To this enchantment I may owe my self-discovery as a woman of words.

Just as the women who prayed for my mother's soul found a way out of isolation, I have found words to ward off the lurking shadow of isolation in books and writing. Isolation is what all of us struggle against; it is the universal curse of humanity, as we are born to be separated from the ones who give us life. We try to find love among strangers, and we invent and reinvent homes to fulfill that yearning.

The isolation I have always felt is not due to homesickness as hers was; I do not long for a particular location. My sense of loss is not for familial love, or for a house, or for a landscape; it is more an existential hueco. I yearn for that place where something I cannot quite identify should be. I have a sense of having been halved.

When grief has made me heavy and slow, only making the difficult walk to my desk and the empty page or screen, only the ritual of putting down words, fills the empty place, but it does not stay full. There is longing like smoke or fog that expands to fill the vacuum; there are the losses wrought by time, distance, and aging; there is sorrow; and there are restless spirits that haunt me, that sneak in during the night and empty the shelf again. There is, always, the hueco. My little altar with its votive candles, pictures of la familia, and rosary beads is now empty again—nada, nada. And every morning, I must start again.

20 *Adiós*

It is 1956, and my mother, who is just twenty, has risen with her mother before dawn to get us ready for the long car ride to San Juan, where we will board a Pan Am airplane to New York. My brother is a toddler and I am three and a half. My mother is wearing a dress that makes a sound like hush, hush as she walks, and high heels that tap-tap on the tile floor. I hear her sobbing softly, and I hear my abuela's voice: Hija. Así es la vida. They are speaking the words I will hear again and again, at departures, bedside vigils, and deaths. This is the way life is. This is a prueba God has given you.

We are leaving behind the blinding primary colors of her Island, the small house that seemed to have enough room for her eight brothers and sisters—and later their wives, husbands, and children. The house whose windows and doors were thrown open at first light so that the sun, wind, rain, and animal and human life were all part of the same experience. My mother was leaving behind the constant presence of the familiar. She will from that day on feel like a migrating bird that has been abandoned by the flock. She will feel separated, out of her element.

Ahead of her: life with a man who has been away most of the time since their wedding. How different he seems each time they reunite after months or years of separation. He is no longer part of the flock. He resists the company of others and talks only about making a new life on their own.

At the bottom of the hill from my grandmother's house a little crowd has gathered. The hired car that will take us over and around the mountain range that runs down the middle of the island is already parked in front of the house, where a little boy has already taken his place as the witness to yet another departure. He is the one who will call my mother one of the heroes of our diaspora at her funeral. This day he is just the curious little boy who takes it all in, wondering why the women are crying so hard, almost wailing. He thinks he would like to be the one going to Nueva York. To fly on an airplane over the sea! To see the city from above like a bird! I am focused on my mother and the pain she is inflicting on me as she unconsciously squeezes my hand. Very tight. I can tell that she is both afraid and sad.

Ahead of her: a last view of the island as it will forever appear in her dreams, the turns and twists over mountains not yet blasted through by American engineers. A full three hours to cross an island spanning less than one hundred miles end to end. On one side of the car is a vertiginous drop to the sea and on the other, the threat of imminent rockslides. She holds us tightly the whole way as if she fears one of us will jump out before she can get us safely to our father. He will be waiting for us with an armload of coats when we land in winter. First we will walk into the freezing cold from the airplane to the gate. She will gasp, "Ay." A cry of pain as if the freezing wind has cut her. She will never recover from that first assault.

Do I remember this, or did I dream it? It doesn't matter now.

Acknowledgments

A selection from *The Cruel Country* appeared in *Brevity.com*, issue 40, Fall 2012. The same selection will be included in *The Bedford Reader* and *The Brief Bedford Reader*, Bedford/St. Martin's Publishers, forthcoming.

"Mothers and Daughters," an excerpt from *The Cruel Country*, is included in the anthology *A Story Larger Than My Own: Women Writers Look Back on Their Lives and Careers*, edited by Janet Burroway, University of Chicago Press, 2014.

"Of Books and Huecos," a selection from *The Cruel Country*, will be included in the anthology *After Montaigne*, edited by David Lazar and Patrick Madden, forthcoming from the University of Georgia Press.

"The Photo" and "Verde: My Mother's Clothes," two selections from *The Cruel Country*, will be included in *The Texas Tech Anthology of New American Writing*, forthcoming.

Gracias

I would like to express my gratitude to the many readers of this book as it progressed through many drafts and versions. I offer profound thanks to my family: to the Morot family on the Island, who gave me their unqualified love and support during a very difficult time; to John, who heard and read every page as I wrote it; and to Tanya, Dory, Rolando, and Diane, for giving my narrative their blessings. For a poet's eye for detail and her abilities in the fine-tuning of language, I thank Ida Stewart. I am most grateful to Ida, who read all versions of this book, palabra by palabra. For his expertise of Puerto Rican culture, I say mil gracias to Dr. Rafael Ocasio. The views of his beloved Old San Juan in this book are dedicated to him. Also to my compañera and fellow native daughter of Hormigueros, Puerto Rico, Dr. Edna Acosta-Belén, who read a late version for accuracy in my depiction of our pueblo. For their suggestions and support I thank Johnny Damm, Bradley Bazzle, Gabrielle Lucille Fuentes, Kathryn Locey, Joy Castro, Brenda Reagan, and Hugh Ruppersburg. My gratitude to Lisa Bayer and the many people at the University of Georgia Press for believing in my work and for dedicating their time and talents to this, our project.

I'd also like to thank the publishers of my books of poetry and prose, which I referenced or quoted in this book.

Selected Sources

Achotegui, Joseba. "Immigrants Living in Extreme Situation: Immigrant Syndrome with Chronic and Multiple Stress (The Ulysses Syndrome)." *Norte (Spanish Association of Neuropsychiatry)*, 7.21 (2004). 39–53. http://www.fhspereclaver.org/migra-salut-mental/Ulises/Ulysses%20text%20 2%20english-1.pdf

Alvarez, Lizette. "Murder Rate and Fear Rise in Puerto Rico." *New York Times,* 20 June 2011.

Barthes, Roland. *Camera Lucida: Reflections on Photography*. Trans. Richard Howard. New York: Hill and Wang, 1981.

———. *A Lover's Discourse: Fragments*. Trans. Richard Howard. New York: Hill and Wang, 1978.

———. *Mourning Diary: October 26, 1977–September 15, 1979*. Annotated by Nathalie Léger. Trans. Richard Howard. New York: Hill and Wang, 2010.

Bougere, Marilyn Hardy. "Culture, Grief, and Bereavement: Applications for Clinical Practice." *Minority Nurse,* Winter 2008. Accessed 1 May 2012. http://www.minoritynurse.com/culture-grief-and-bereavement-applications-clinical-practice.

Cancer Caregiving A to Z. Atlanta, Ga.: American Cancer Society, 2007.

The Collins Thesaurus of the English Language: Complete and Unabridged. 2nd ed. London: HarperCollins, 2002.

Dickinson, Emily. "550." *The Poems of Emily Dickinson*. Ed. R.W. Franklin. Cambridge: Harvard University Press, 1999. 248.

Didion, Joan. *The Year of Magical Thinking*. New York: A. A. Knopf, 2005.

Eliot, T. S. "Ash-Wednesday." *Collected Poems, 1909–1962*. New York: Harcourt, Brace, and World, 1963.

Gherovici, Patricia. *The Puerto Rican Syndrome*. New York: Other Press, 2003.

Ginsberg, Allen. *The Collected Poems of Allen Ginsberg, 1947–1997*. New York: HarperCollins, 2006. 48–49.

"A Guide to Grief." *Hospice,* 1 May 2012. http://www.hospicenet.org/html /grief_guide.html

The Holy Bible. King James Version.

McLean, Don. "American Pie." *American Pie,* 1971.

Mukherjee, Siddhartha. *The Emperor of All Maladies: A Biography of Cancer.* New York: Scribner, 2010.

Nuland, Sherwin B. *How We Die: Reflections on Life's Final Chapter.* New York: A. A. Knopf, 1994.

O'Connor, Flannery. *The Habit of Being: Letters of Flannery O'Connor.* New York: Macmillan, 1988.

———. *Mystery and Manners: Occasional Prose.* New York: Farrar, Straus, and Giroux, 1969.

———. *Wise Blood. New York:* Farrar, Straus, and Giroux, 2007.

Palmer, Robert. "I've got a bad case of loving you (Doctor, Doctor)." *Secrets,* 1979.

Piven, Joshua, and David Borgenicht. *The Worst-Case Scenario Survival Handbook.* San Francisco, Calif.: Chronicle Books, 1999.

Sontag, Susan. *Illness As Metaphor.* New York: Farrar, Straus, and Giroux, 1978.

Thomas, Dylan. "Do Not Go Gentle into That Good Night." *The Poems of Dylan Thomas.* New York: New Directions, 1971.

Thomas of Celano. *Dies Irae.* Trans. William Josiah Irons. 1849.

Vega, Ana Lydia. *Mirada de doble filo.* San Juan, Puerto Rico: La Editorial, Universidad de Puerto Rico, 2008.

Williams, Tennessee. "Time is the longest distance between two places." Line from *The Glass Menagerie.* 1944.

Williams, William Carlos. *Paterson.* 1963.

Welty, Eudora. *One Writer's Beginnings.* Cambridge, Mass.: Harvard University Press, 1984.

Woolf, Virginia. *A Room of One's Own.* San Diego: Harcourt Brace Jovanovich, 1989.

Judith Ortiz Cofer: Works Cited and Excerpted

Excerpts from the following books are reprinted by permission of the University of Georgia Press: "Here Is a Picture of Me" and "Anniversary," poems, from *The Latin Deli: Prose and Poetry*, 1993; "A Theory of Chaos," "Dominoes: A Meditation on the Game," "Beans: An Apologia for Not Loving to Cook," "Before the Storm," and "To Understand El Azul," from *A Love Song Beginning in Spanish: Poetry*, 2005; "Woman in Front of the Sun" and "My Rosetta," essays, from *Woman in Front of the Sun: On Becoming a Writer*, 2000.

Excerpts from "The Way My Mother Walked," "Quinceañera," poems, and "The Black Virgin," essay, are reprinted with permission from the publisher of *Silent Dancing: A Partial Remembrance of a Puerto Rican Childhood* by Judith Ortiz Cofer (© 1990 Arte Público Press, University of Houston).

Excerpts from "Word Hunger," essay, first appeared in *Lessons from a Writer's Life: Readings and Resources for Teachers and Students* (Portsmouth, N.H.: Heinemann, 2011).

Individual works published in journals and anthologies: "The Aging Maria," in *Image* (2007): 56, reprinted in *The Best Spiritual Writing*, 2010; "Give Us This Day" in *North American Review*; and "Listen" in *Afro-American Review*.